the cover up

hans fahrmeyer

HAMBURG GROUP

First published in the United States of America in 2017
by HAMBURG GROUP, INC New York, NY

Design by Werner Redman

Forward by Trevor Briggs

Hans Fahrmeyer's images are bold, colorful and unabashedly sensual in his latest photographic experiment, *The Cover-Up*. The intent is to evoke desire, and it's evident in the eyes of the models on each page. The energy is palpable through his use of vibrant colors, unique body poses and positions, as well as his creative editing. Hans channels the energy into images drenched in both intensity and urgency.

Born in Germany, Hans worked throughout Europe prior to immigrating to the United States in 1979. Although his European influences are evident within his vision, the glamour and energy embedded in his images are erotically rooted in his passion for his home in New York City's West Village. And like Hans, so many of the men who journey to his studio are foreign born as well. Yet through his skill and creativity, in front of Hans' lens, they embody and channel the electricity and creativity of the both the artist, and the city.

In in his last book, The Naked Truth, Hans unveiled an extensive collection of breathtaking images of a multitude of men that Hans has photographed throughout his career. Each image, and each page, revealed models completely bare, with nothing to hide behind, nothing to mask or conceal their own raw truths.

Why then, would Hans follow-up *The Naked Truth* with *The Cover-Up*? Why physically expose his models only to then cover them up? The art of reveal is one of Hans greatest skills as an artist. Although many of the models in *The Cover-Up* are partially covered, the bits of fashion are used to highlight and accentuate the body and specific body parts.

Viewers will enjoy the voyeuristic tease Hans creates with the creative uncovering of models. with a variation of textile and transparent materials. But the viewer is rewarded with what is revealed and then, what is left to the imagination.

Underwear, jock-straps and jeans are worn to cover and protect, they cling directly to our bodies like a second layer of skin. The uncovering of garments highlights and illuminates the male form exposing it in exciting and unique ways. Like the frame of a painting, Hans uses *The Cover-Up* to focus our eye and to spotlight a piece of the painting, or a part of the body, creating an erotic transparency that would not be possible if the model was completely nude.

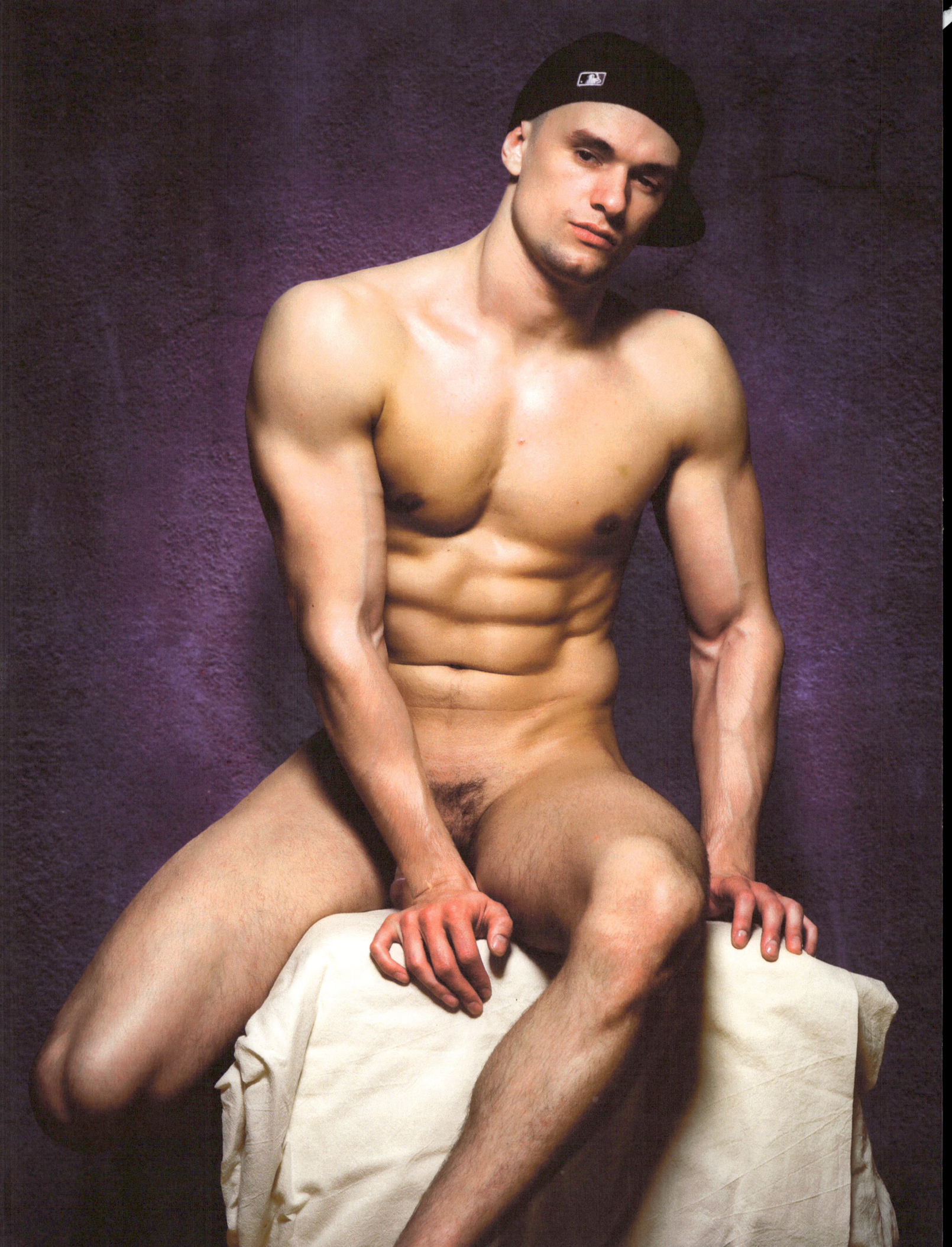

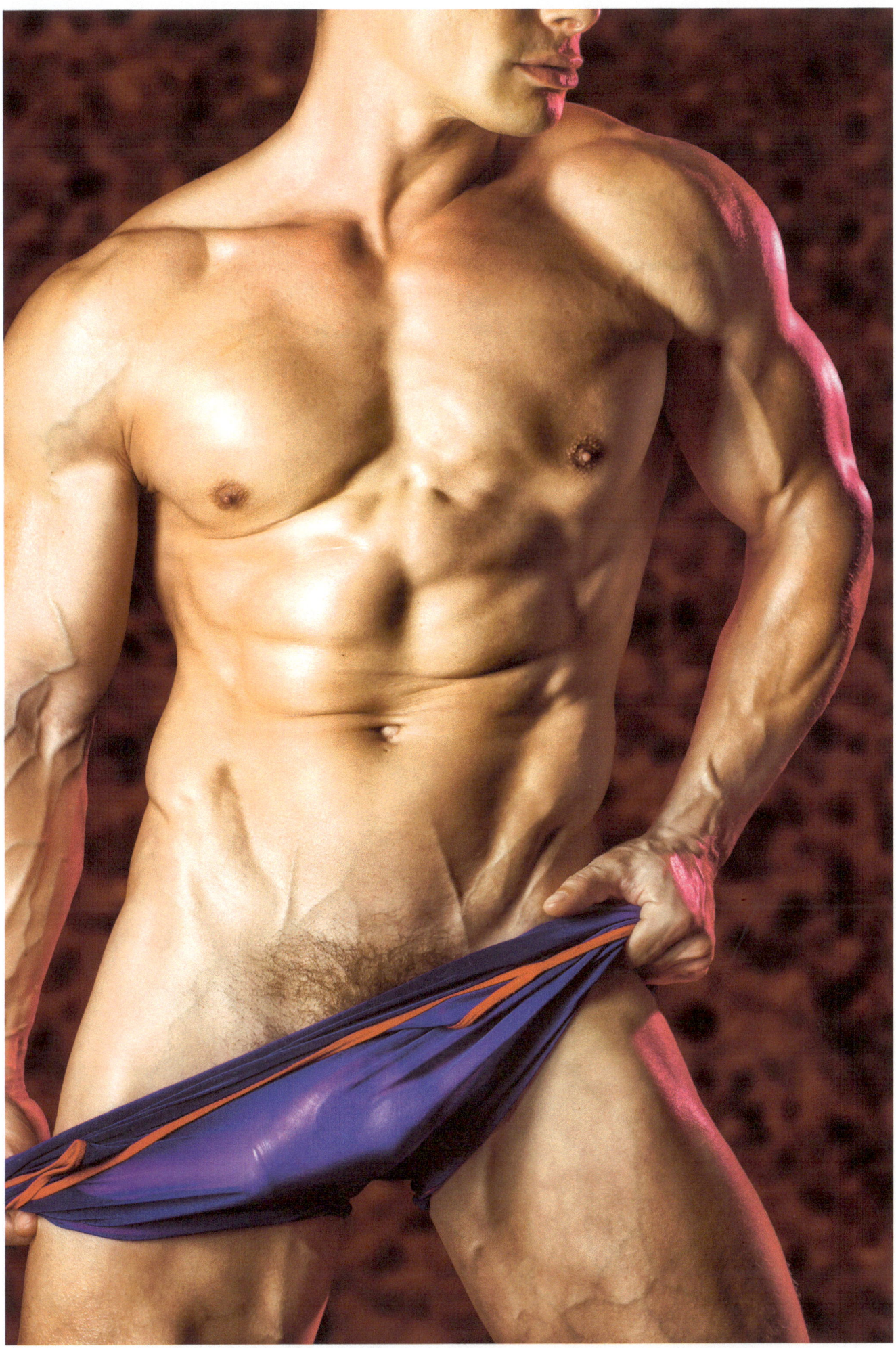

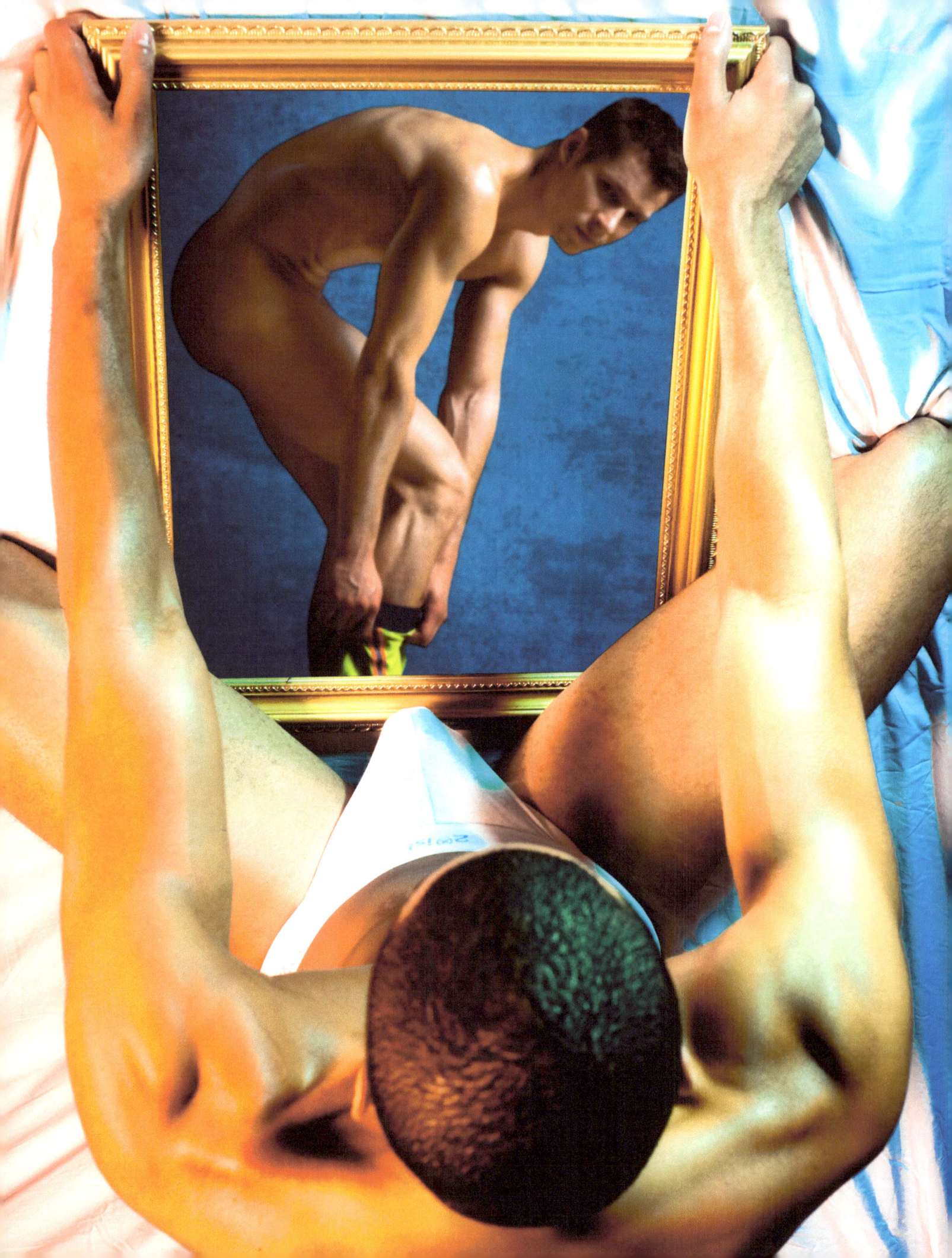

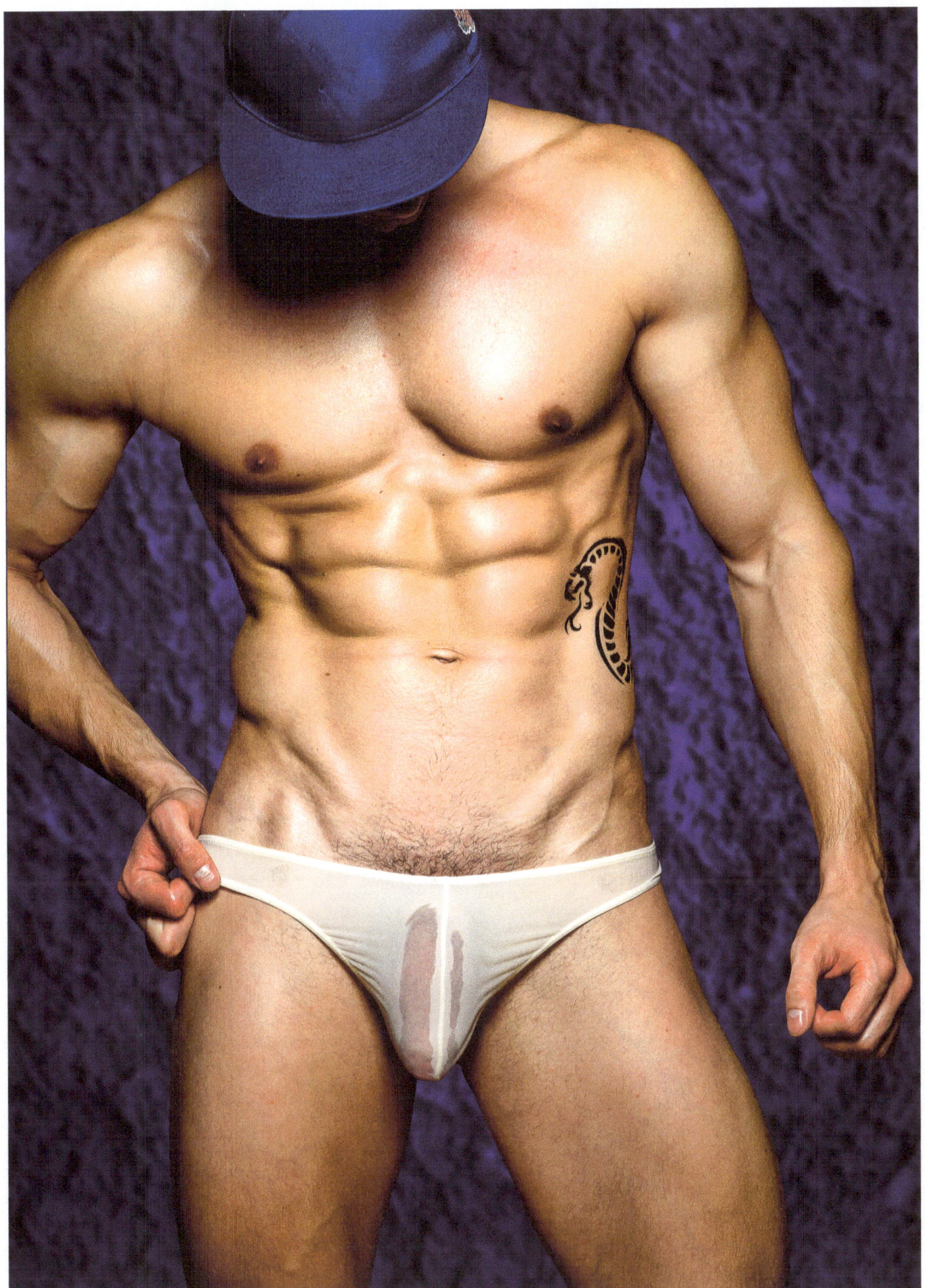

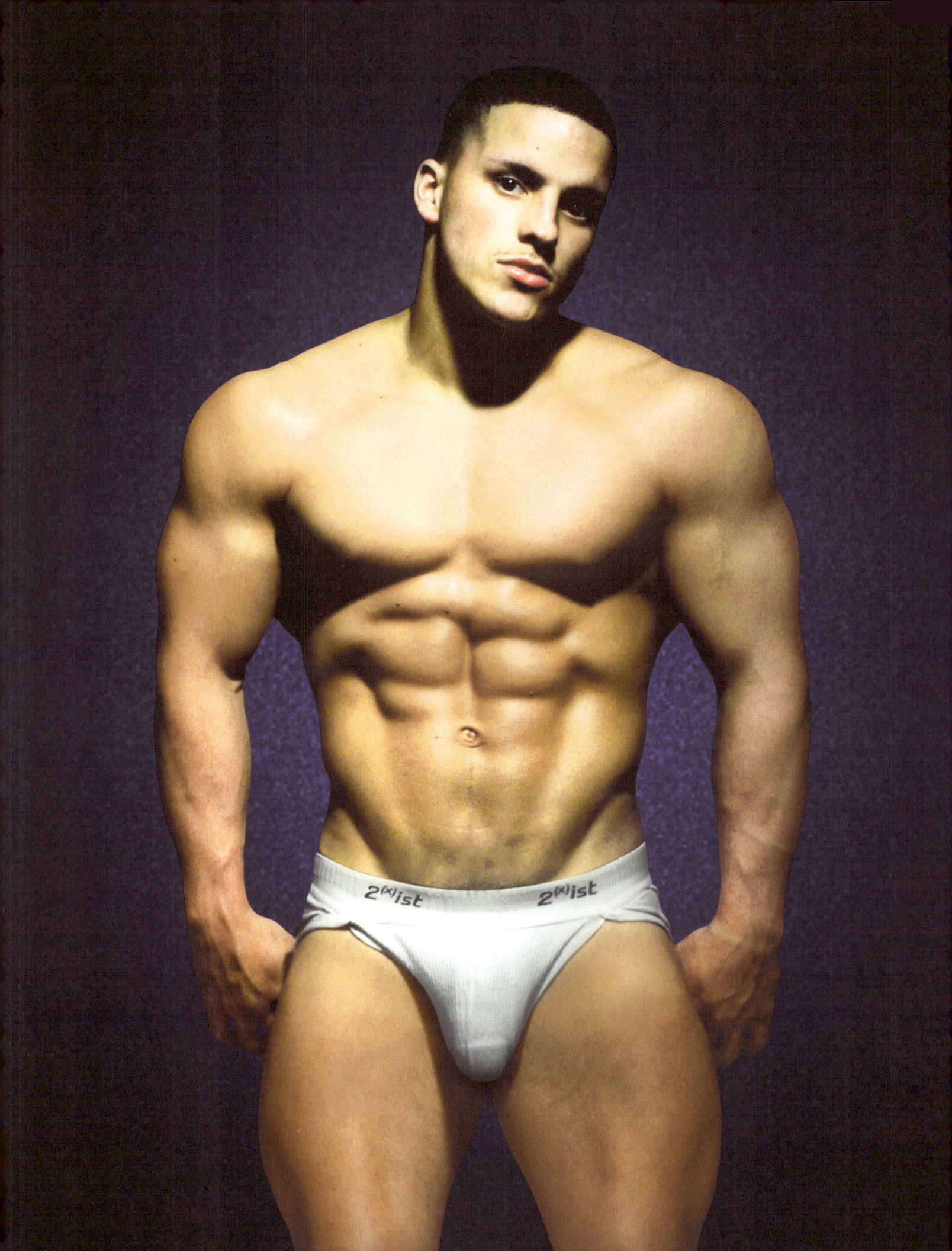

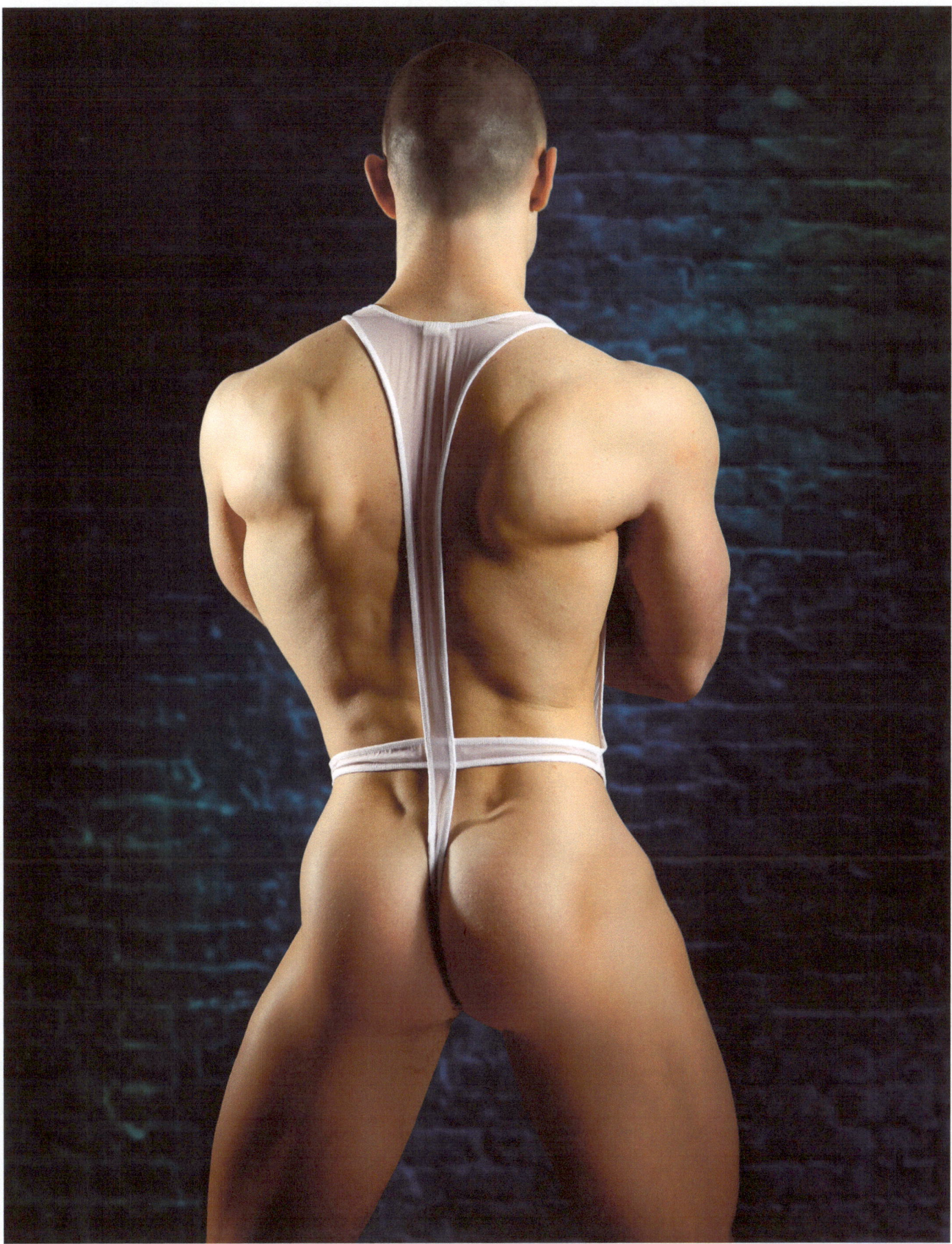

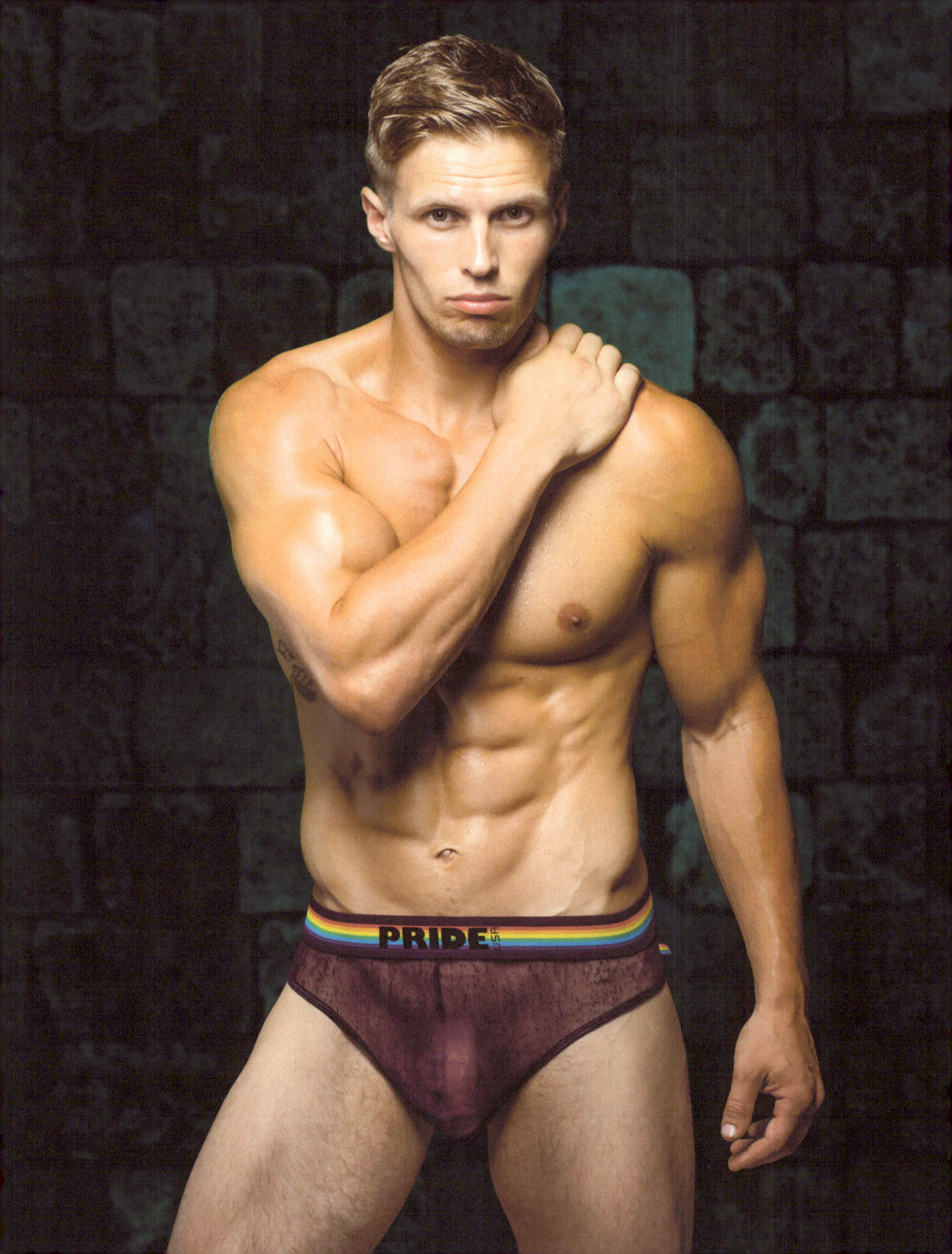

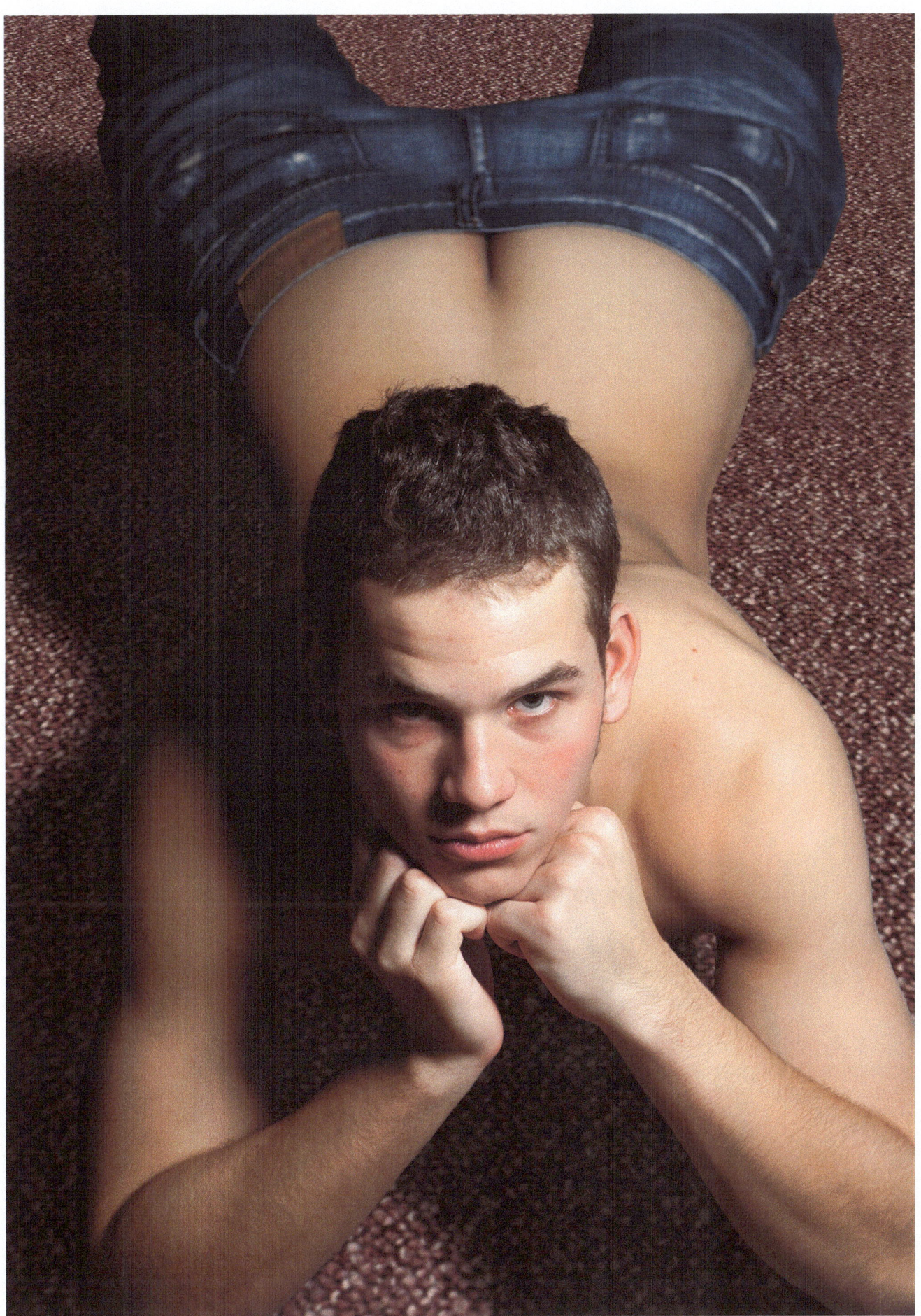

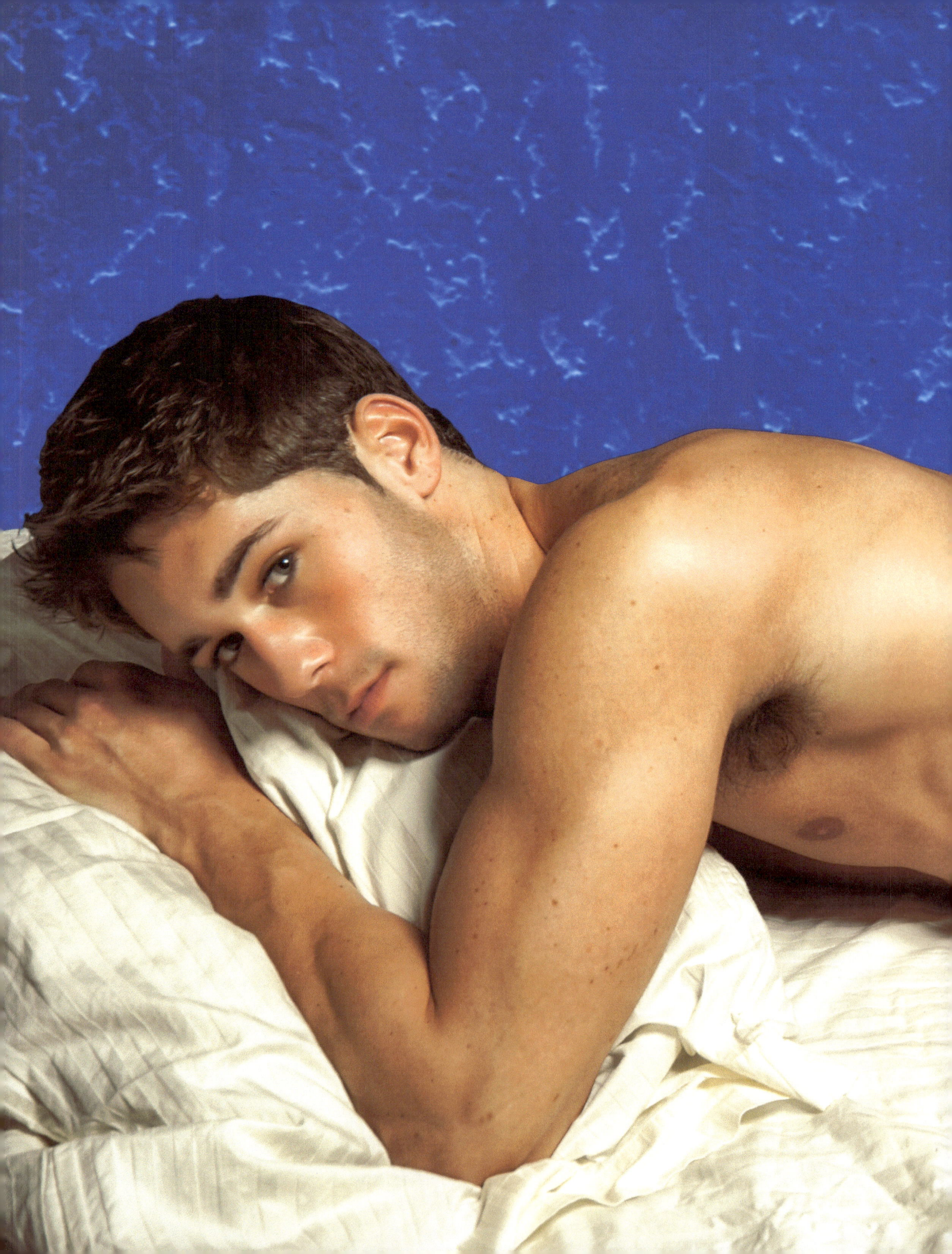

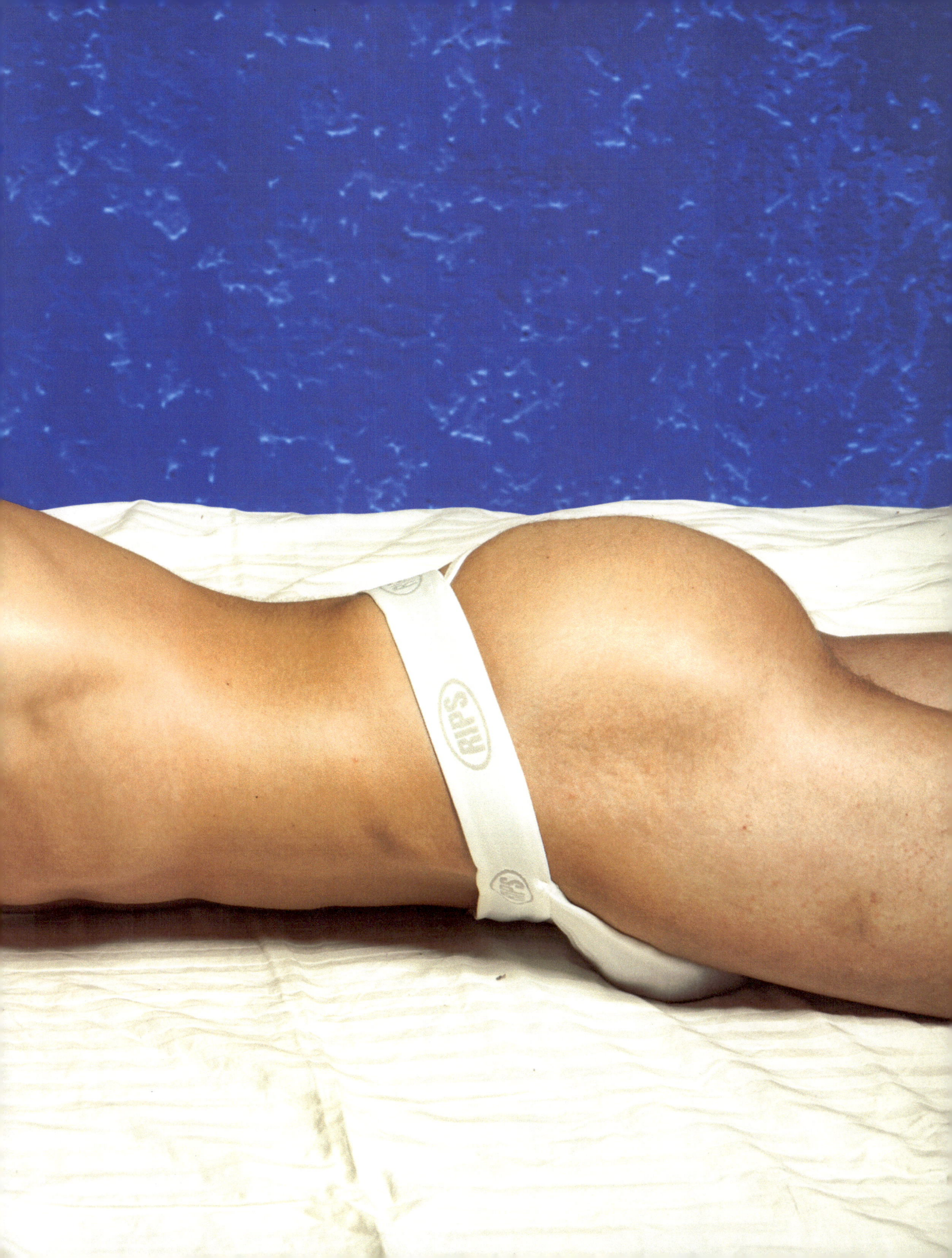

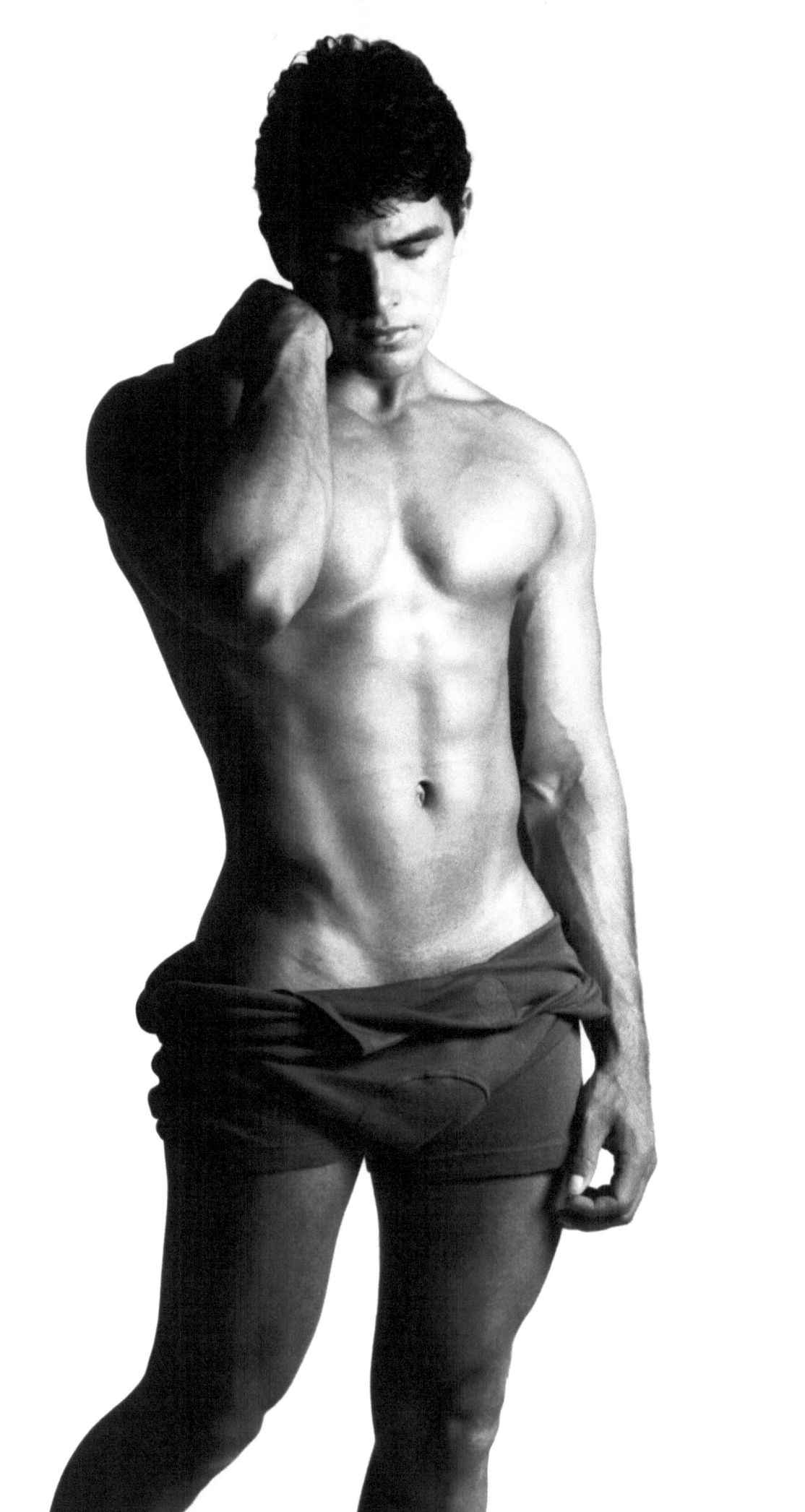

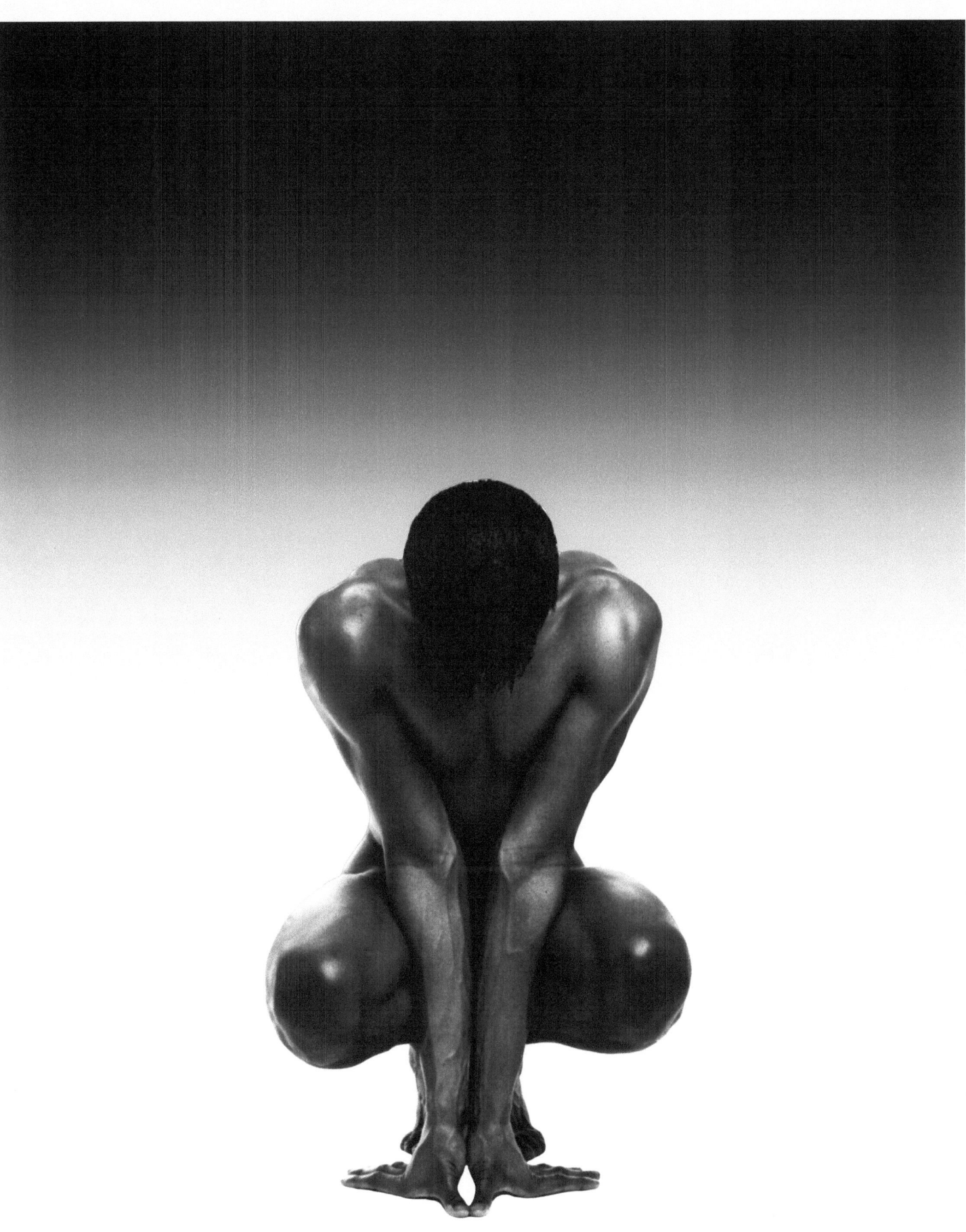

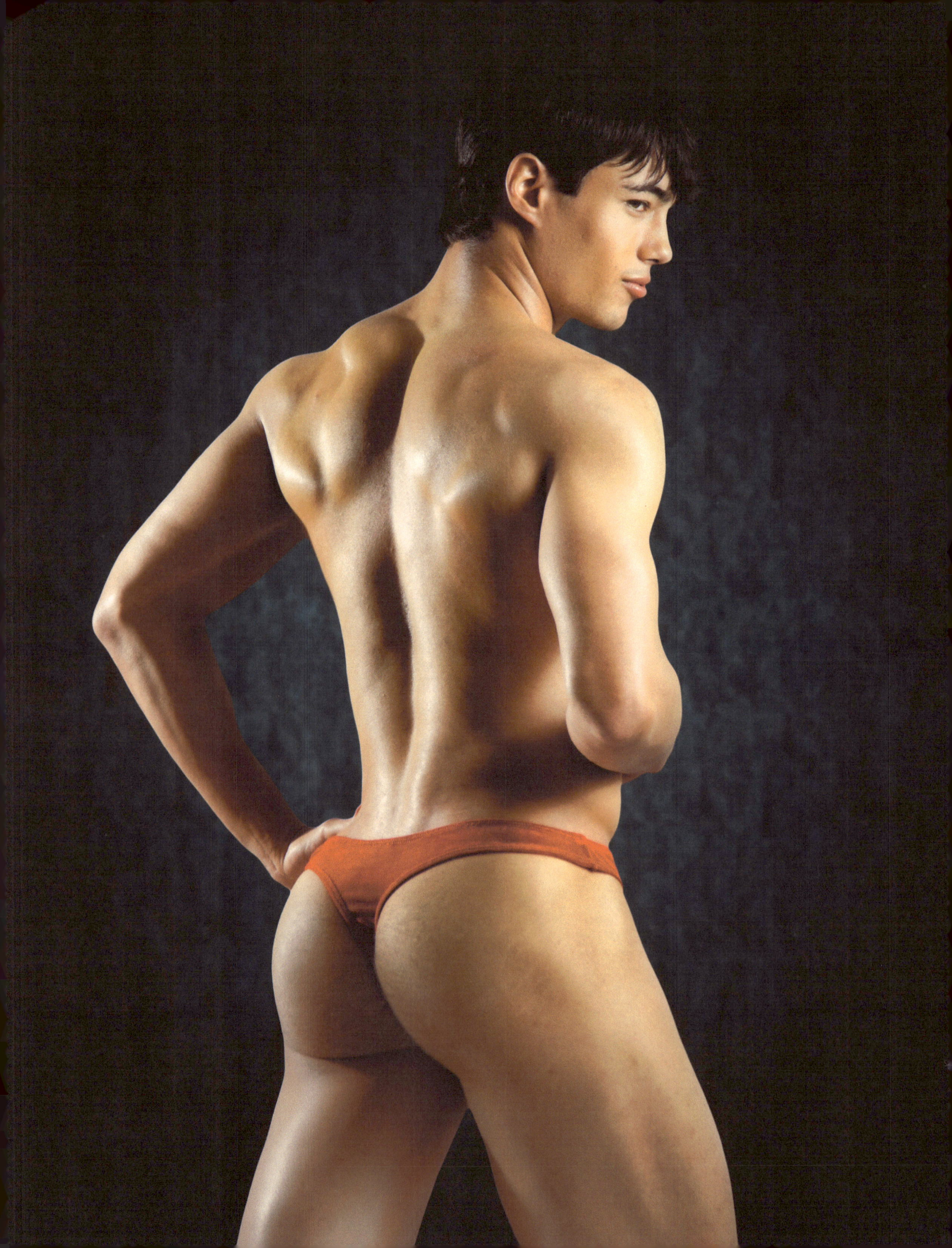

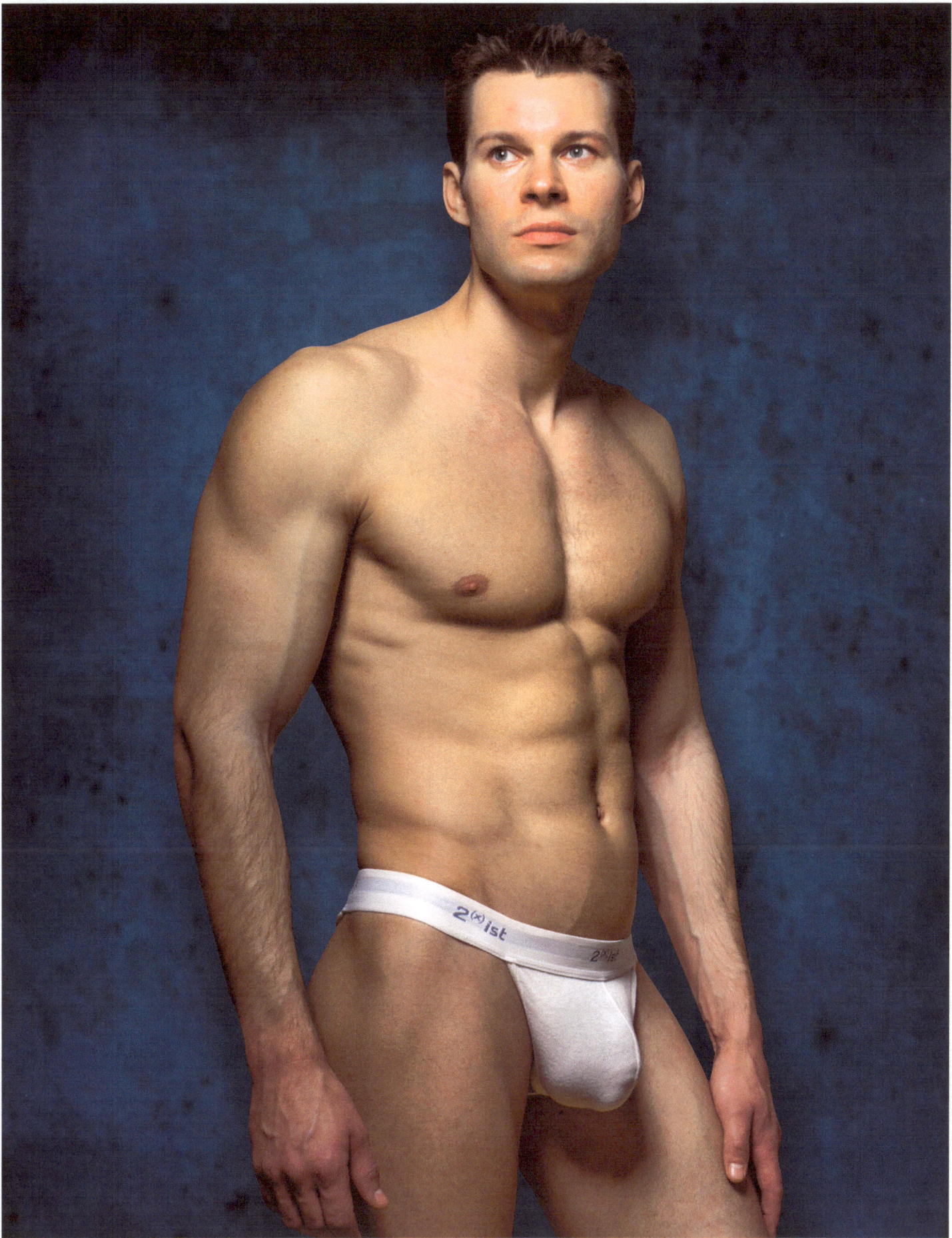

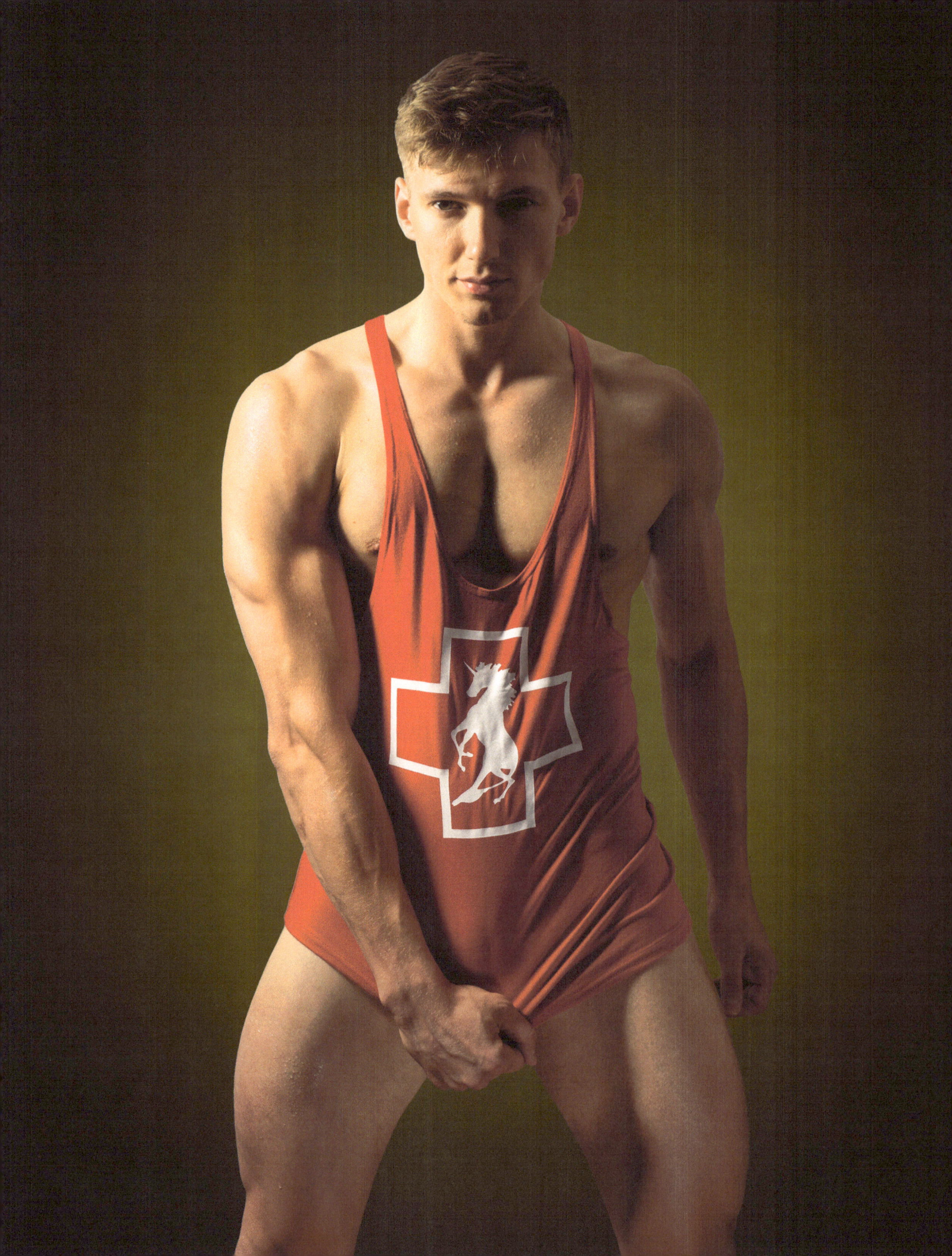

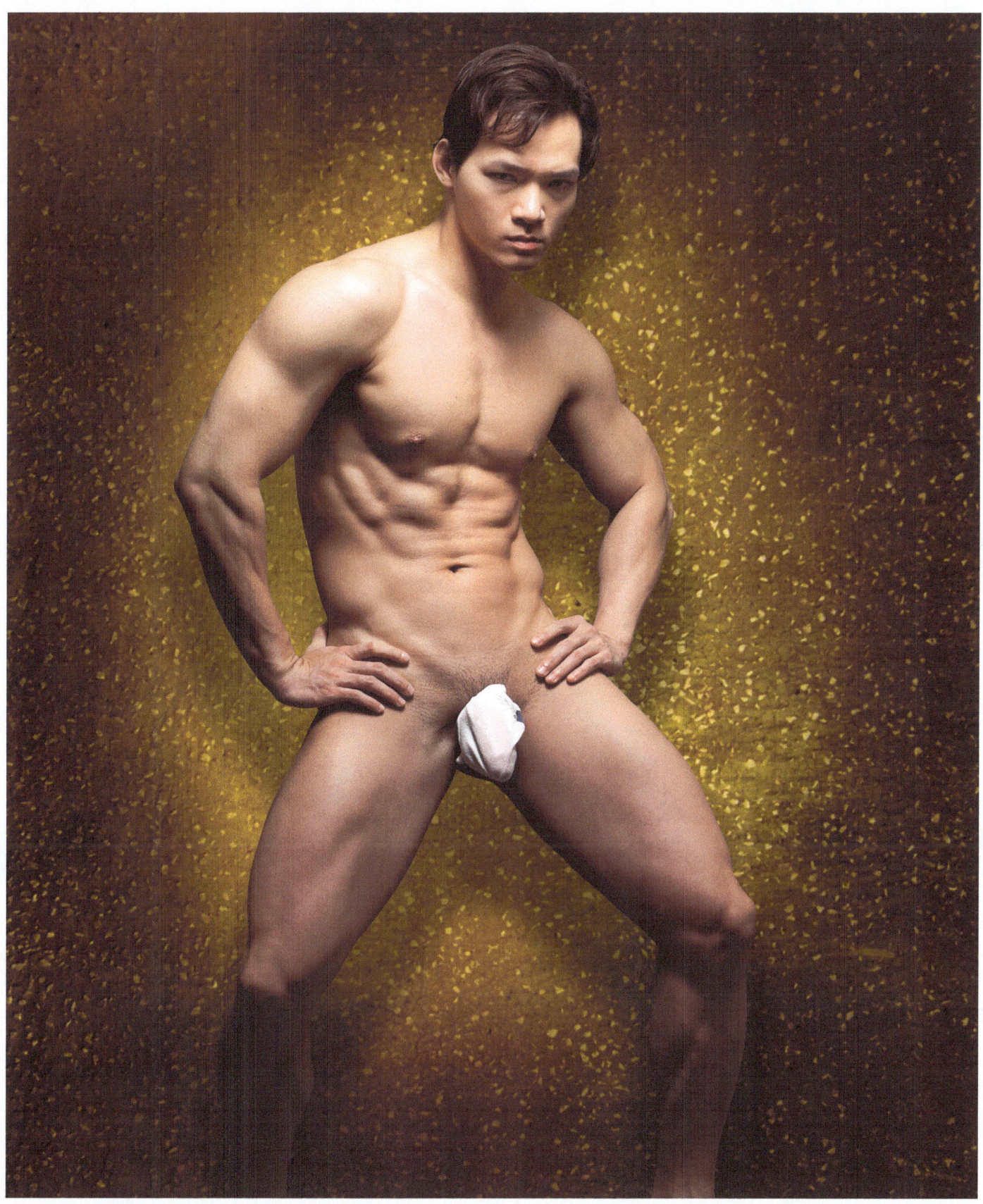

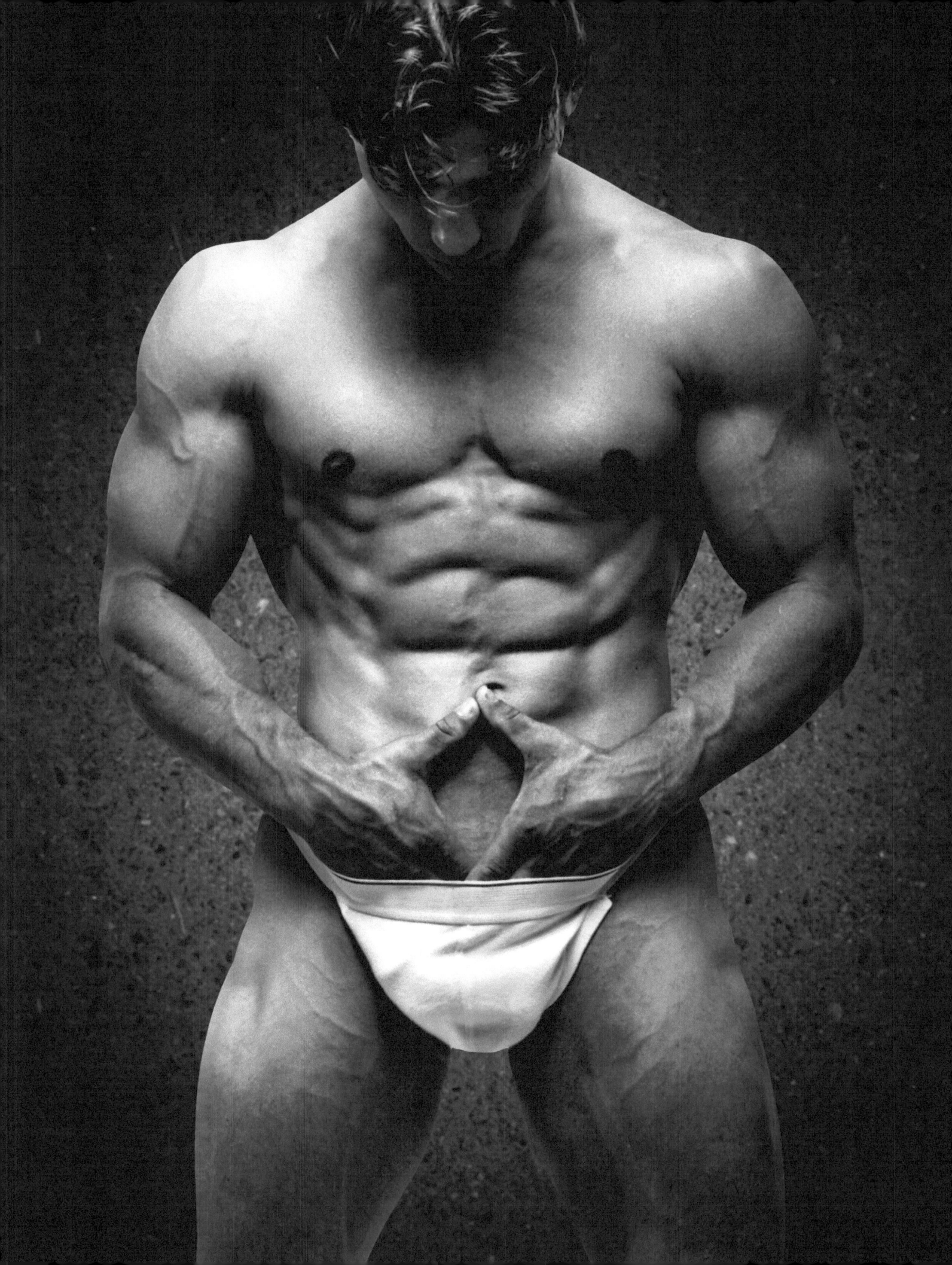

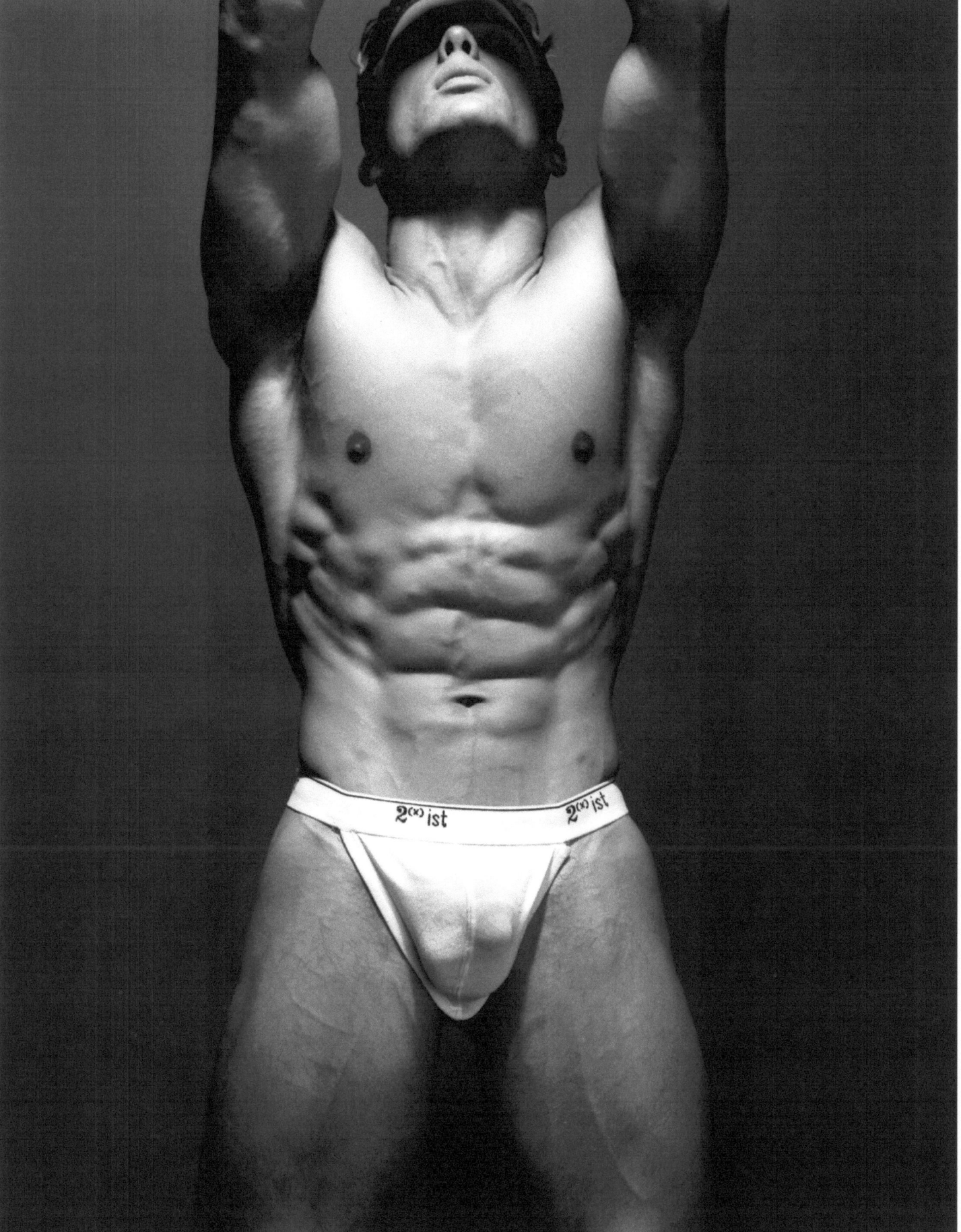

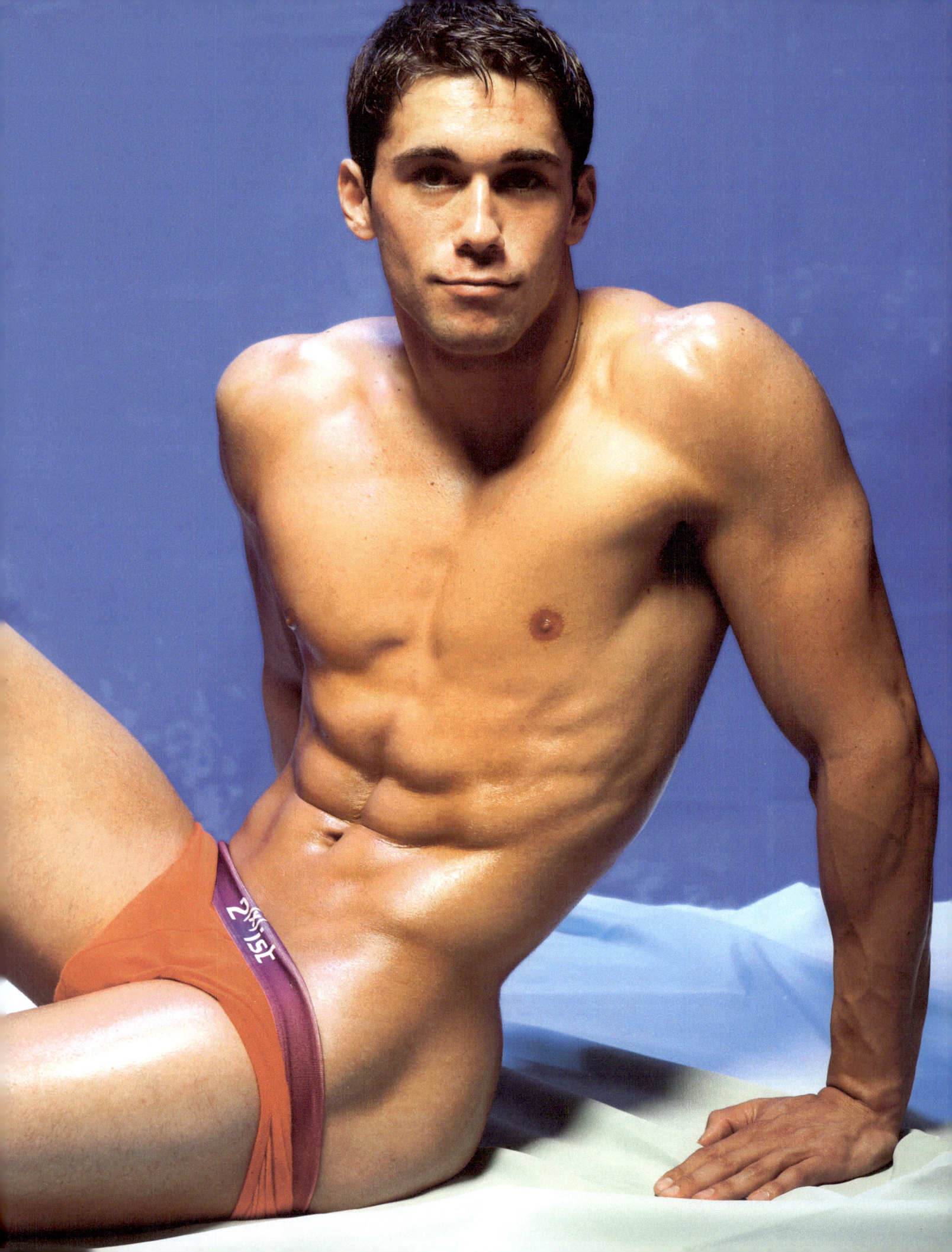

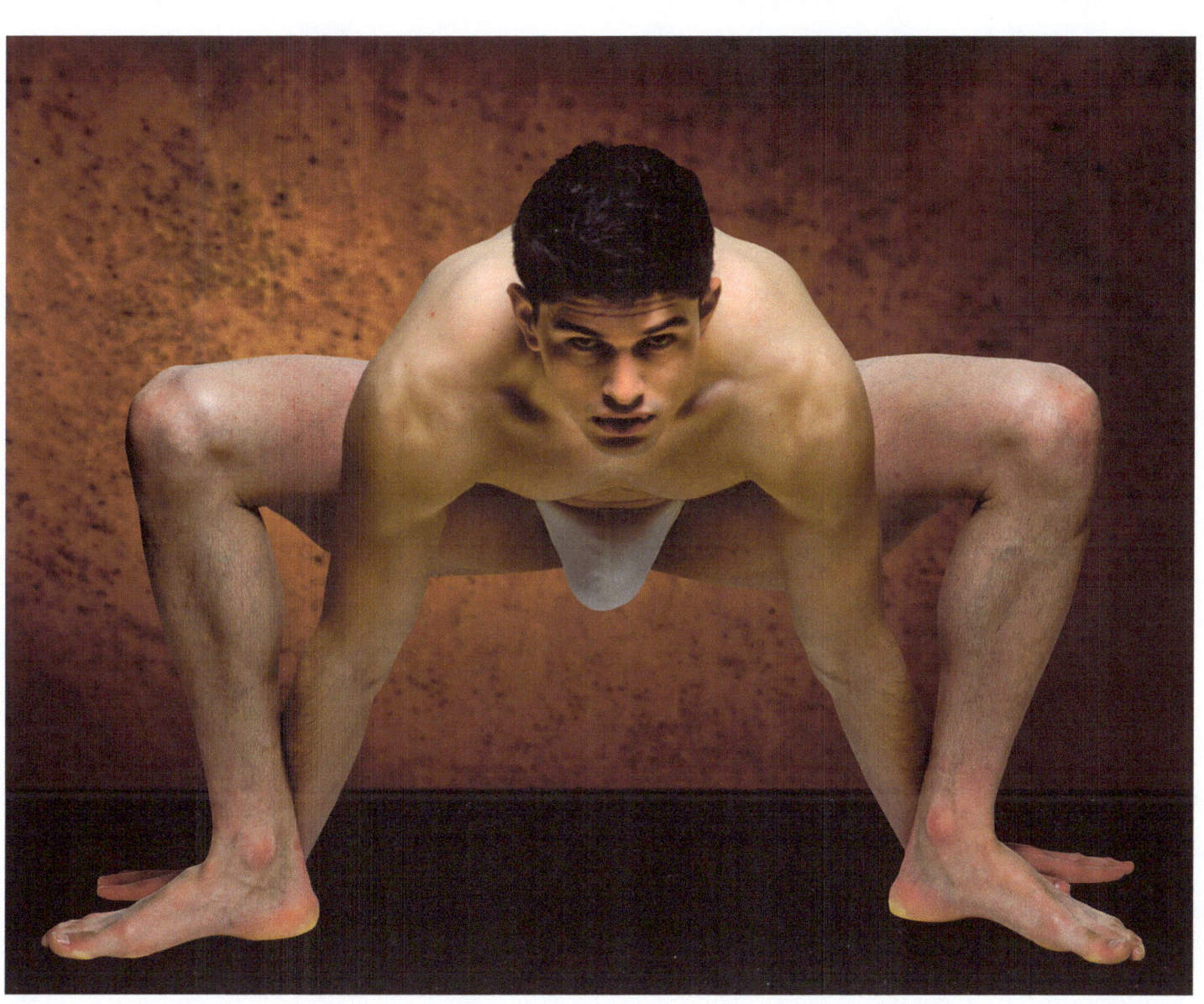

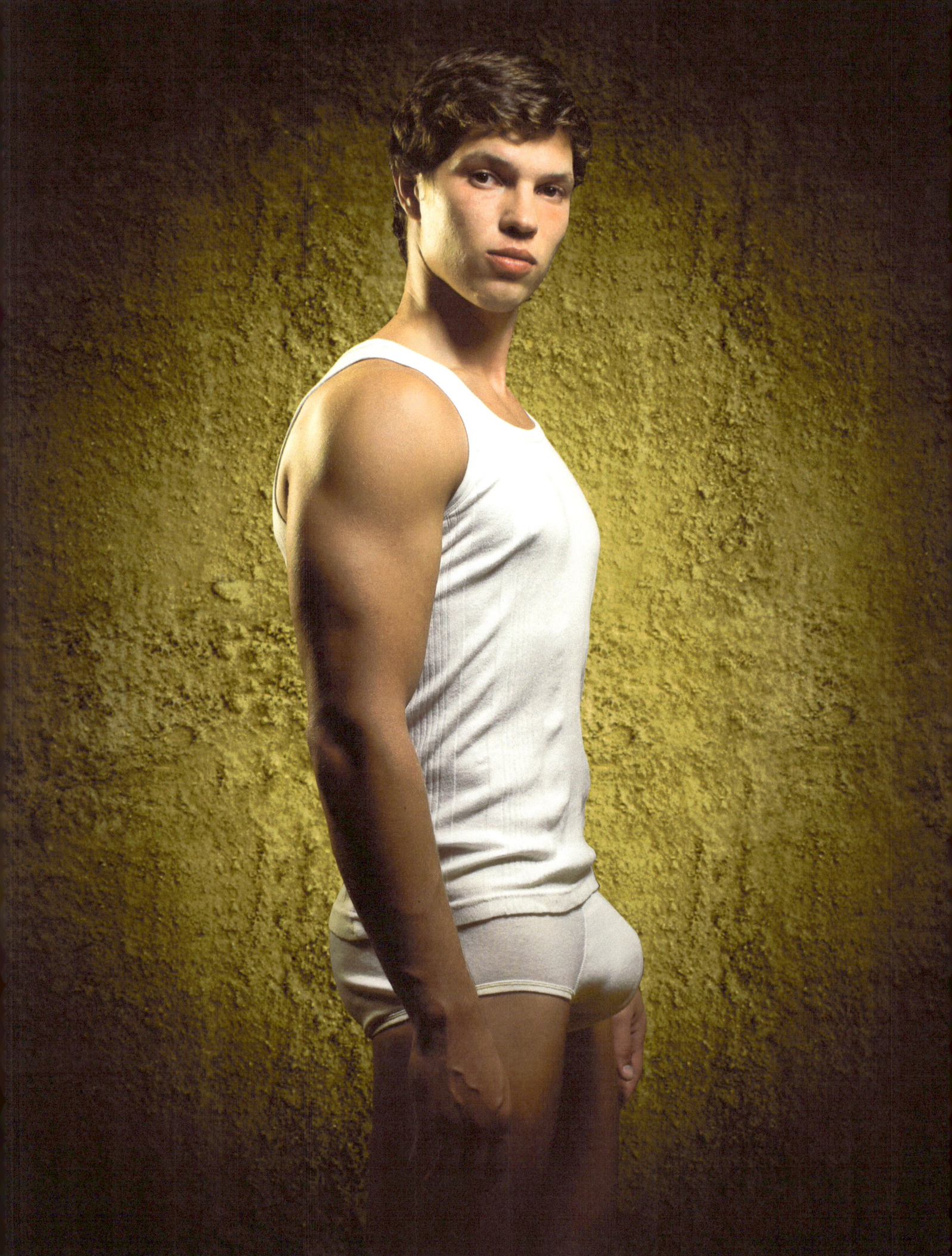

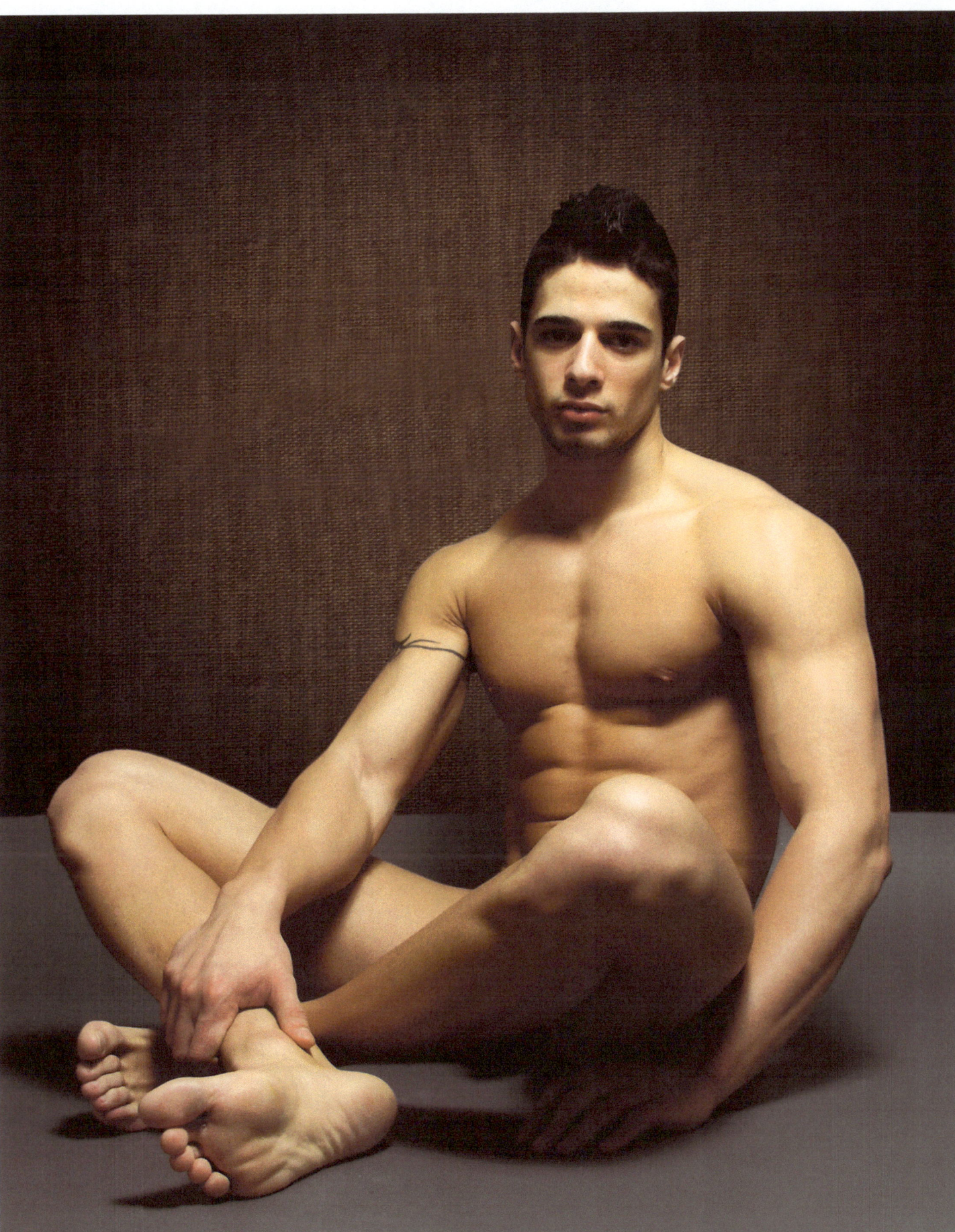

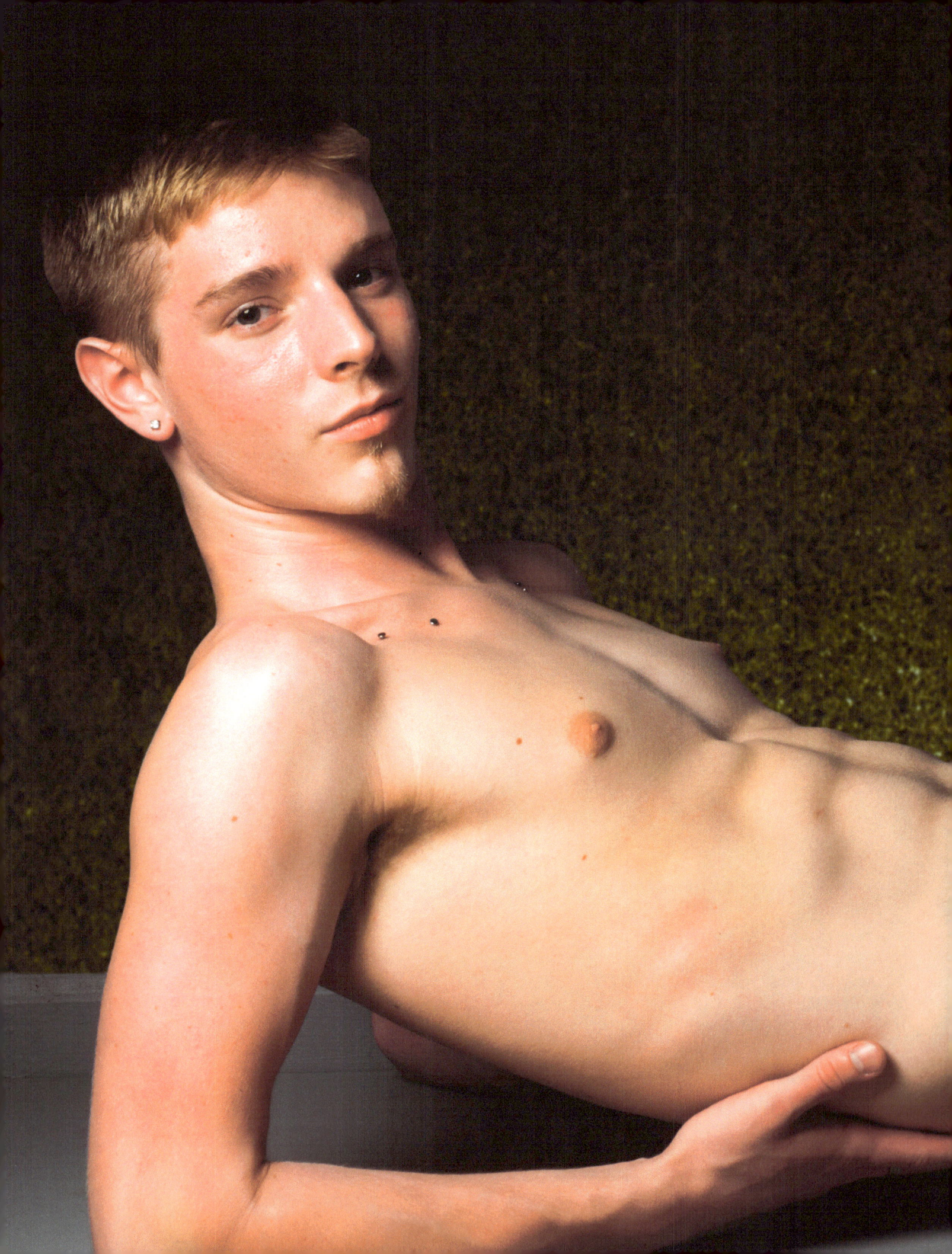

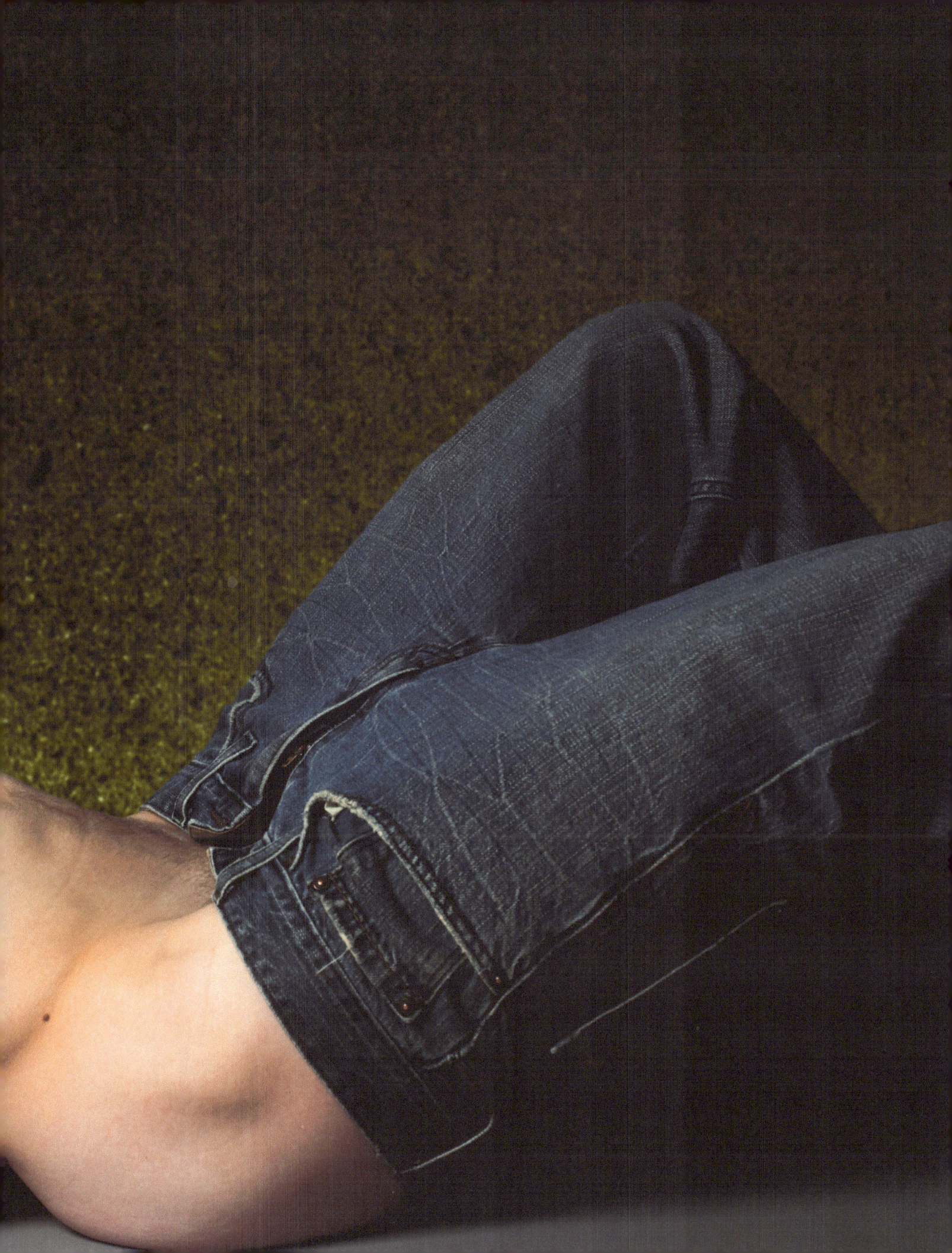

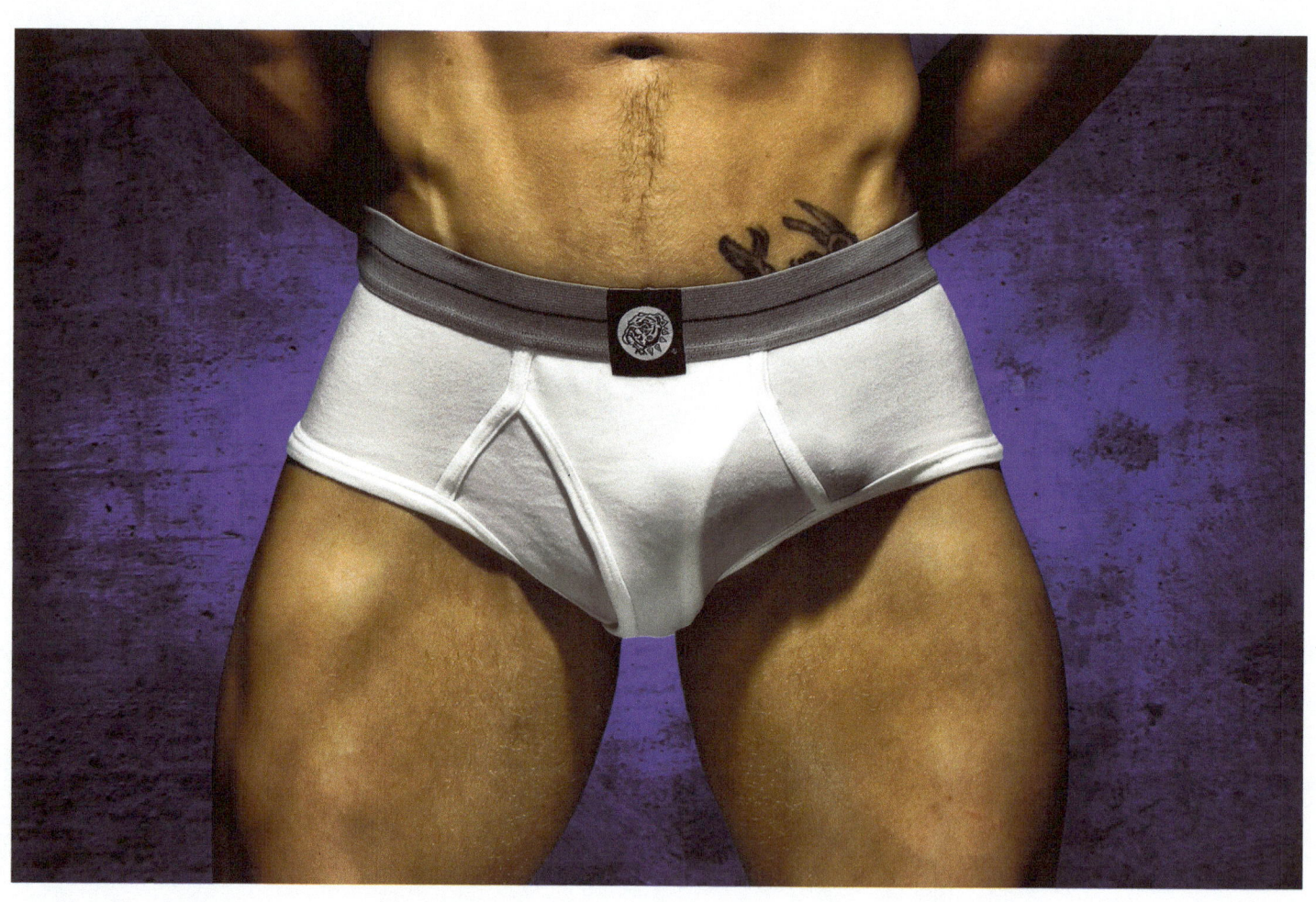

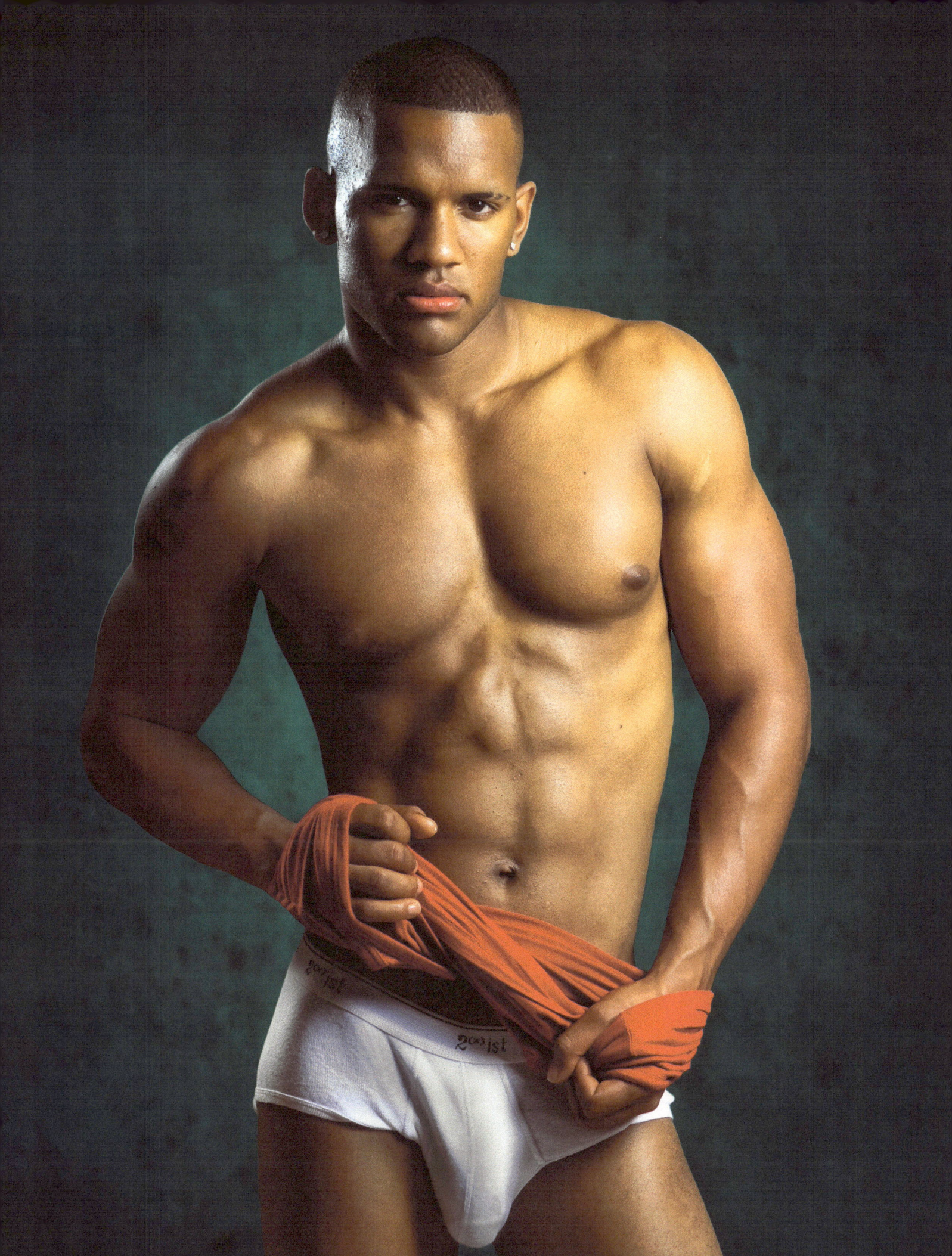

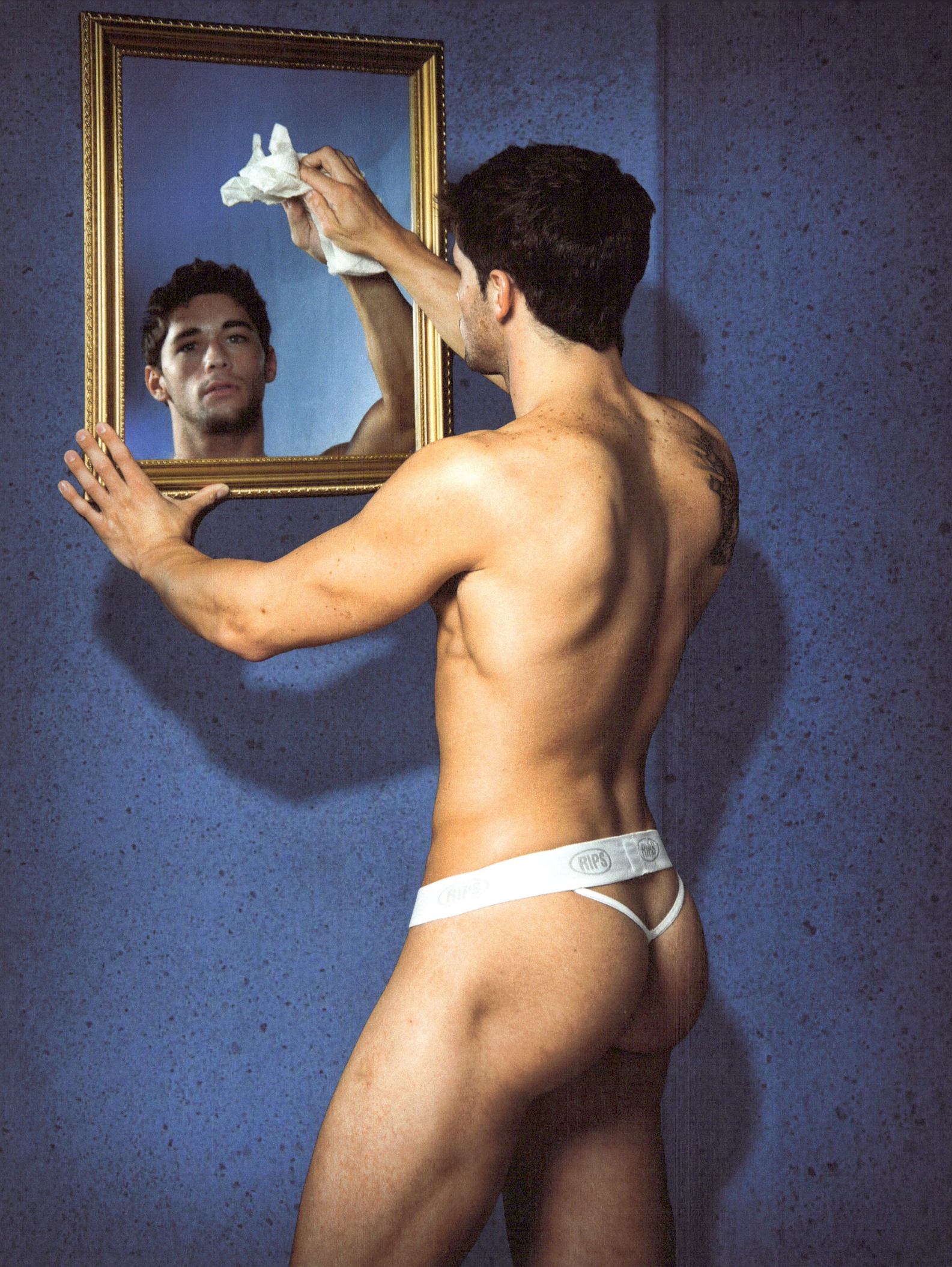

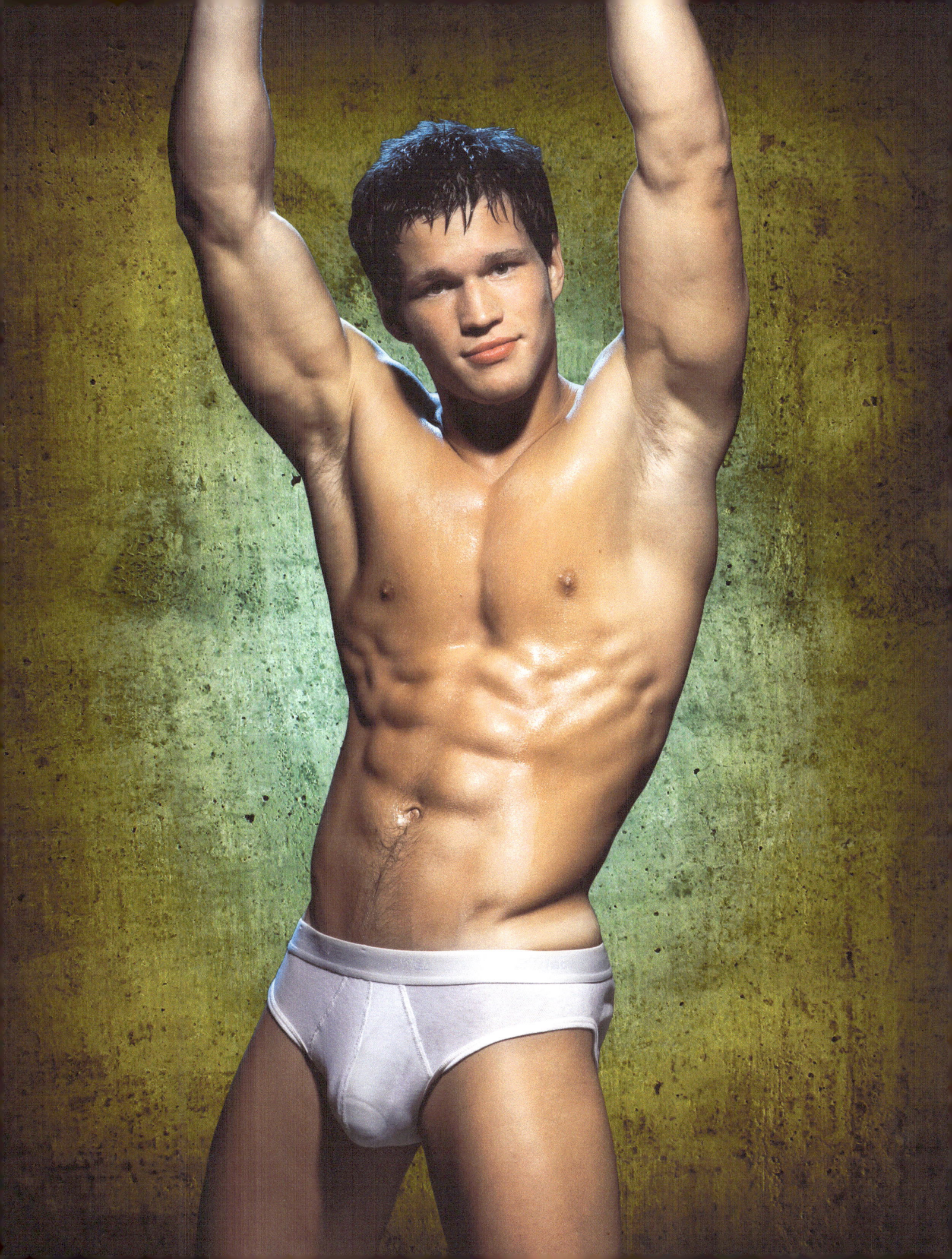

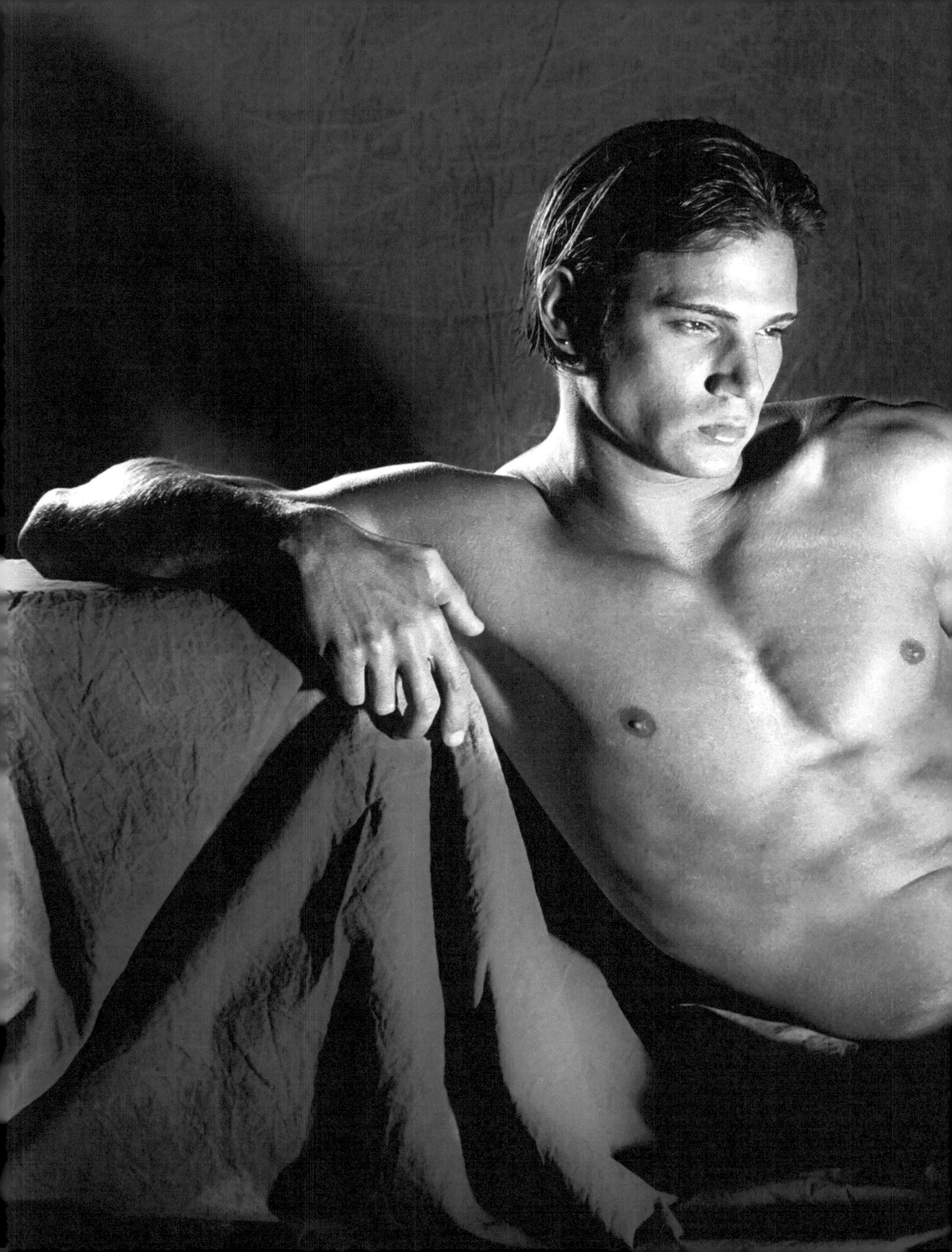

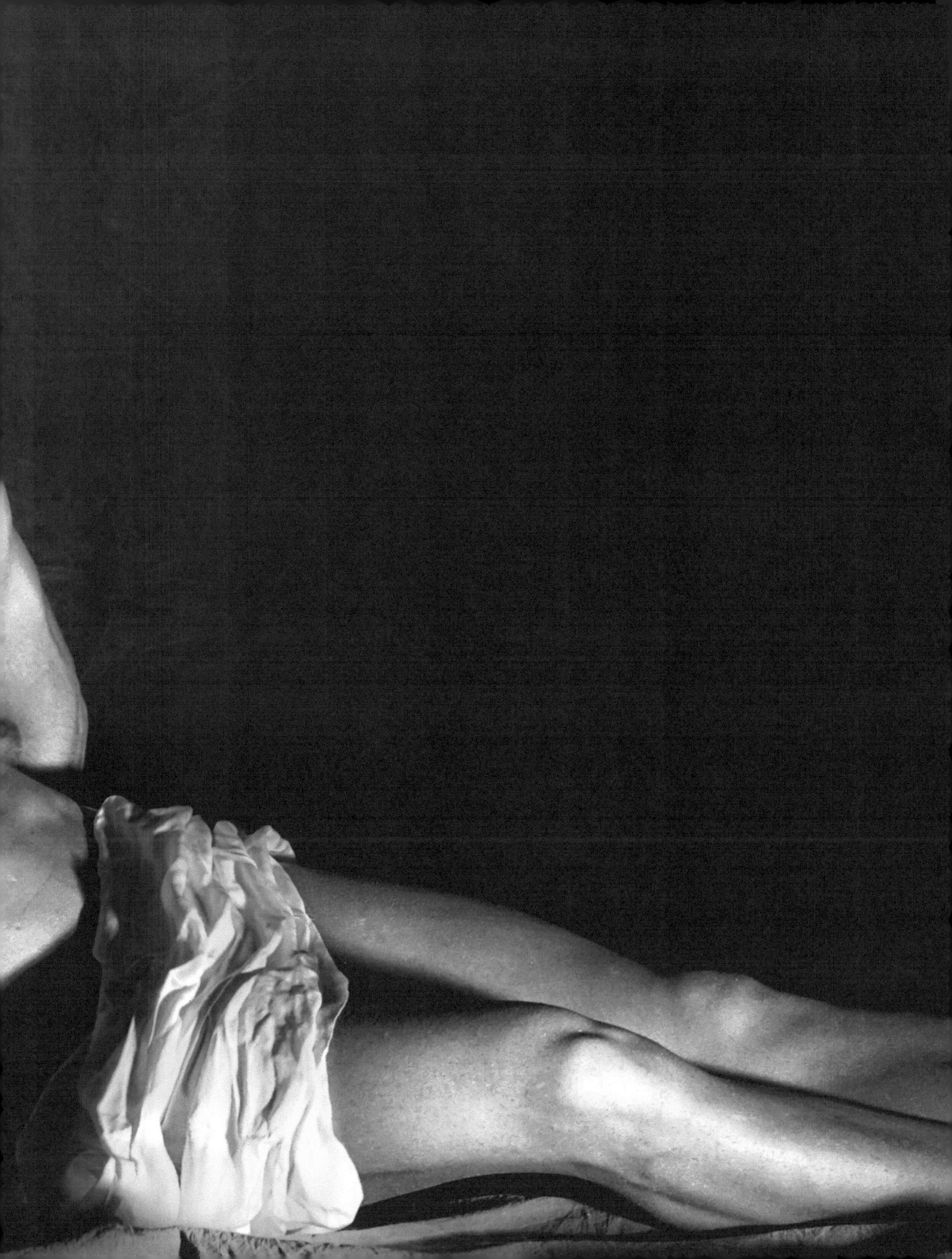

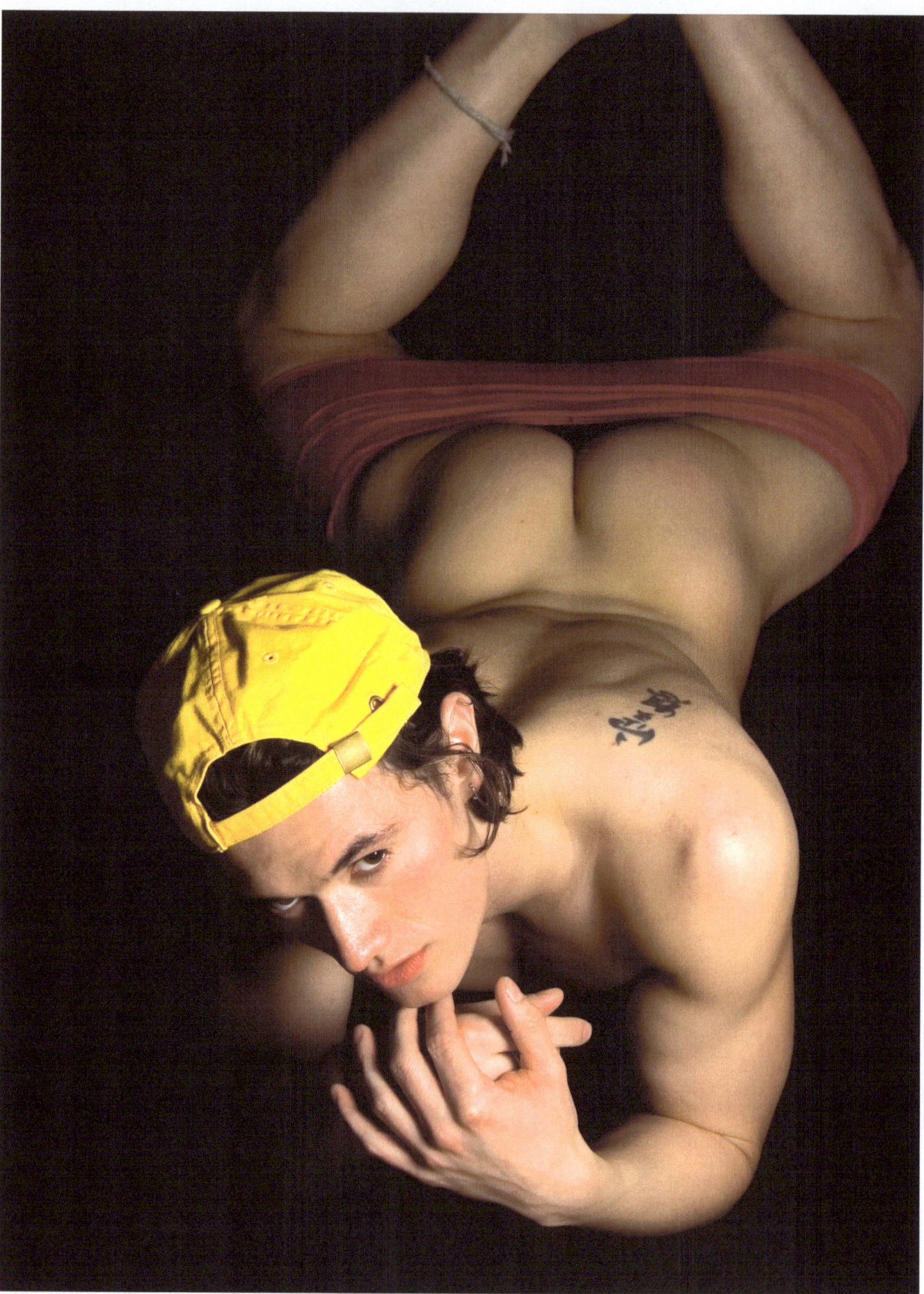

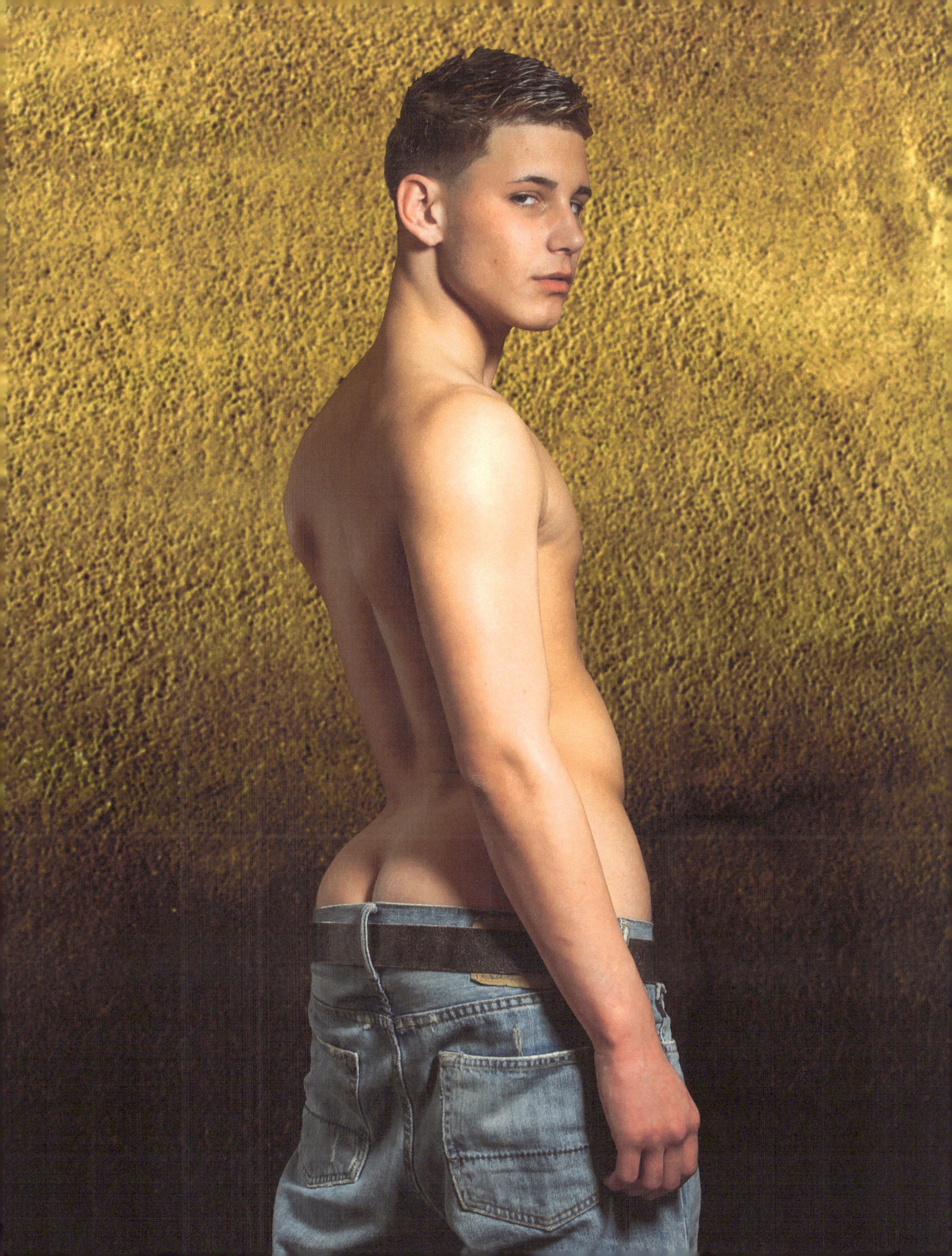

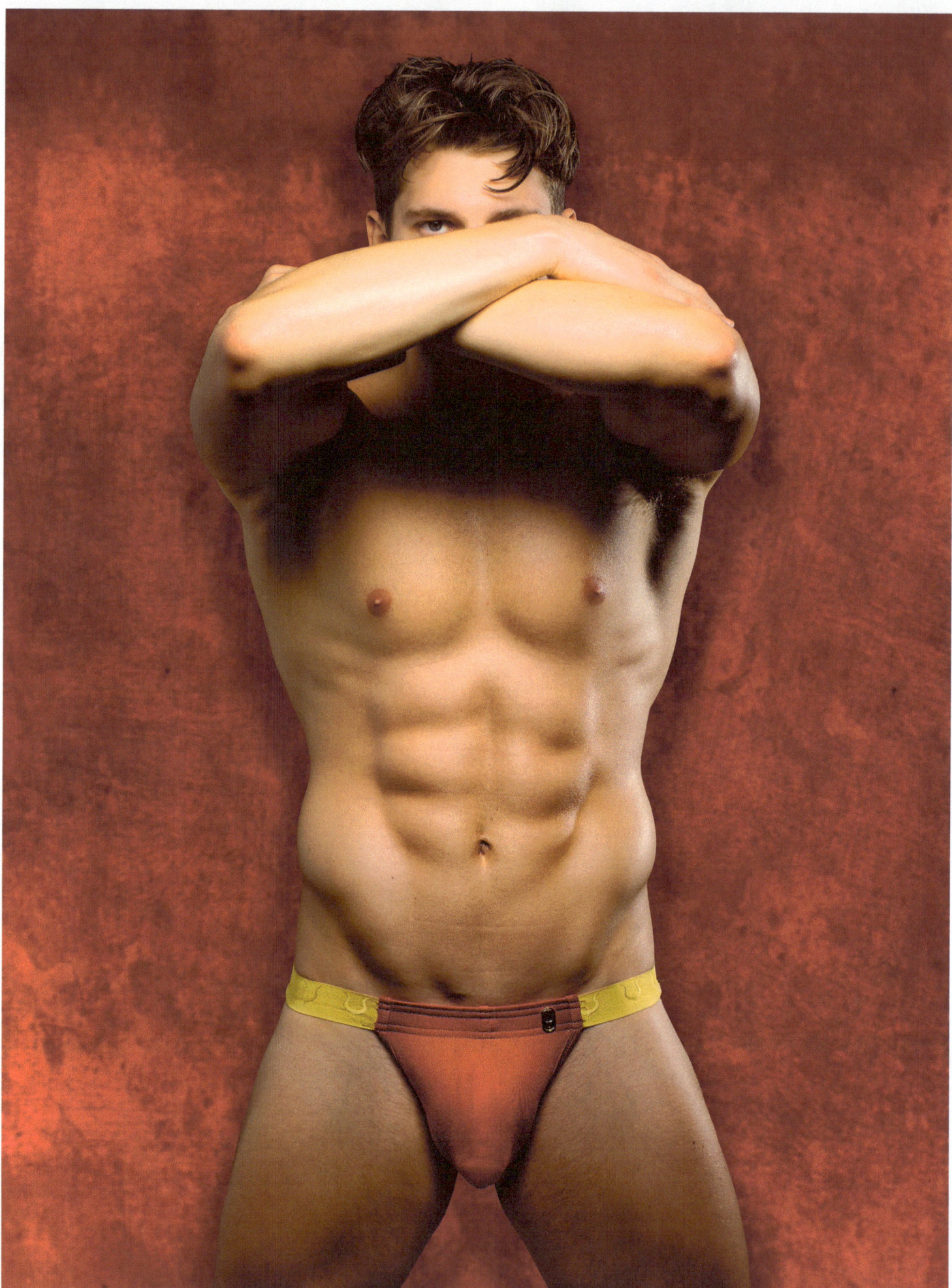

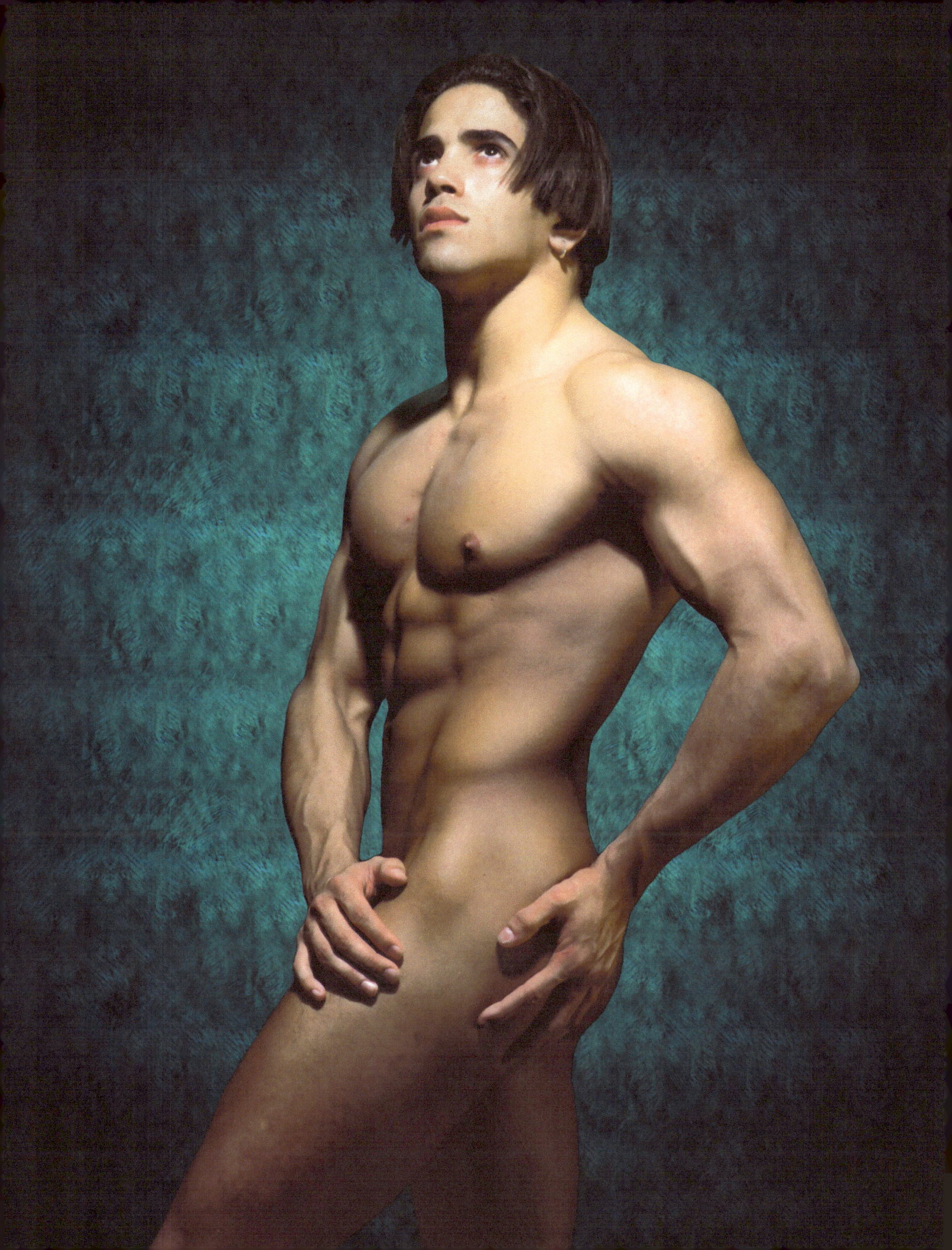

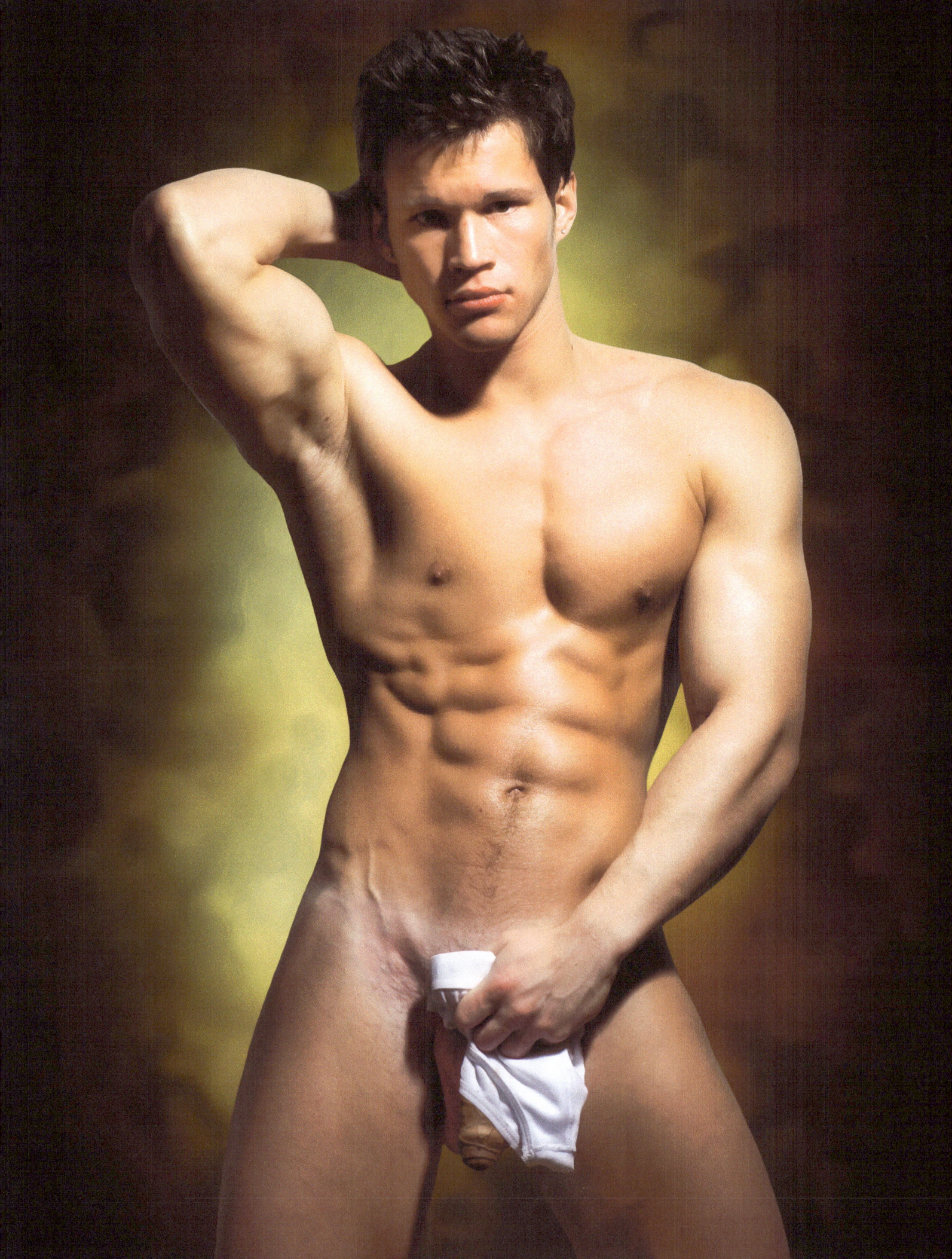

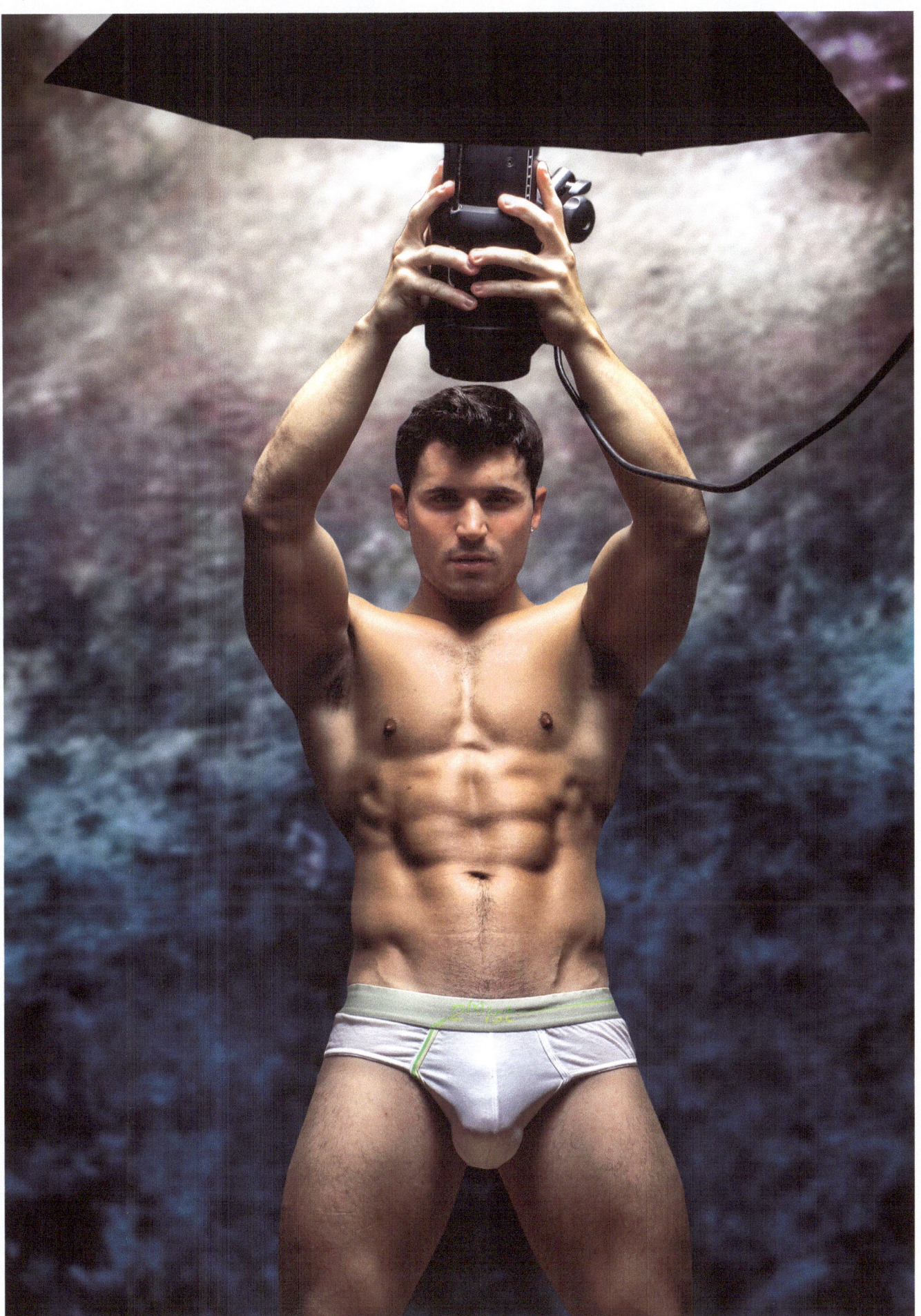

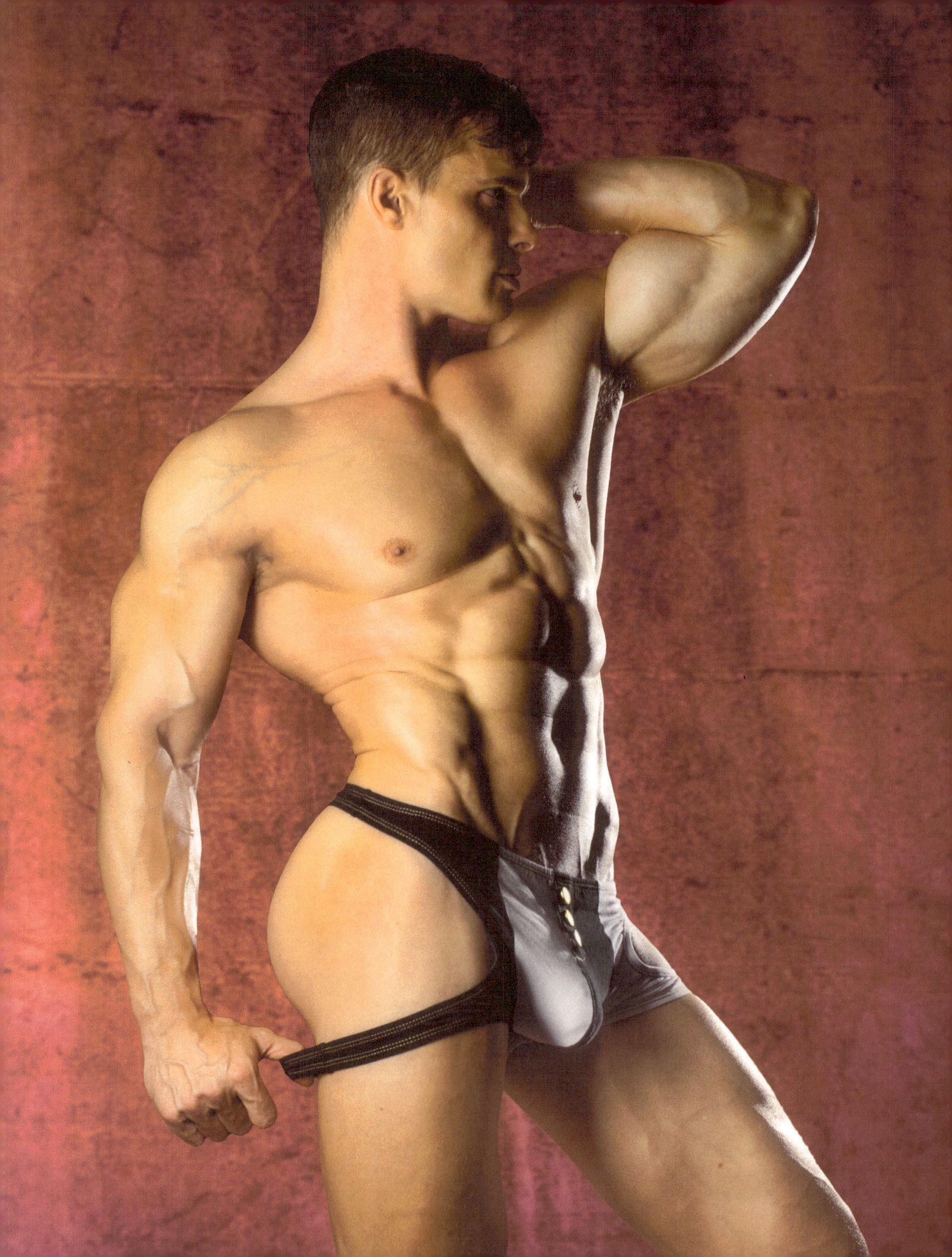

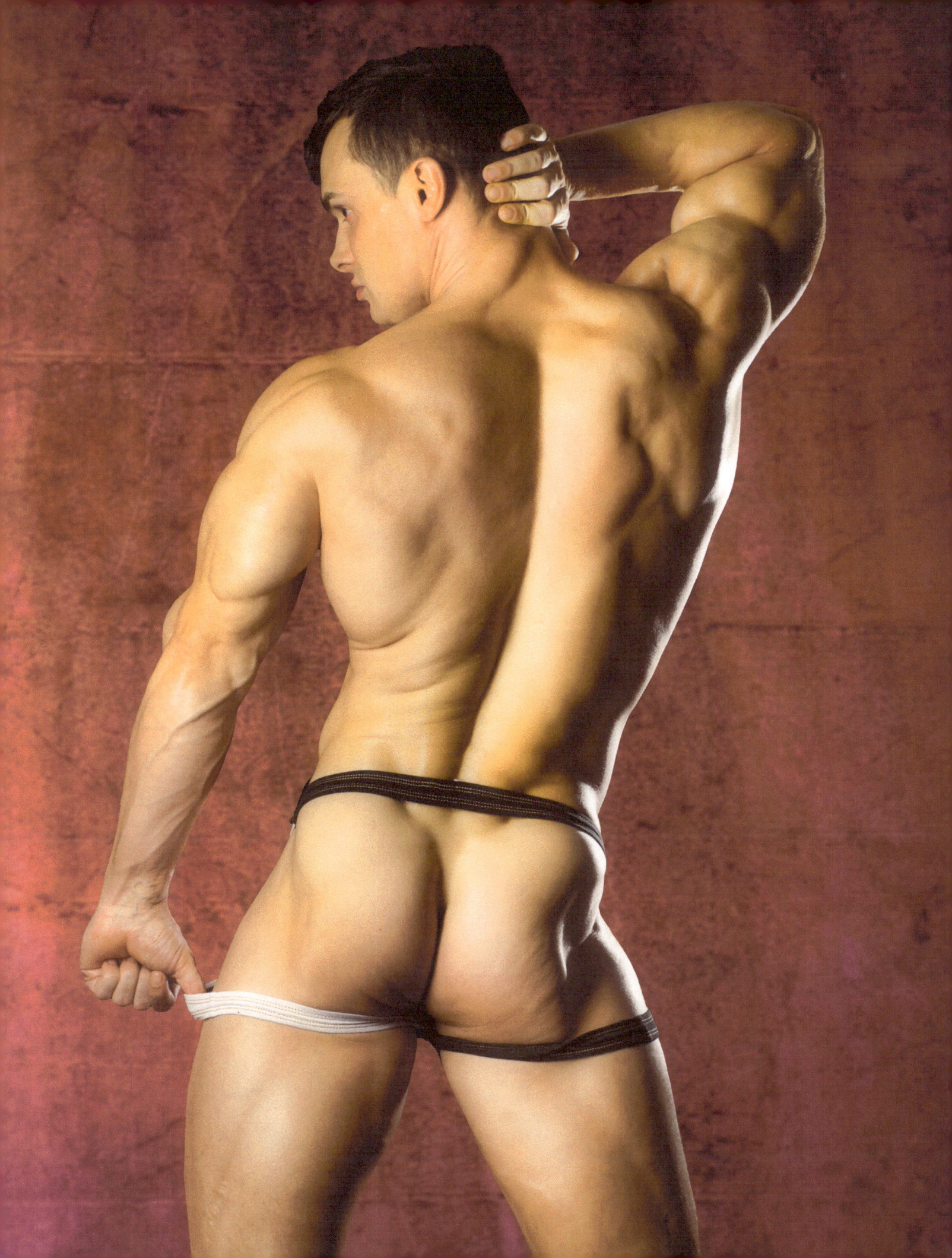

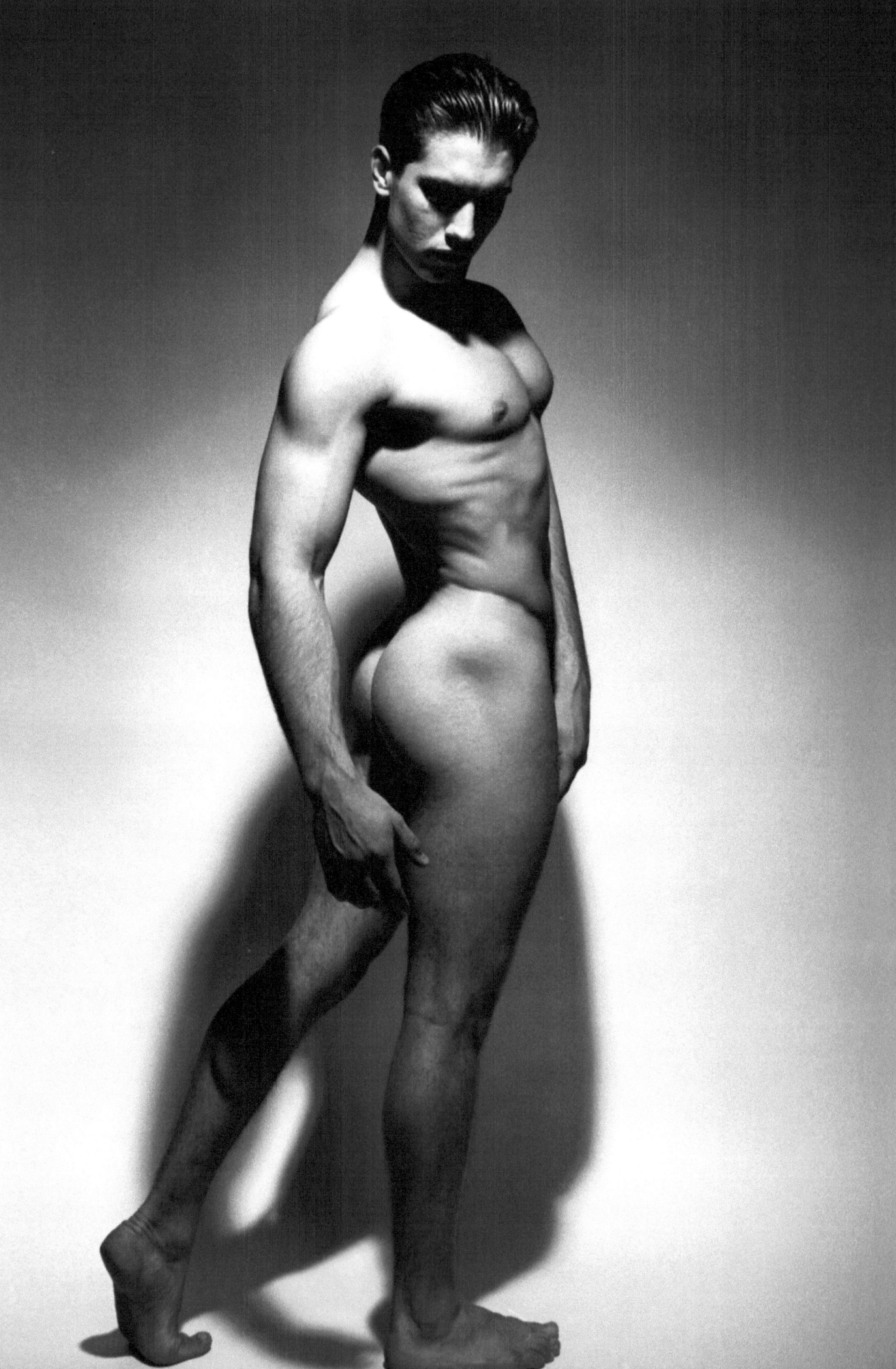

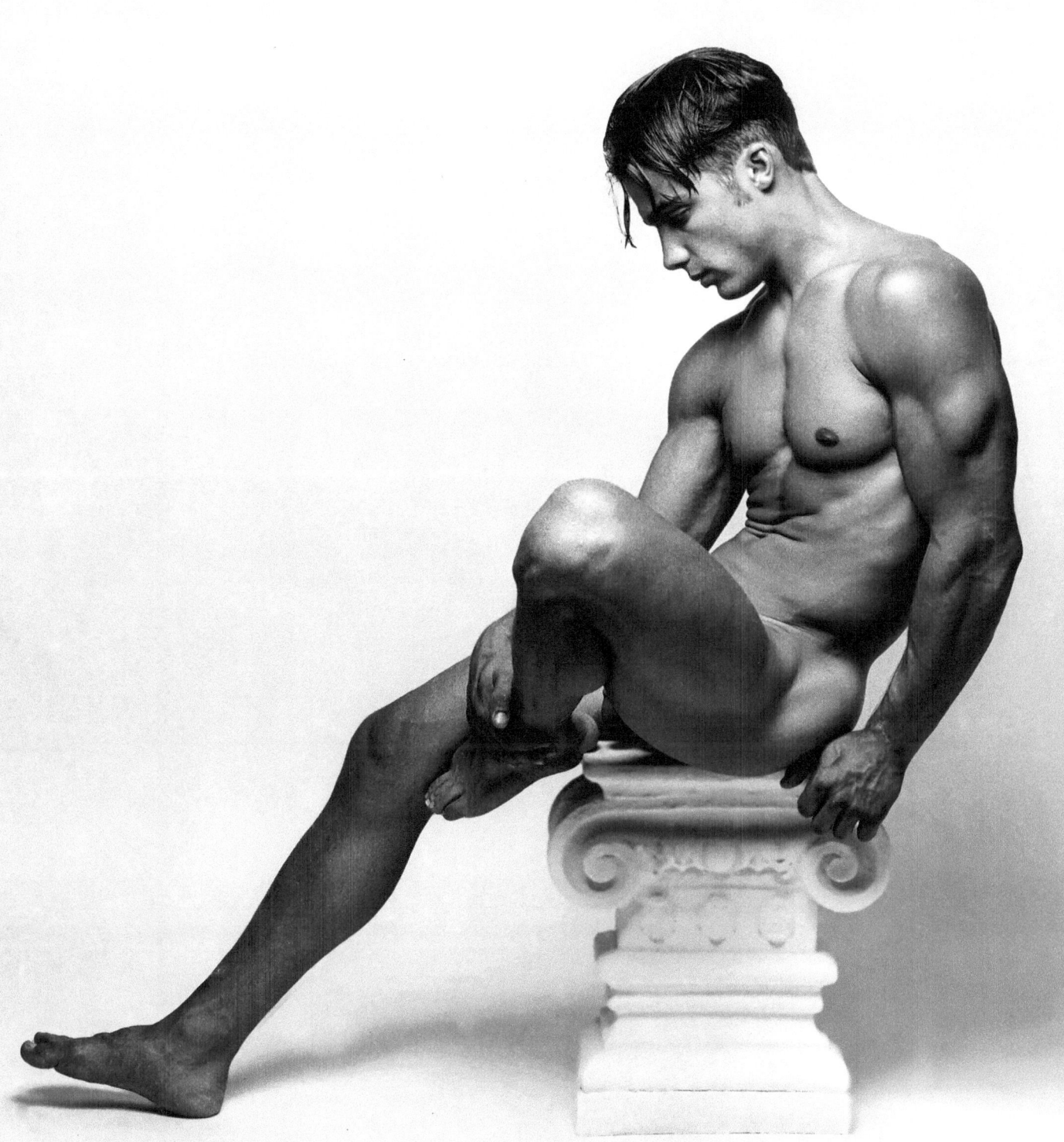

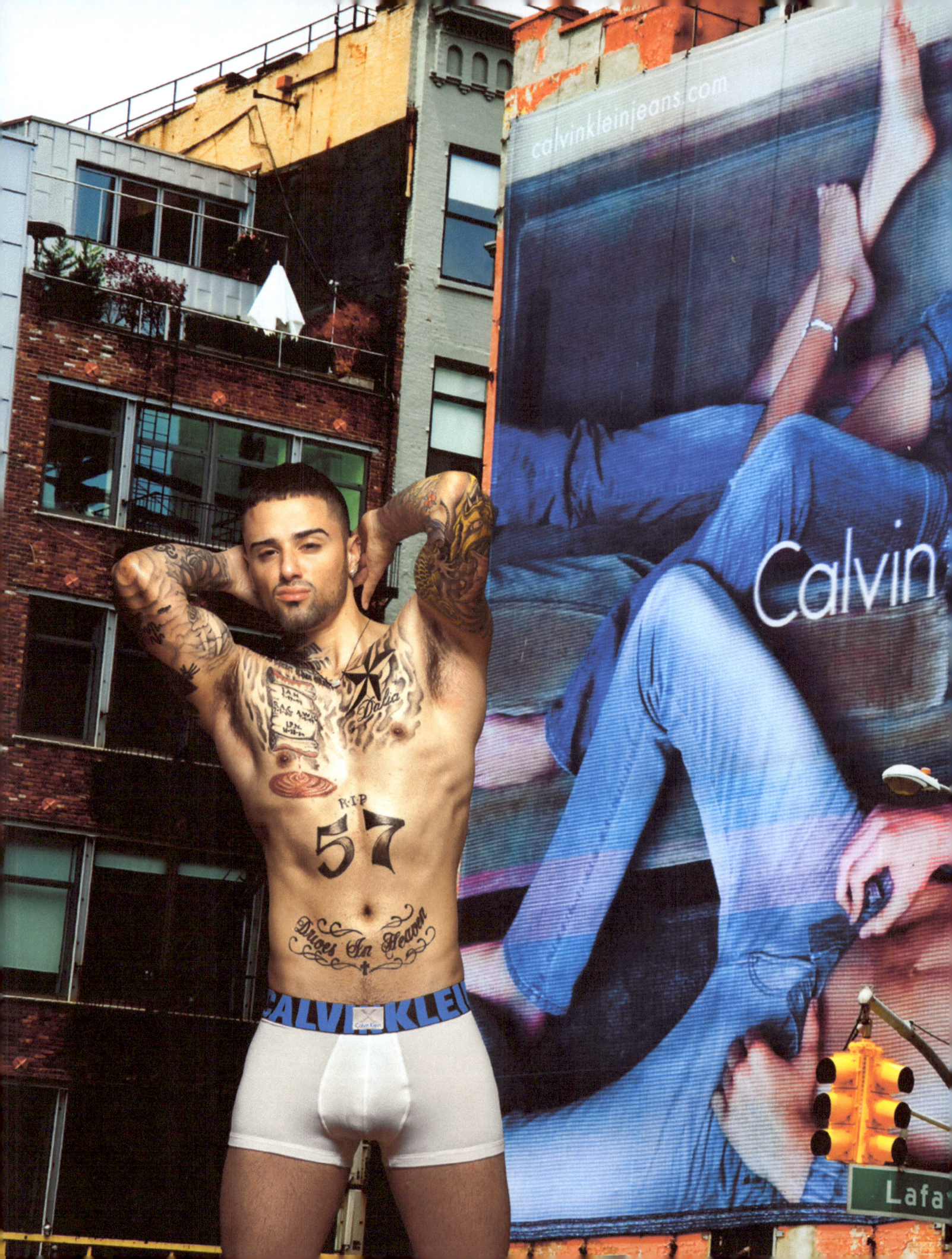

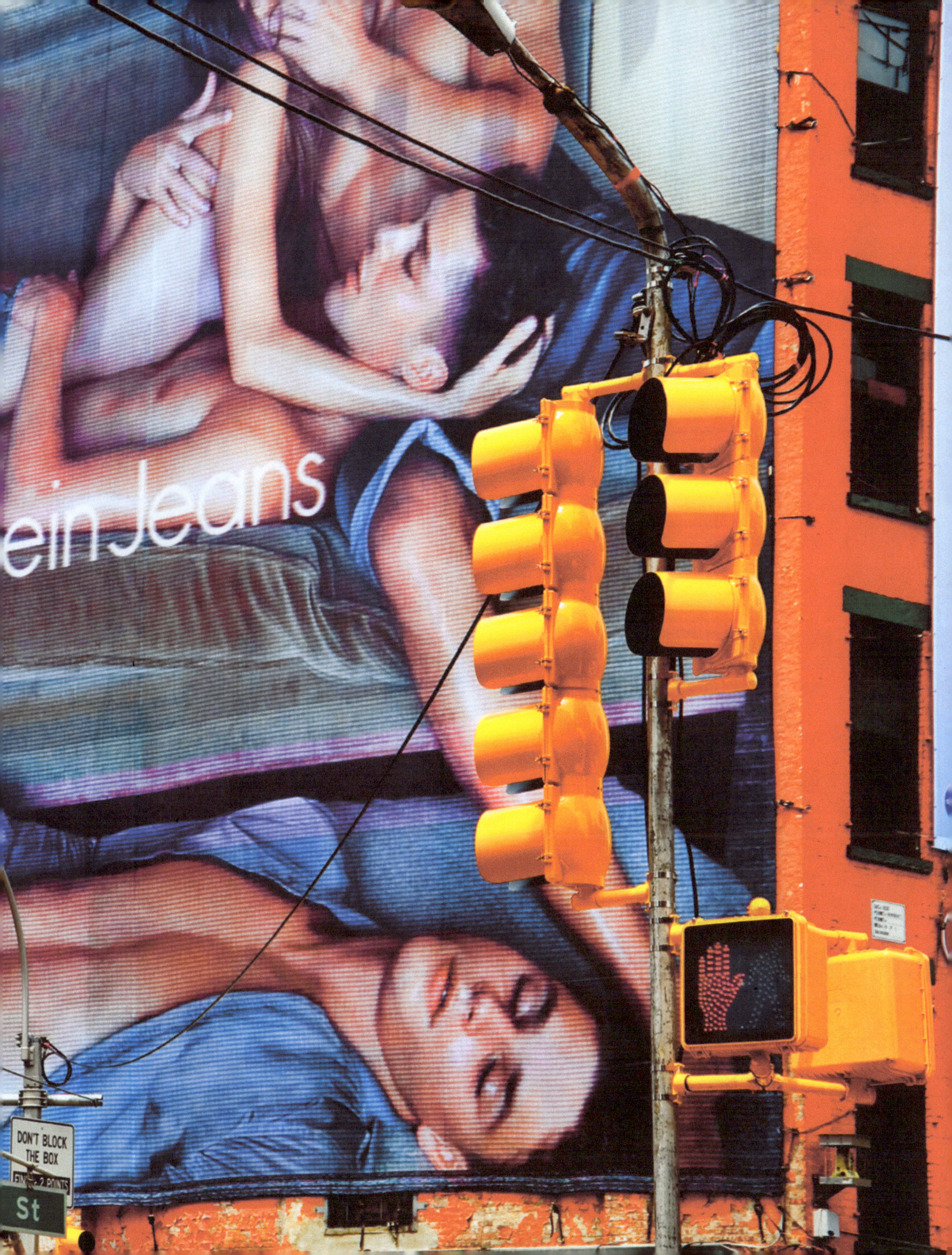

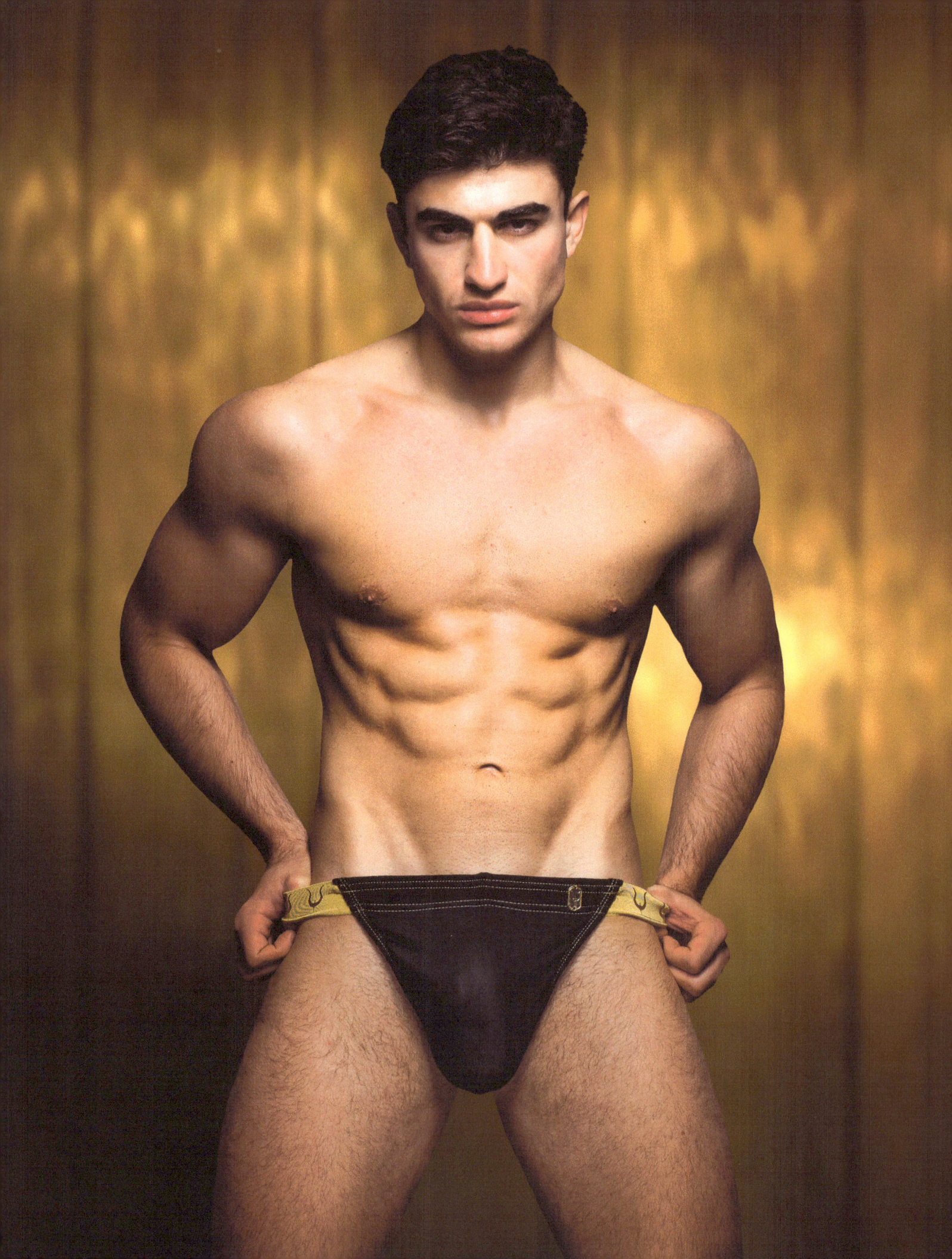

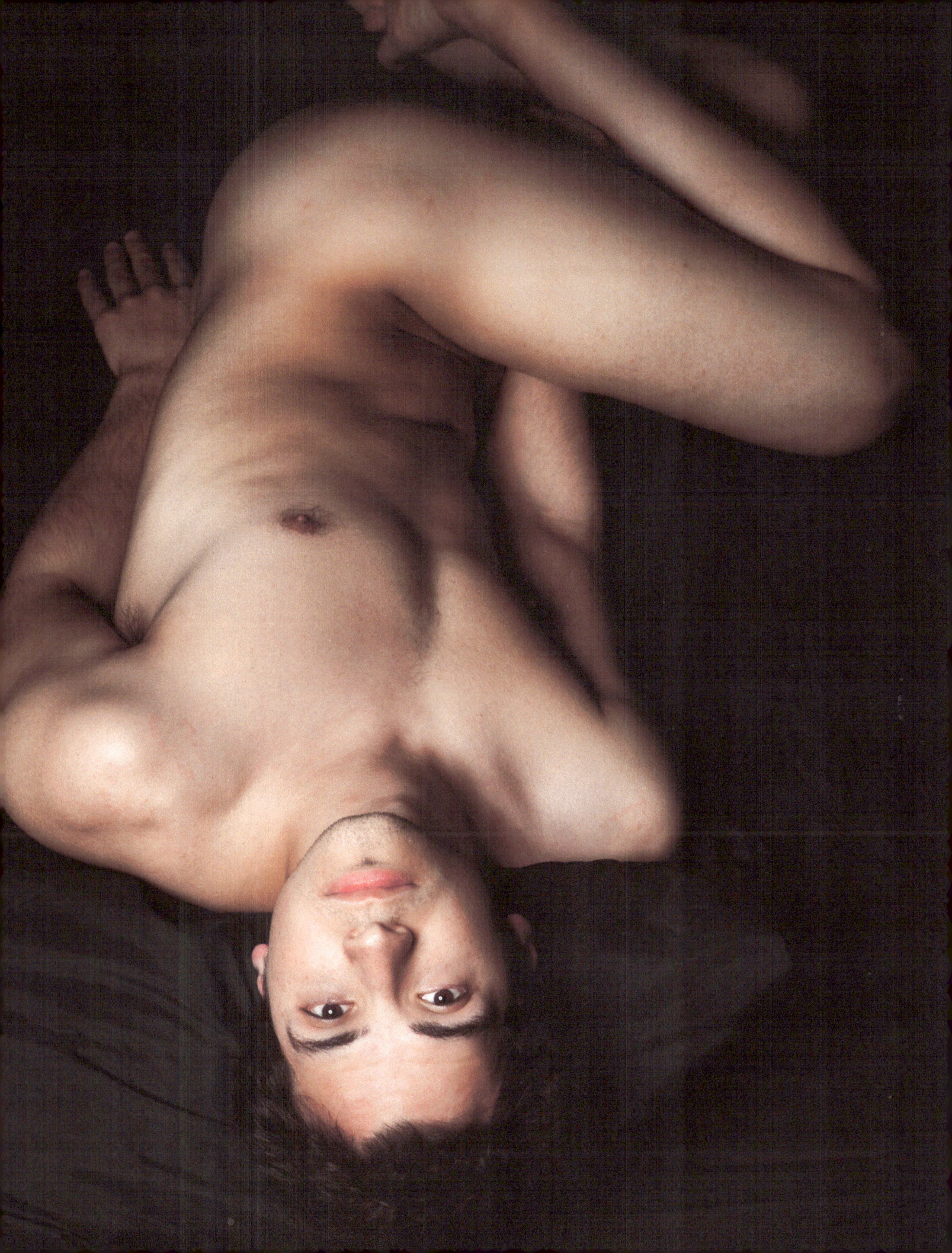

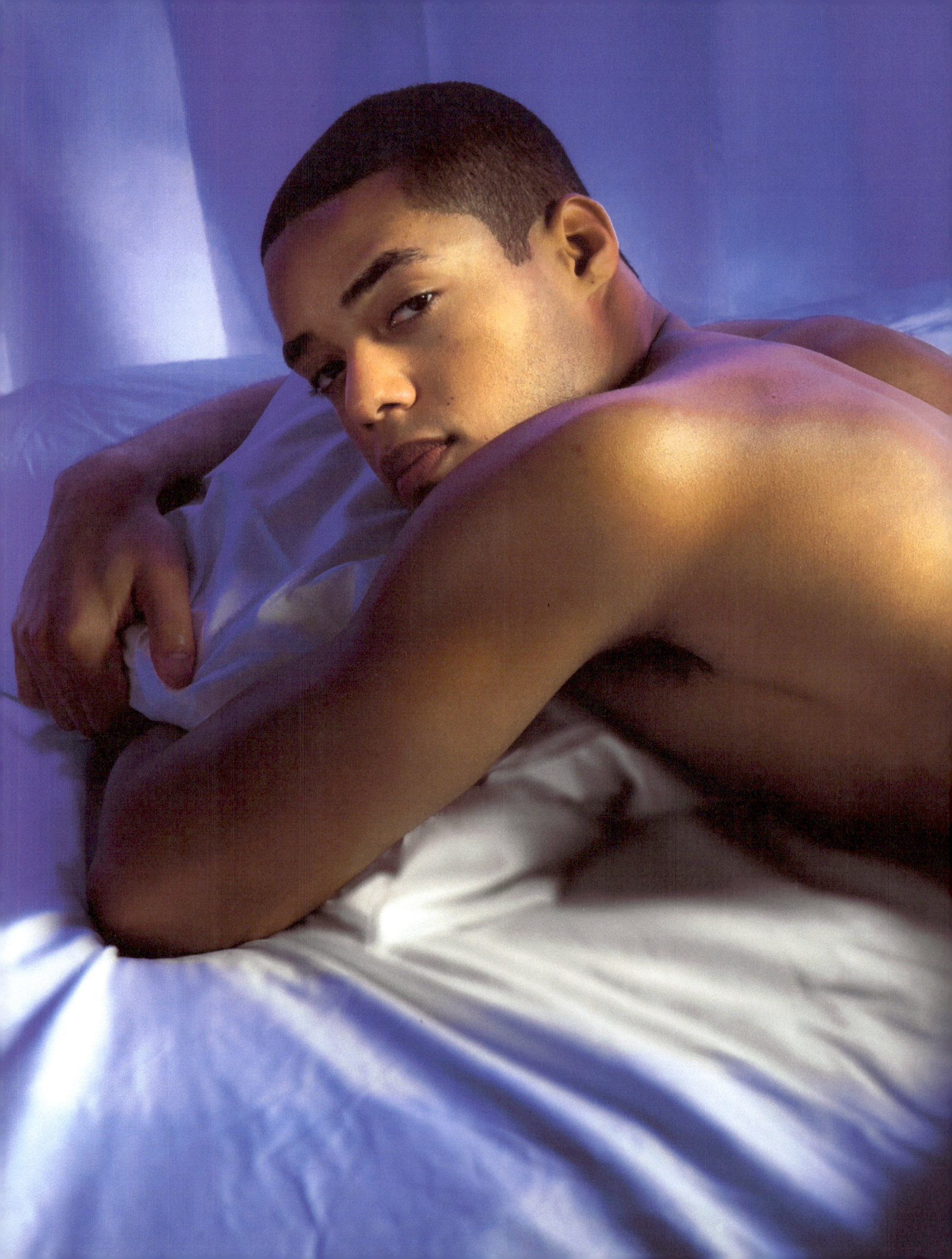

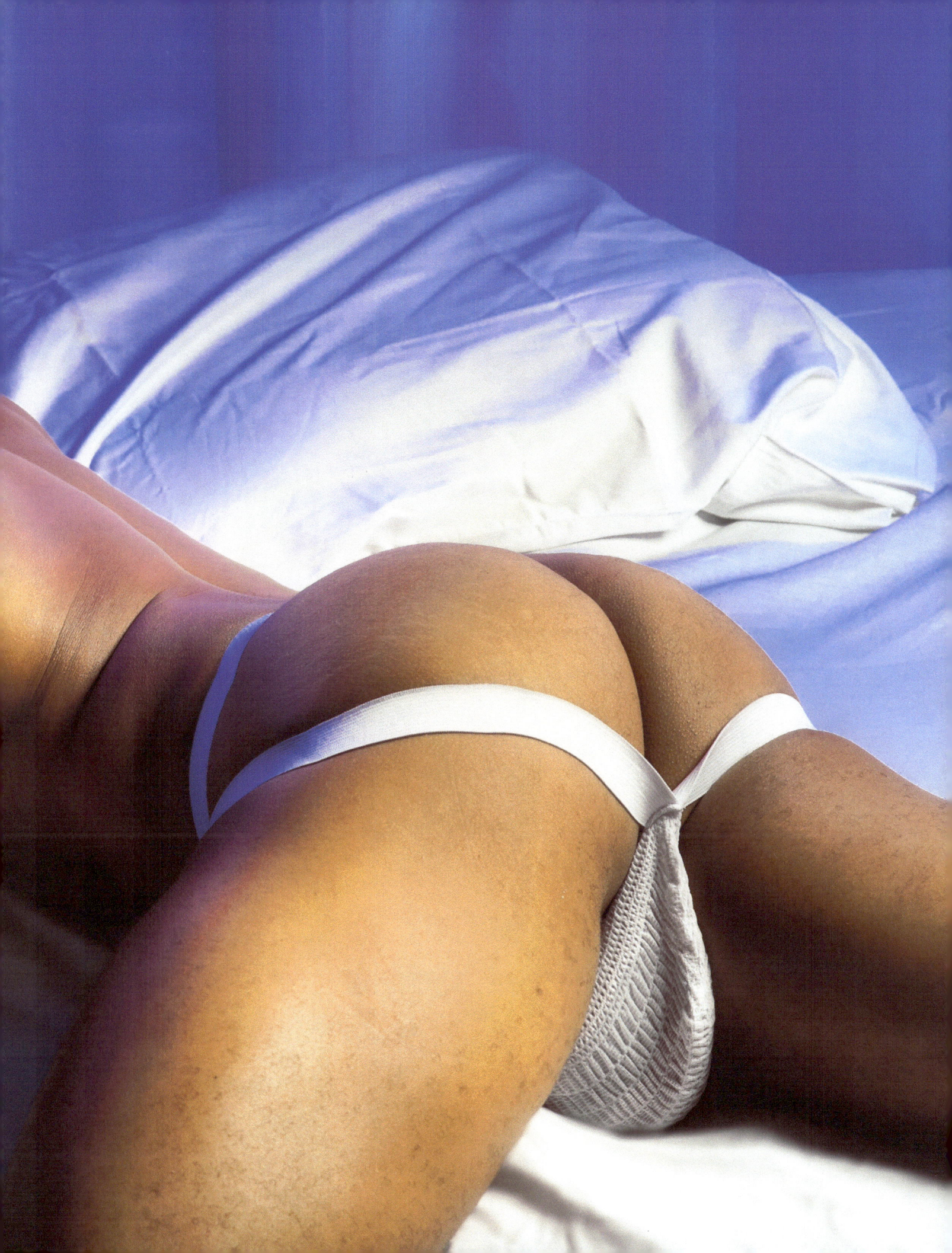

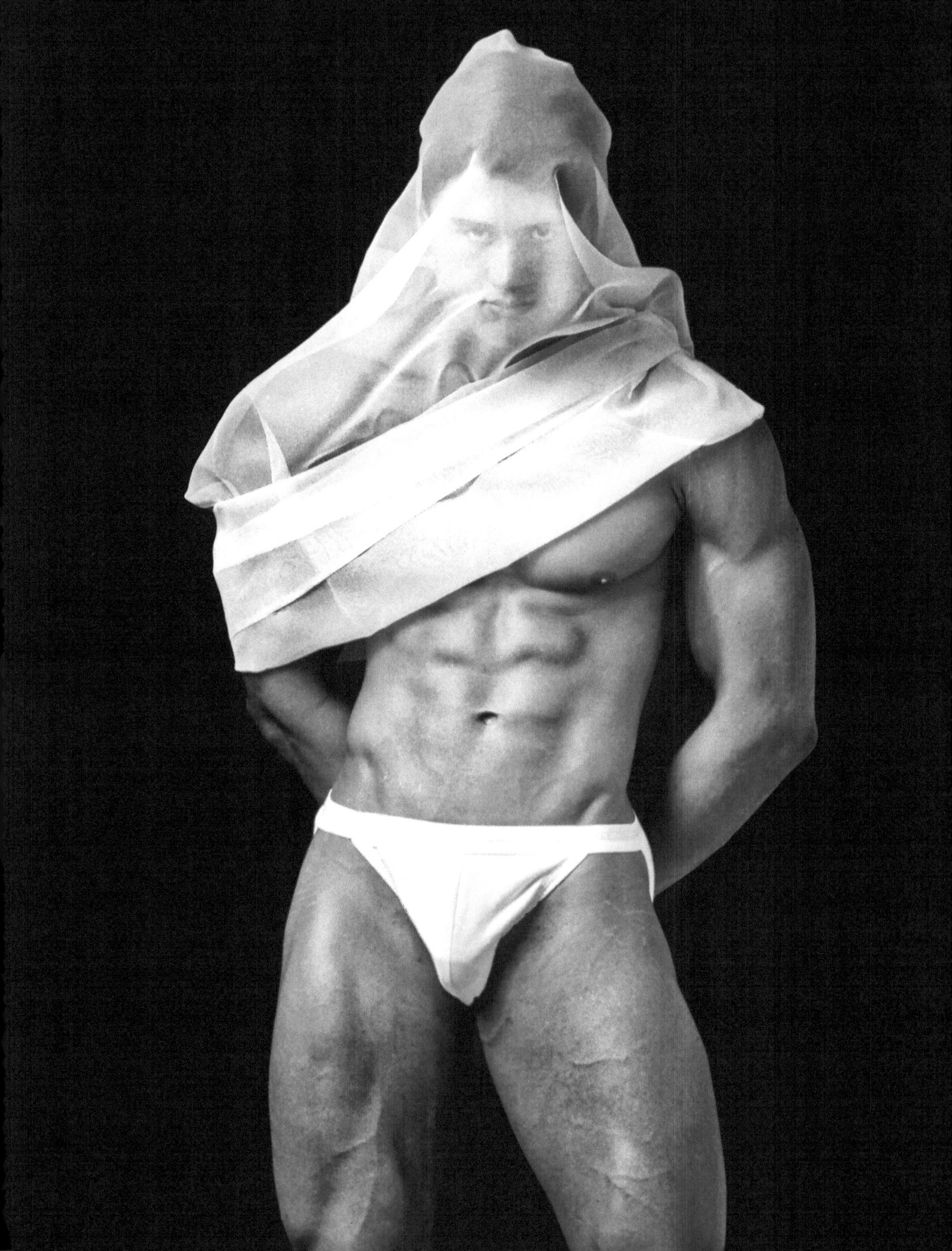

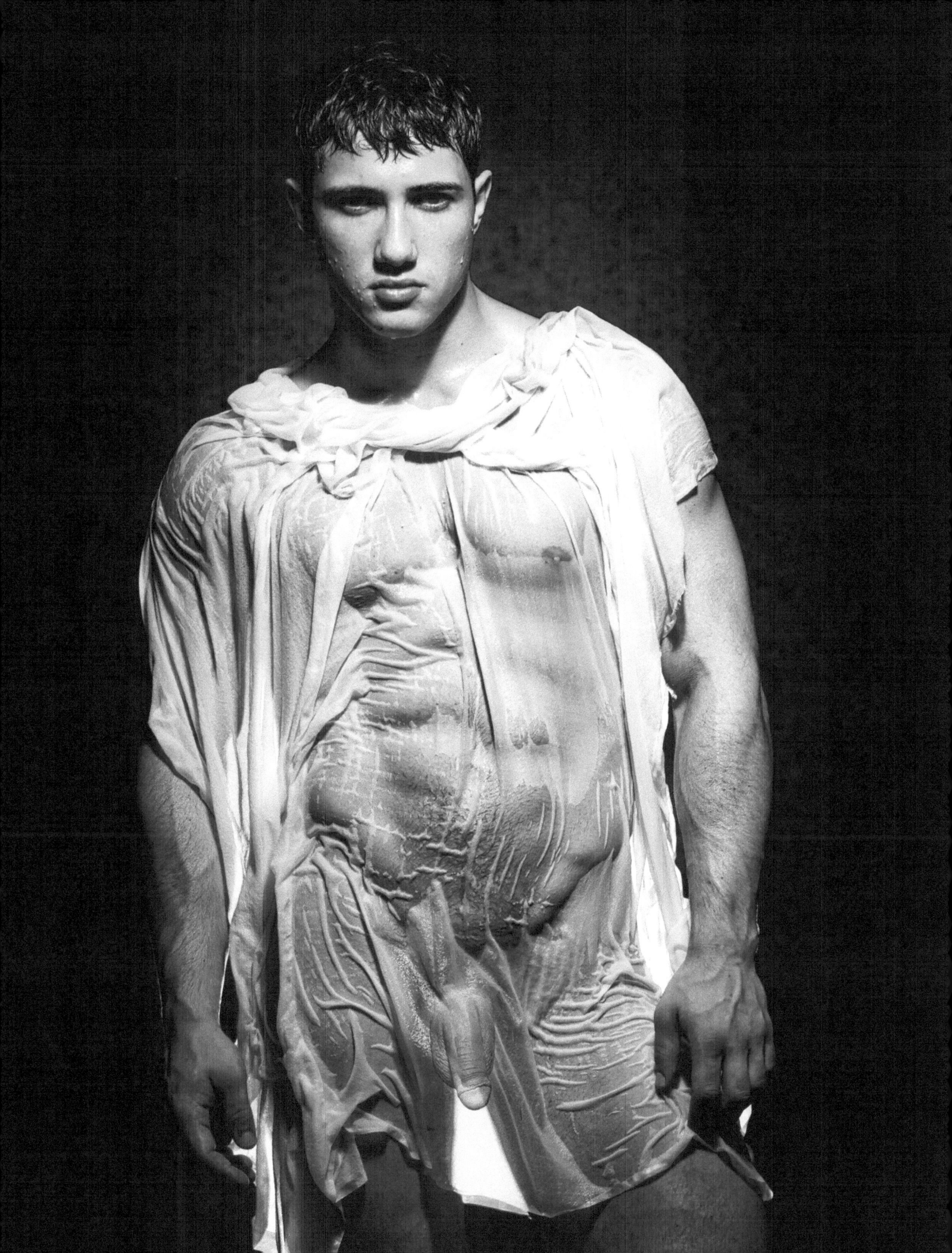

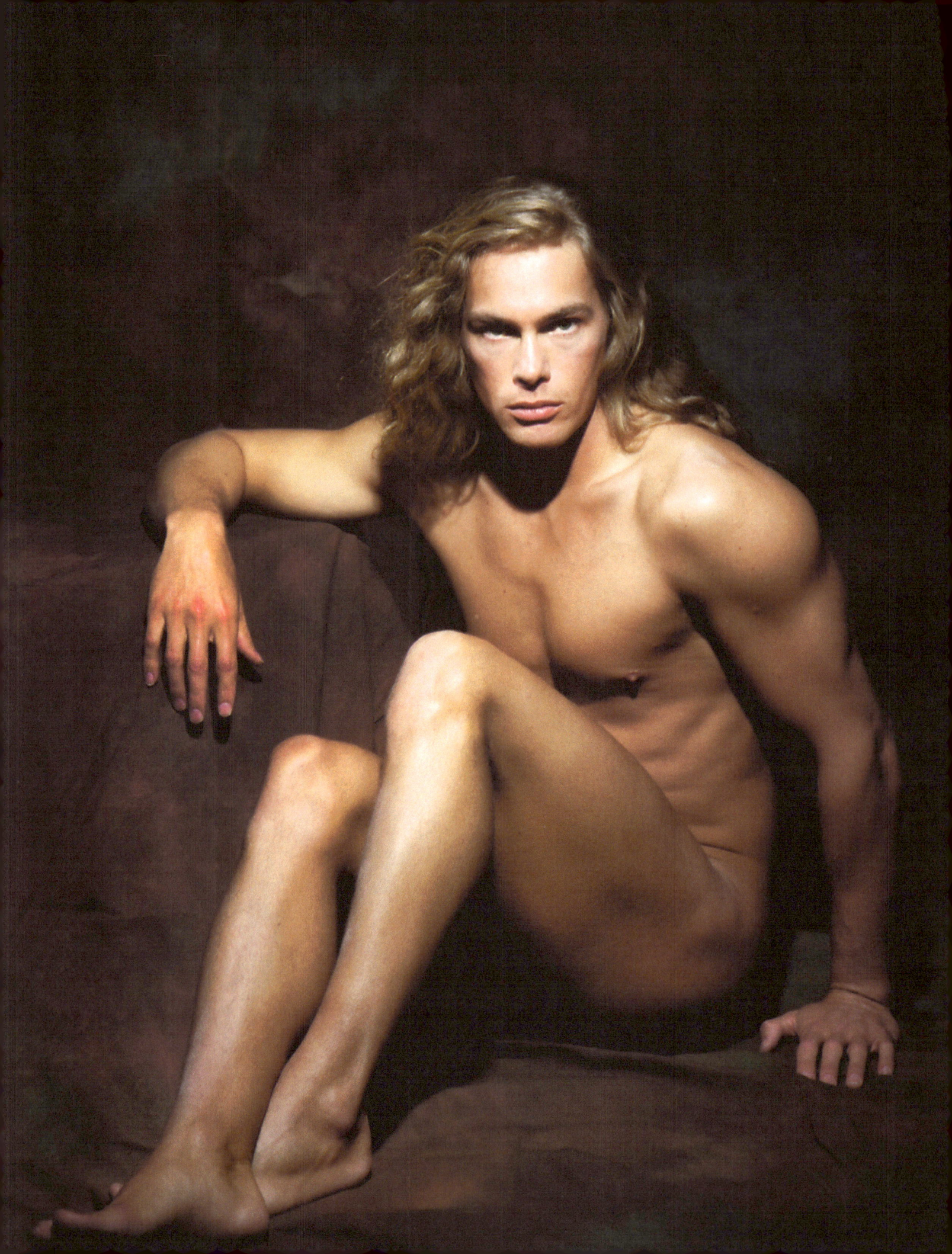

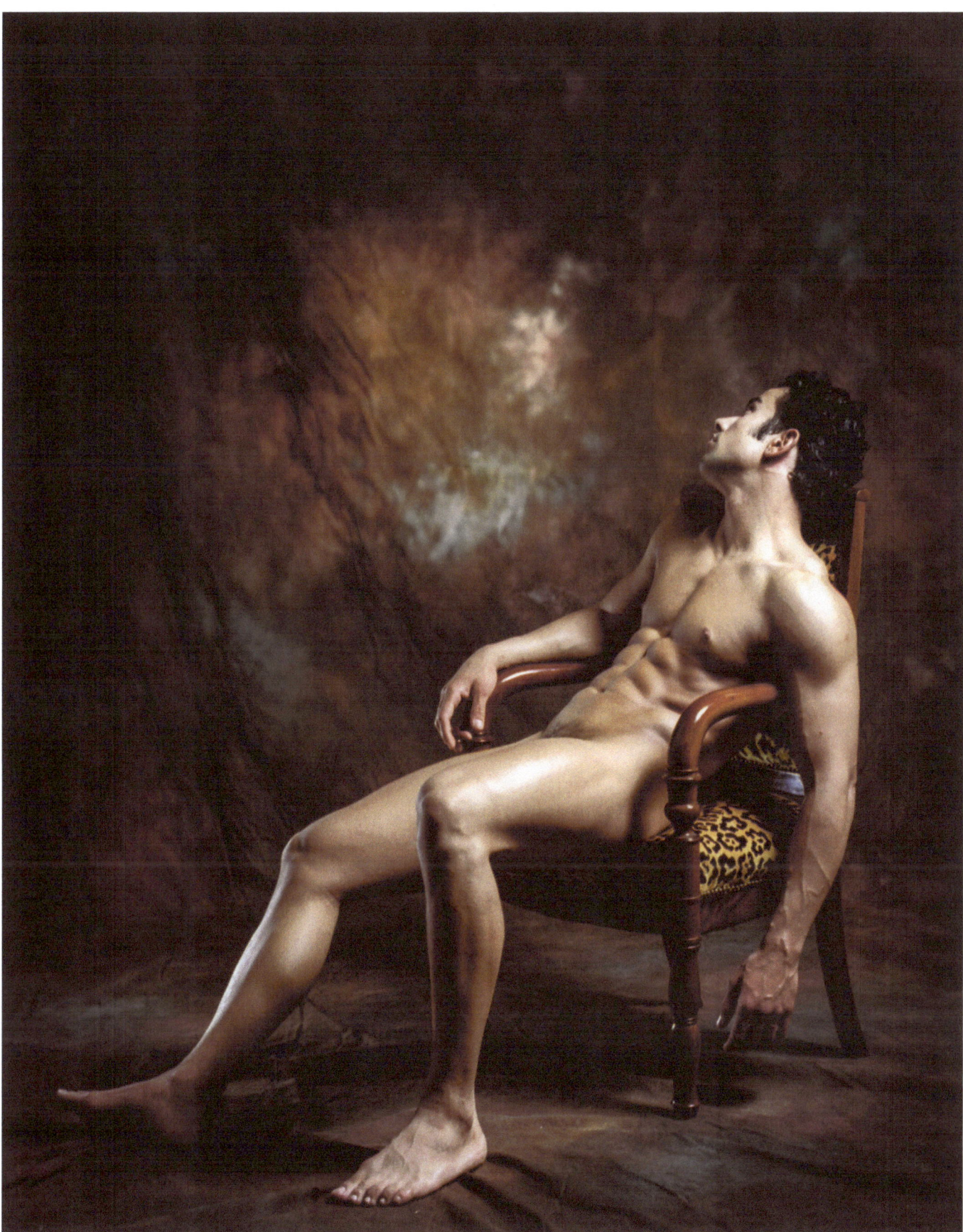

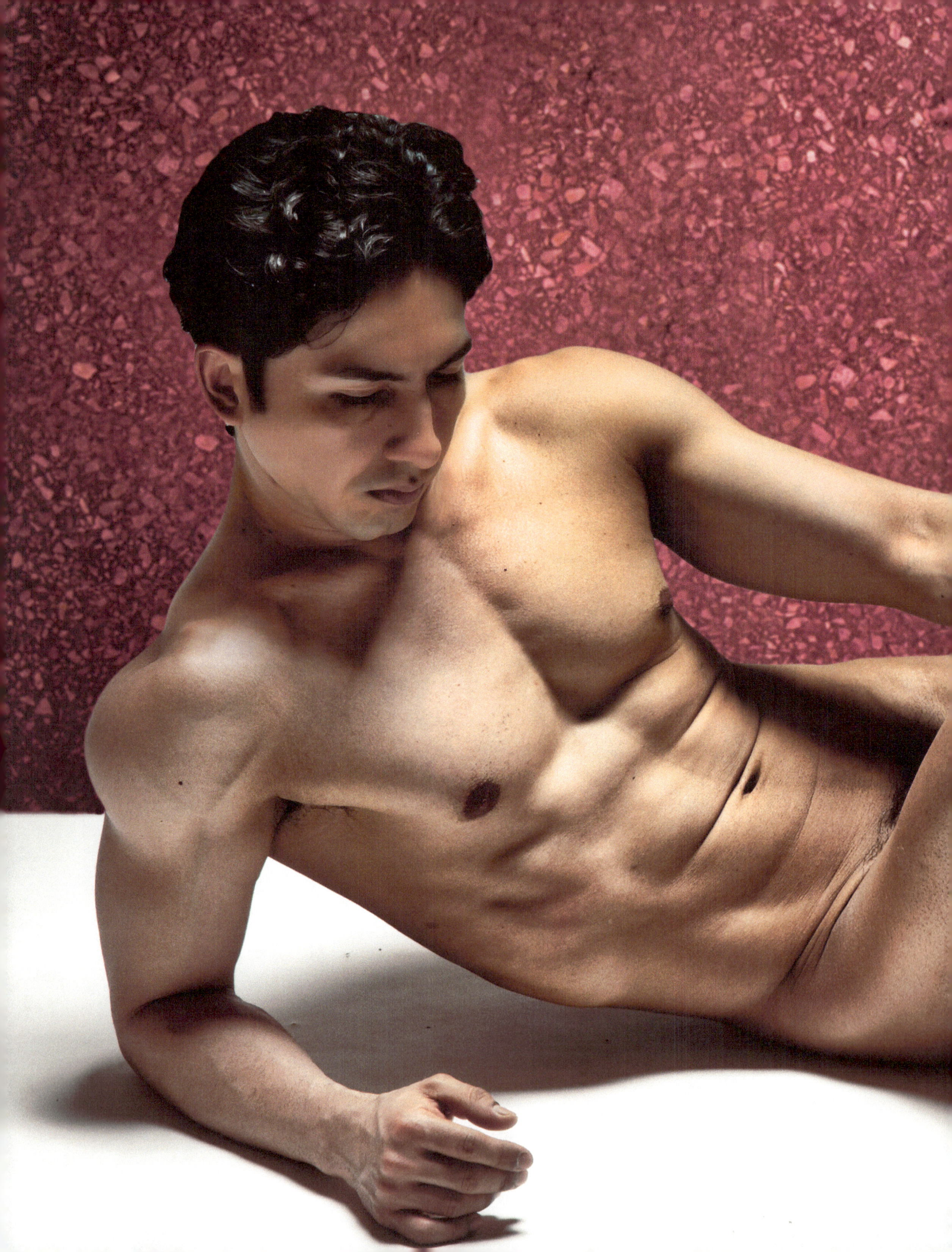

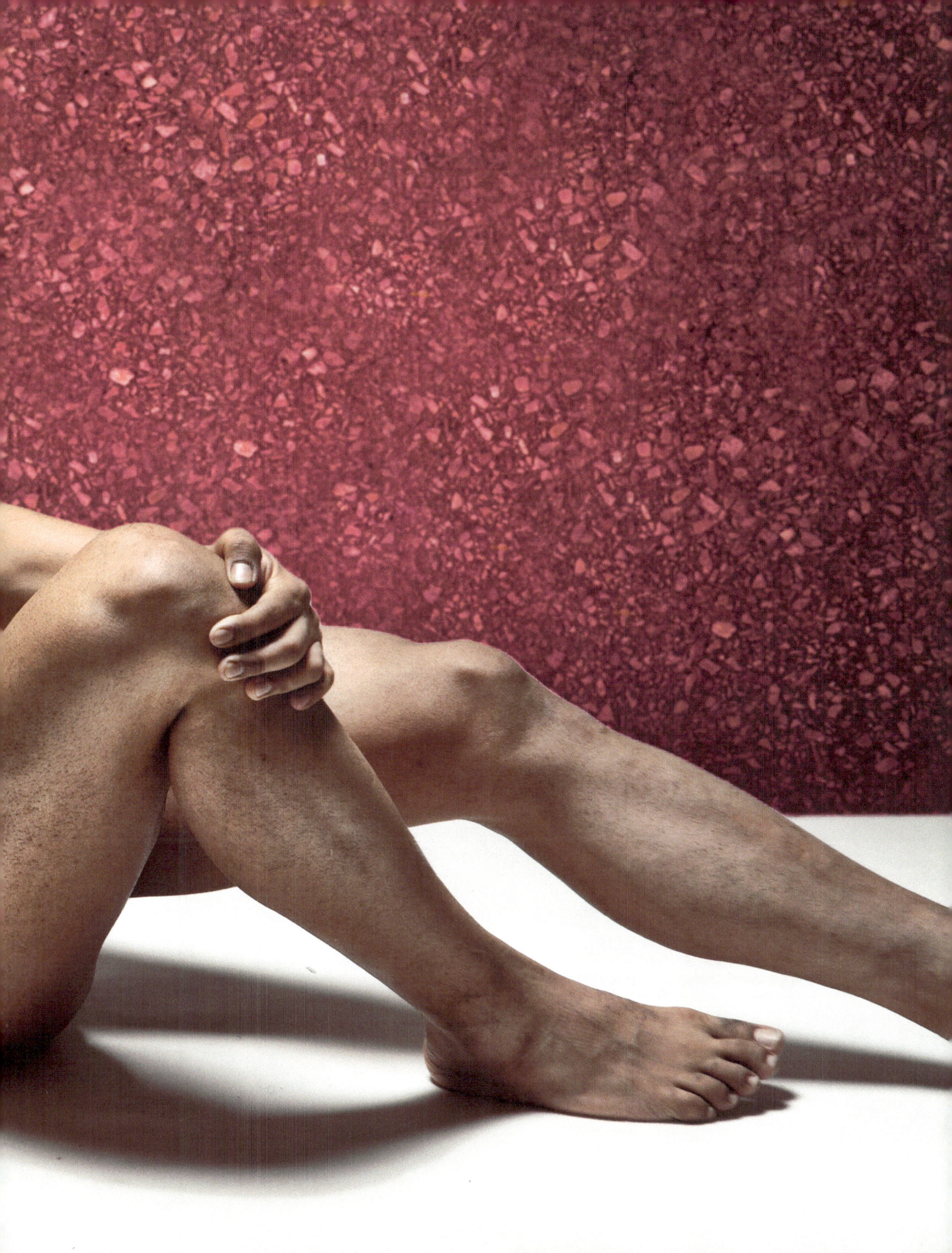

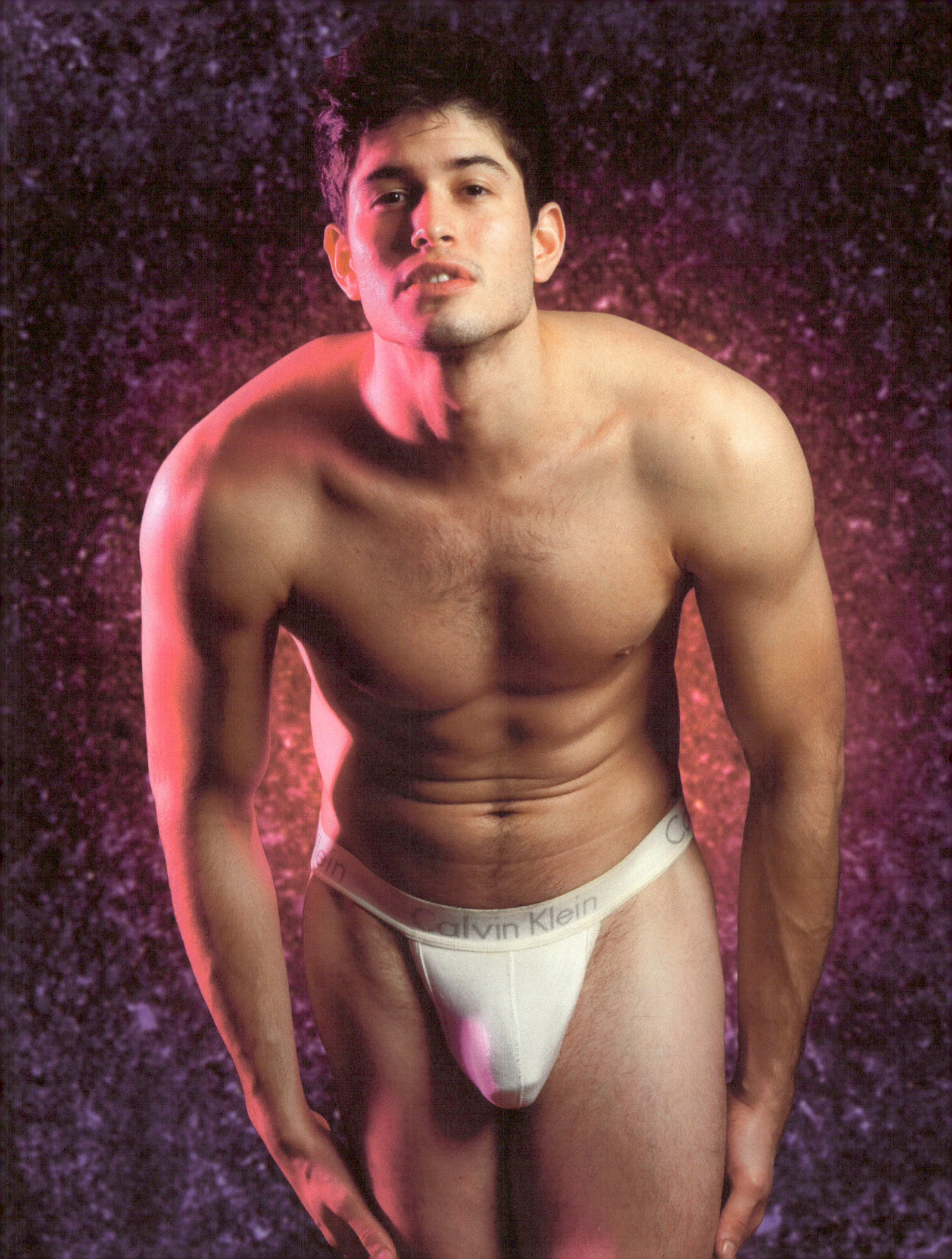

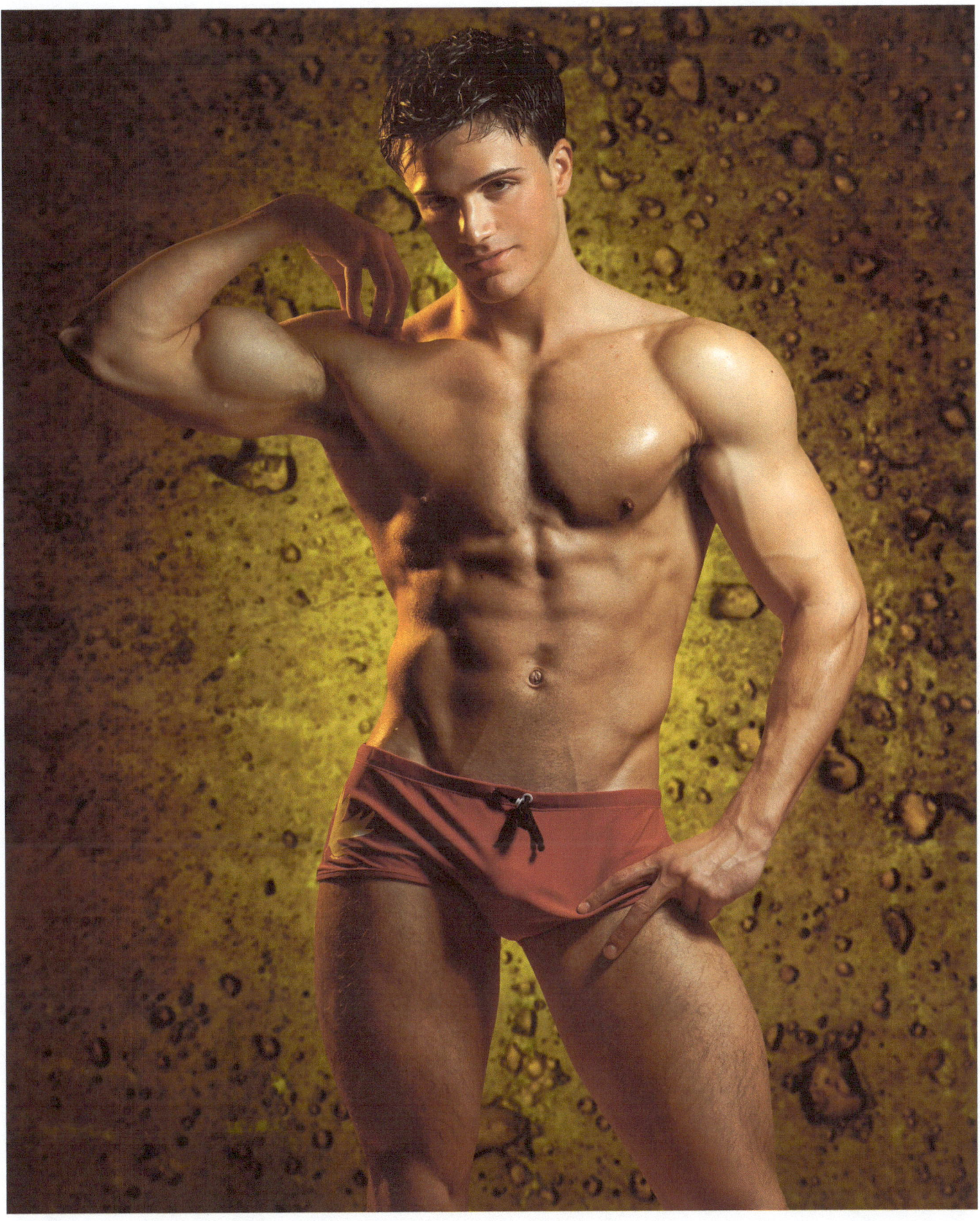

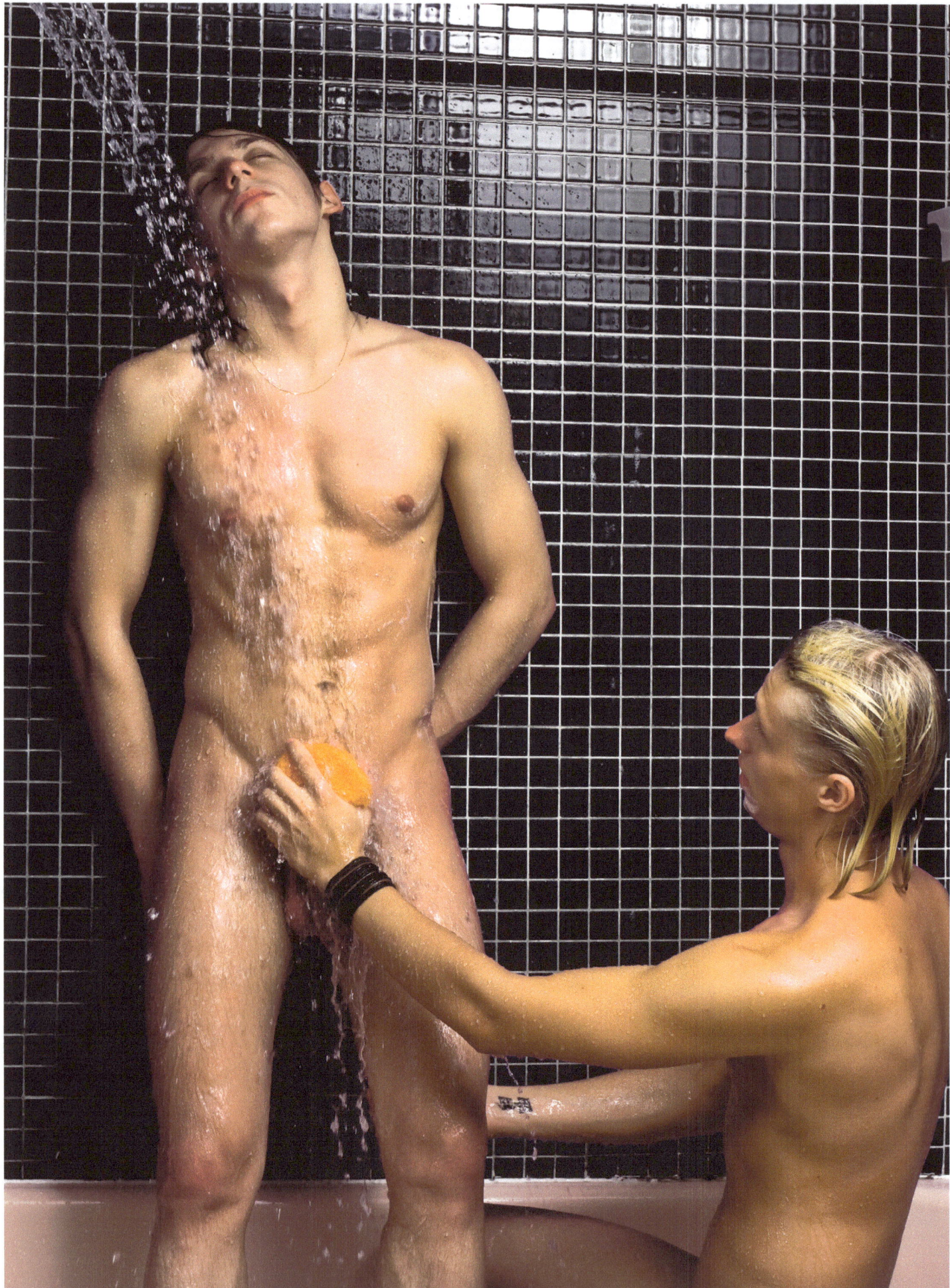

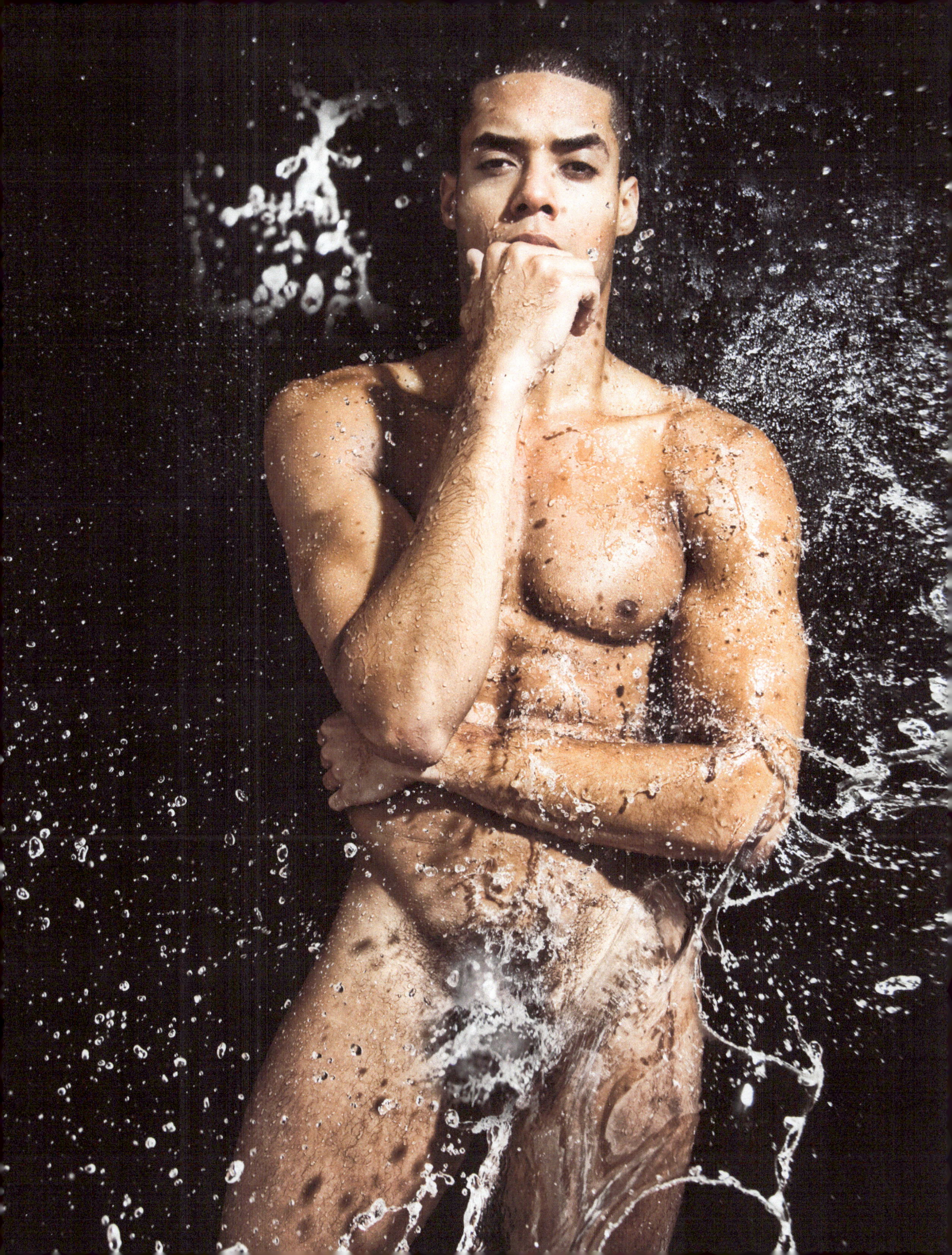

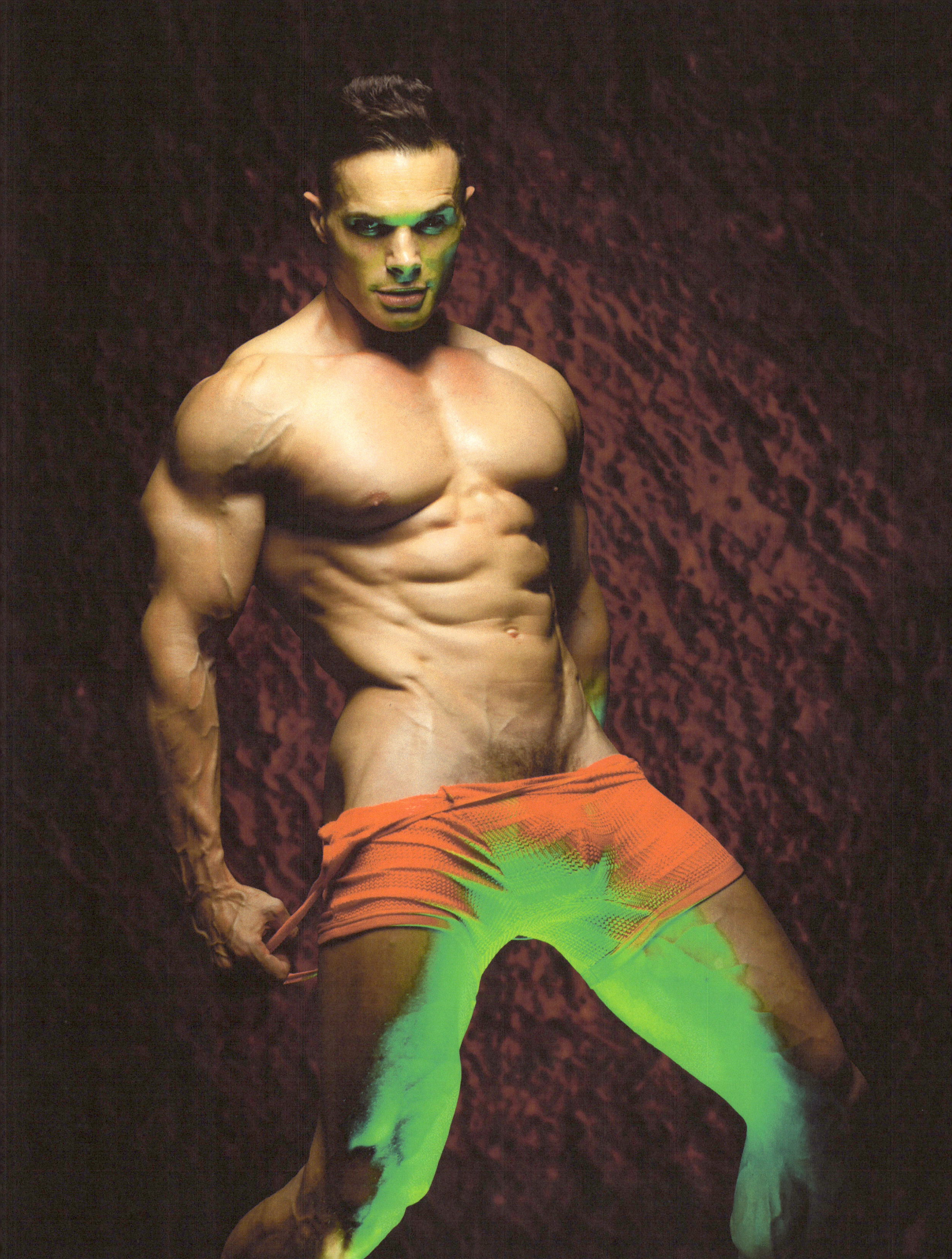

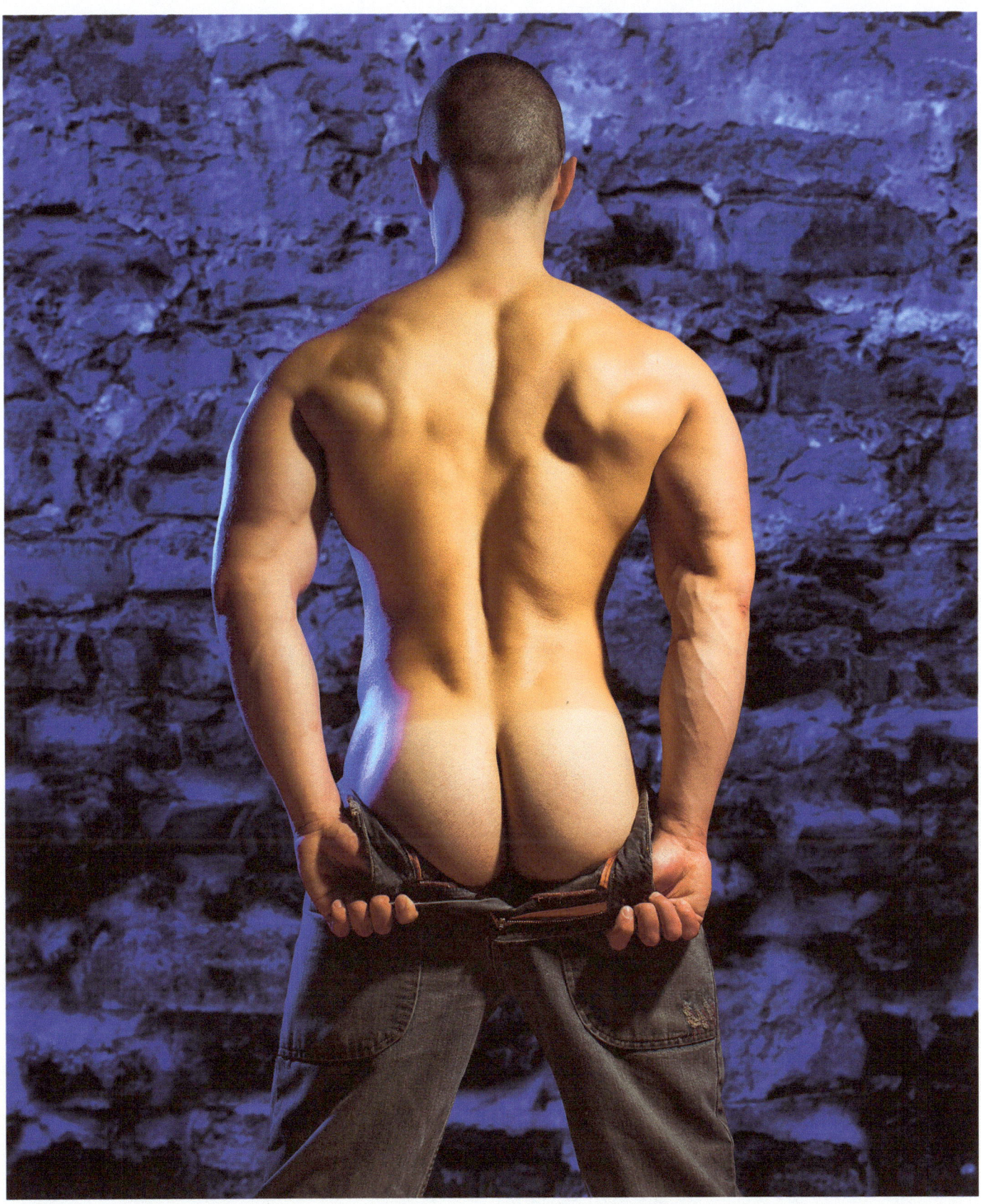

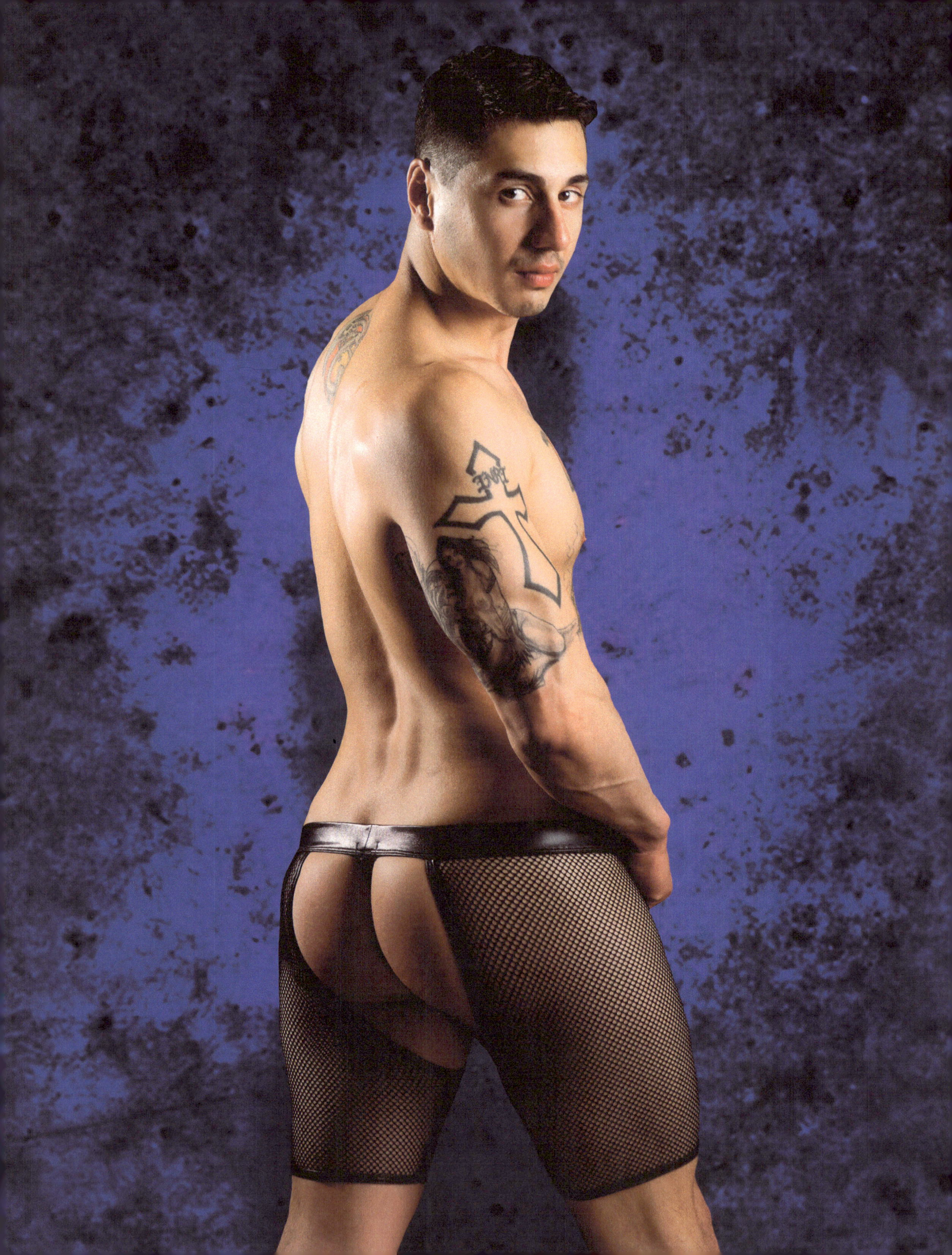

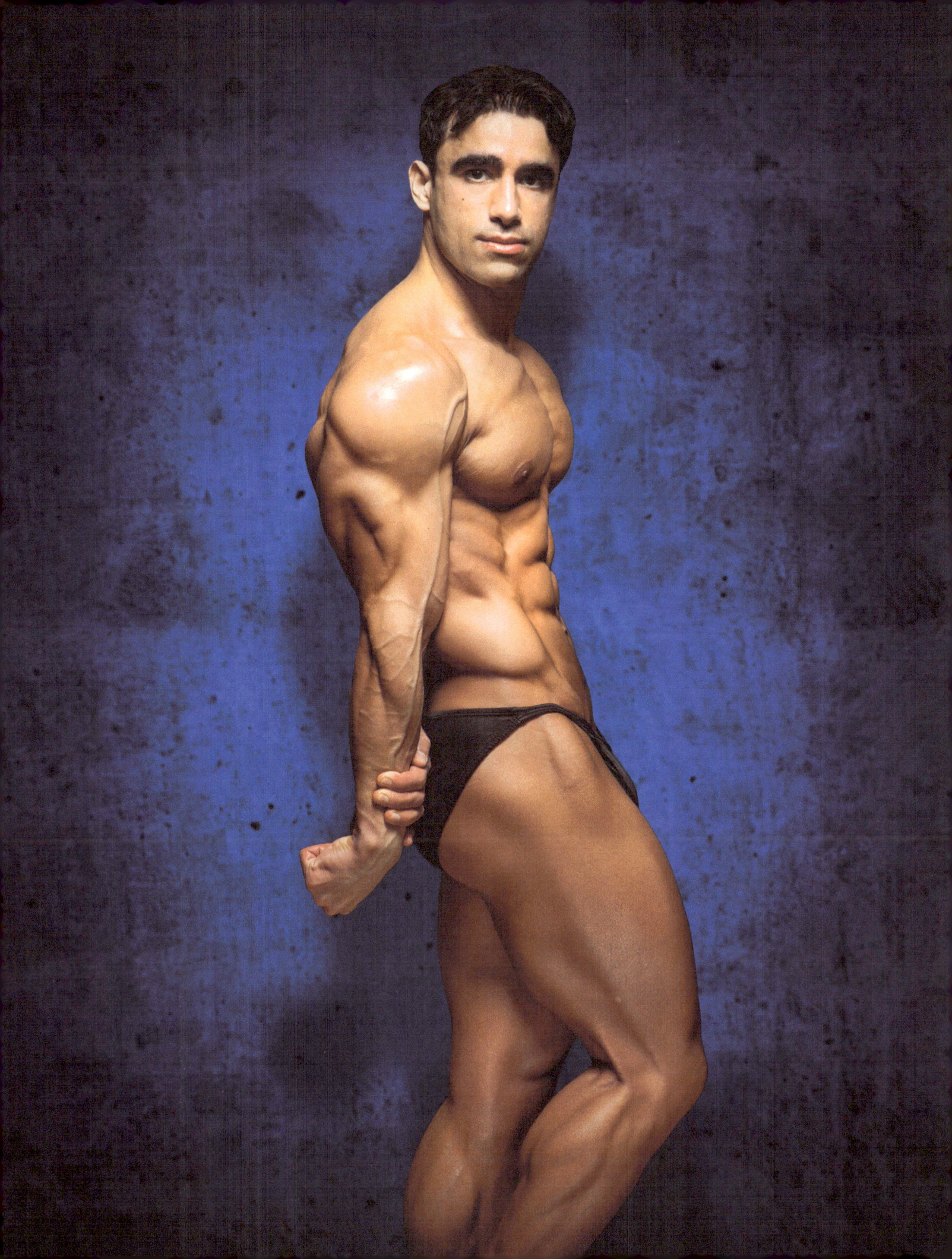

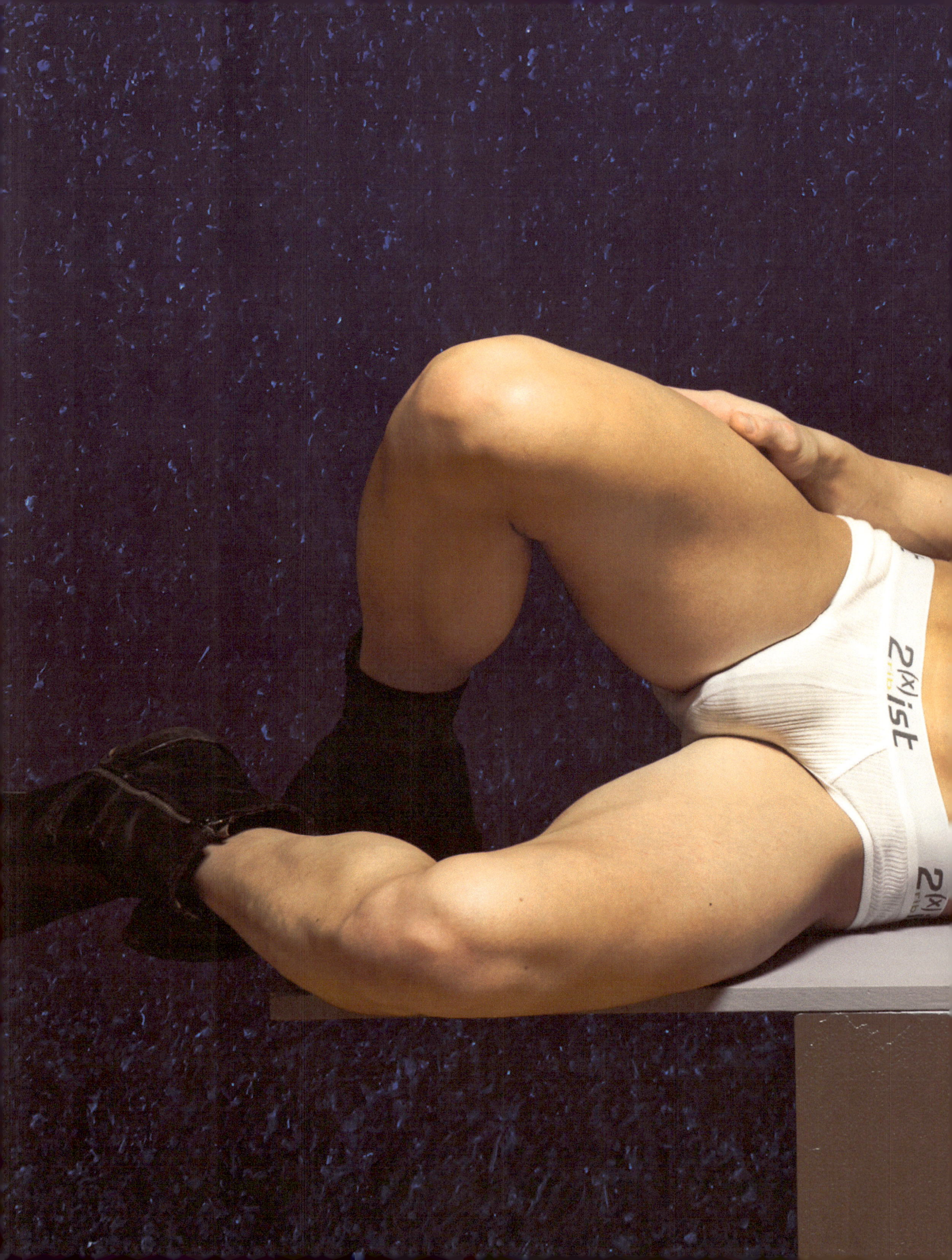

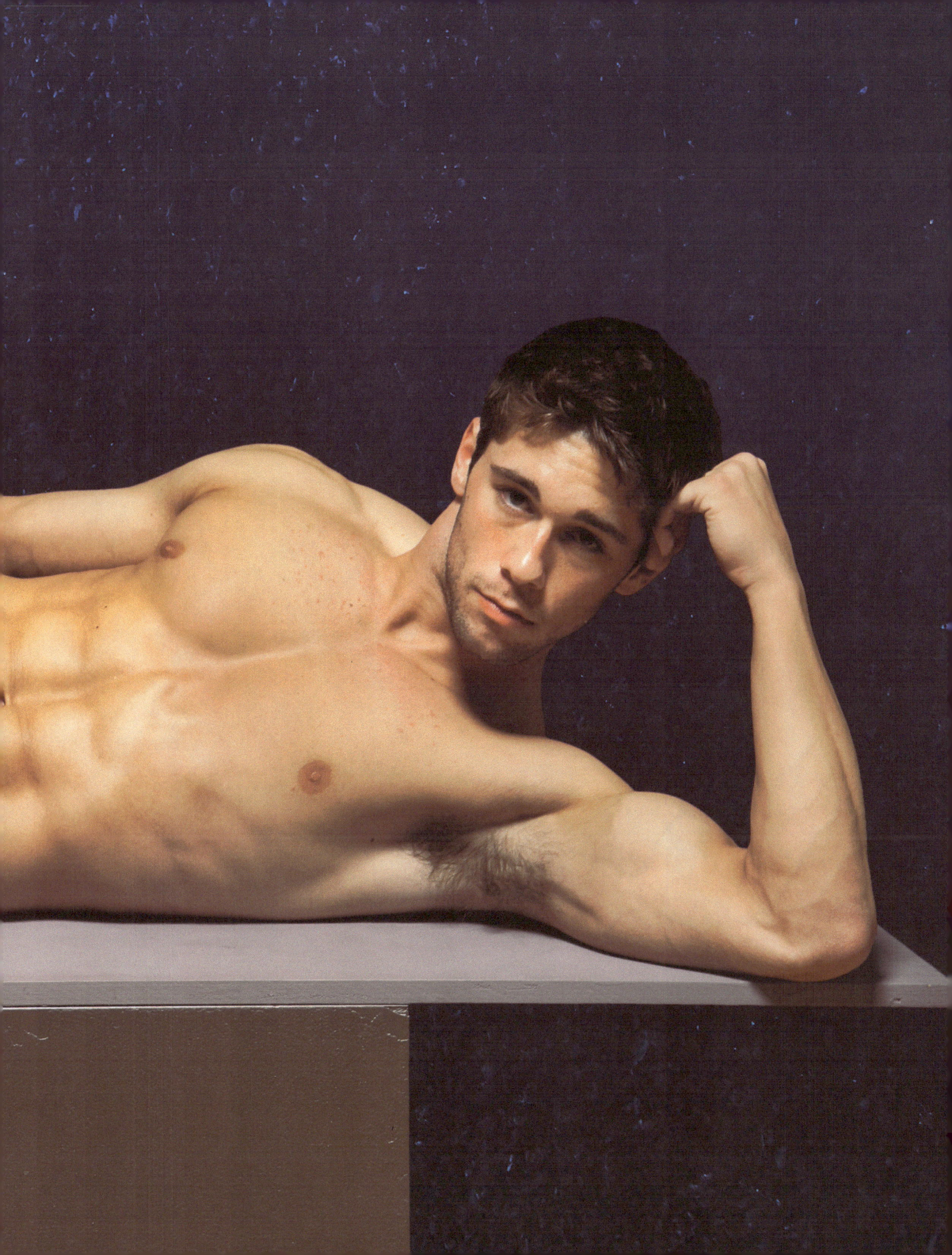

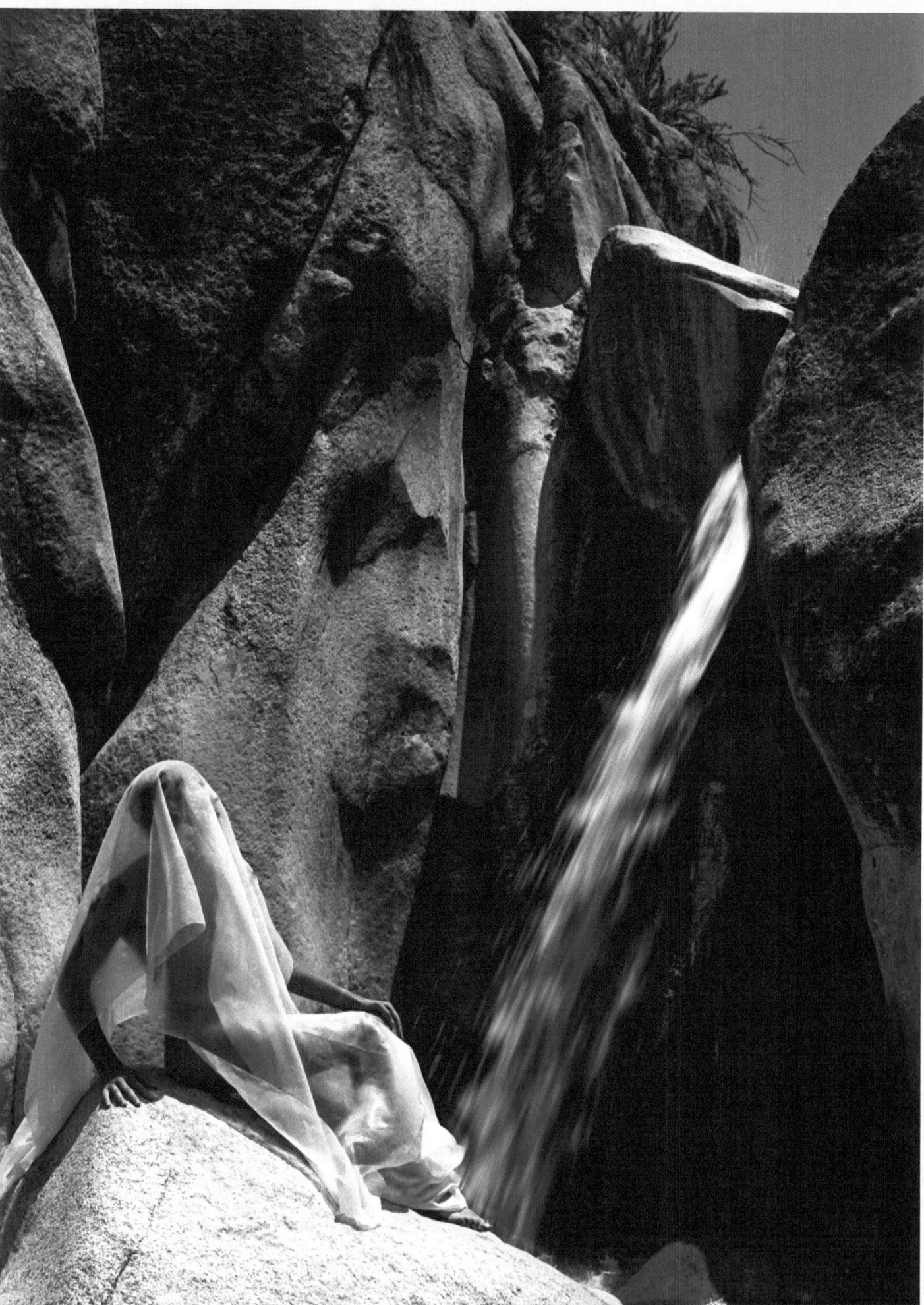

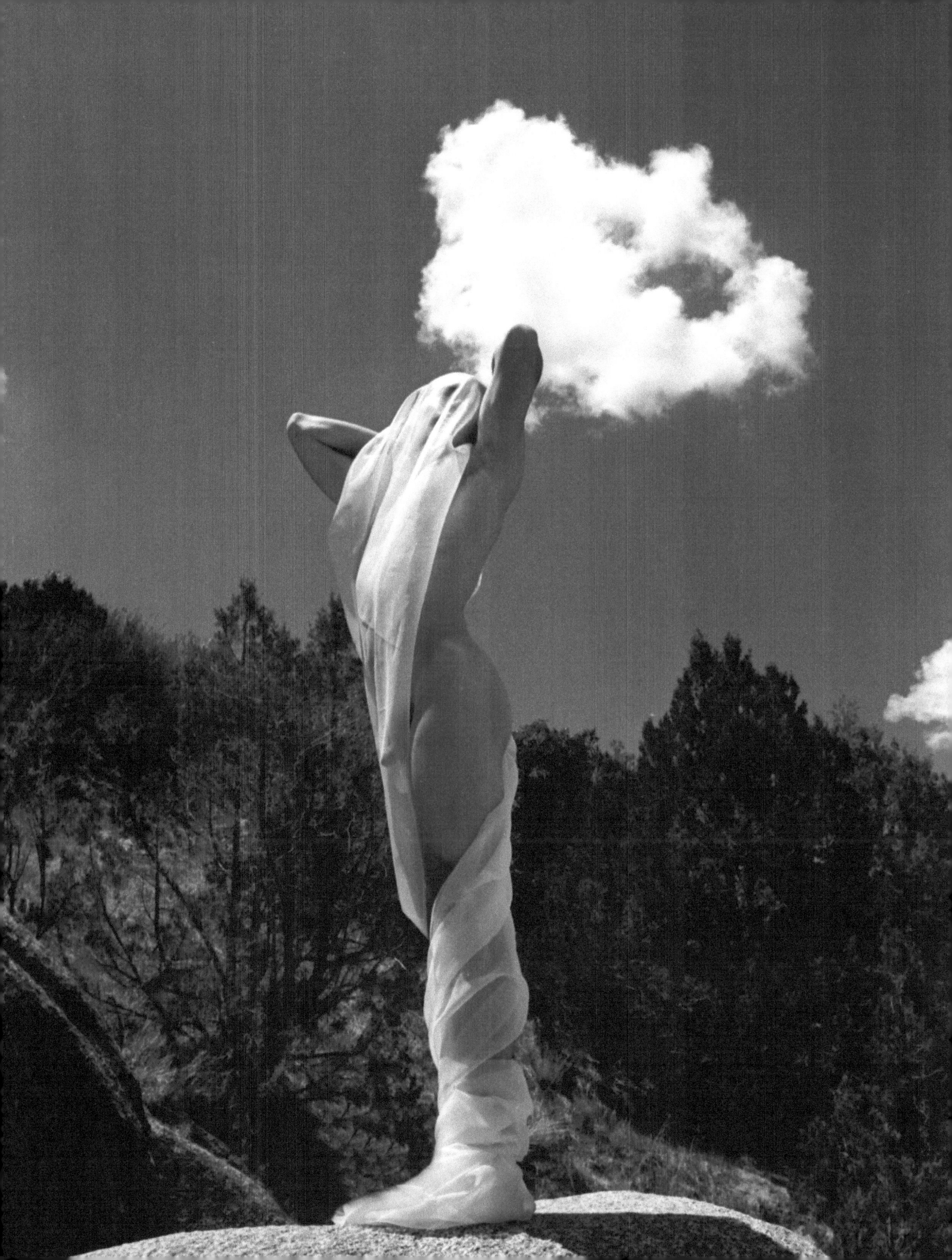

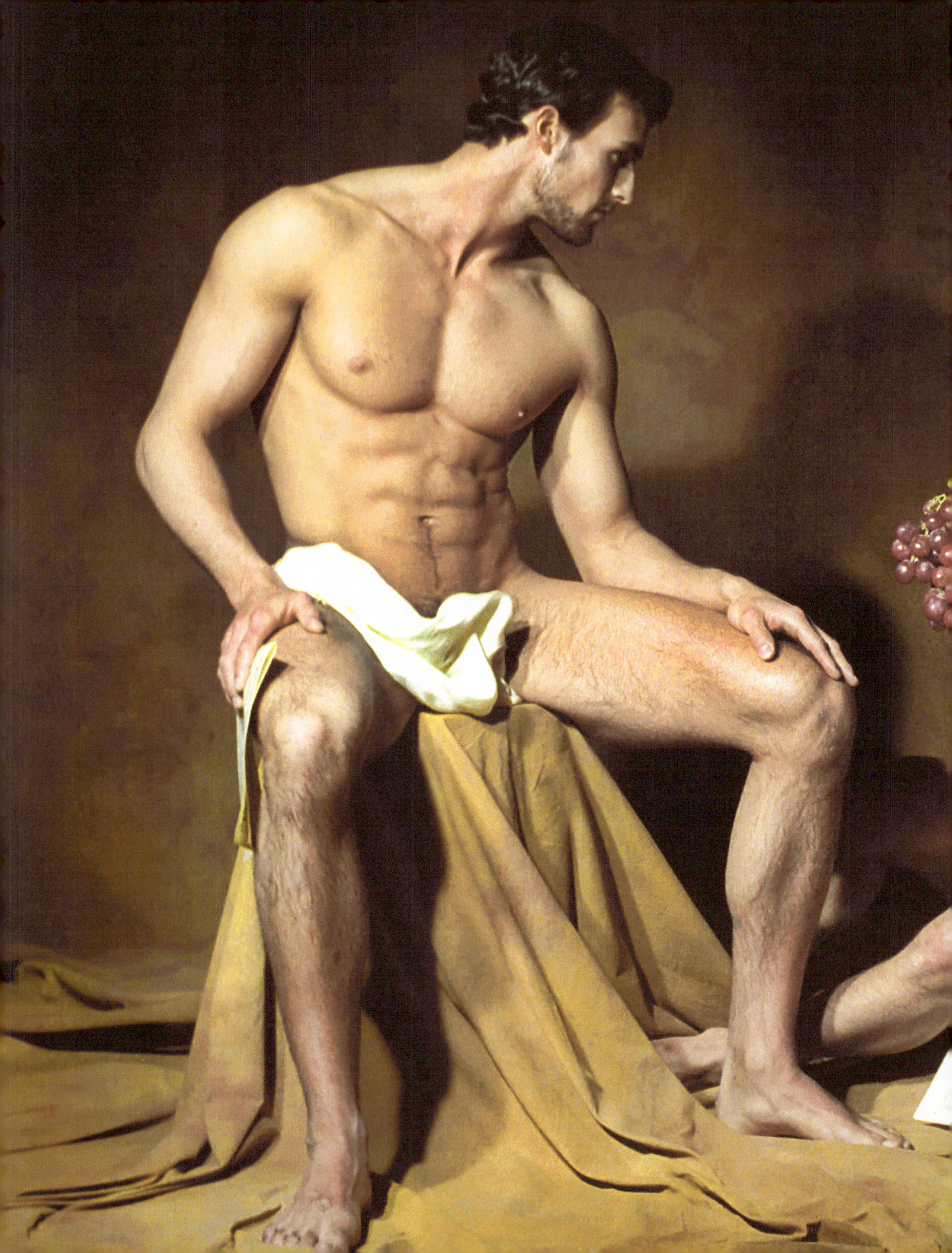

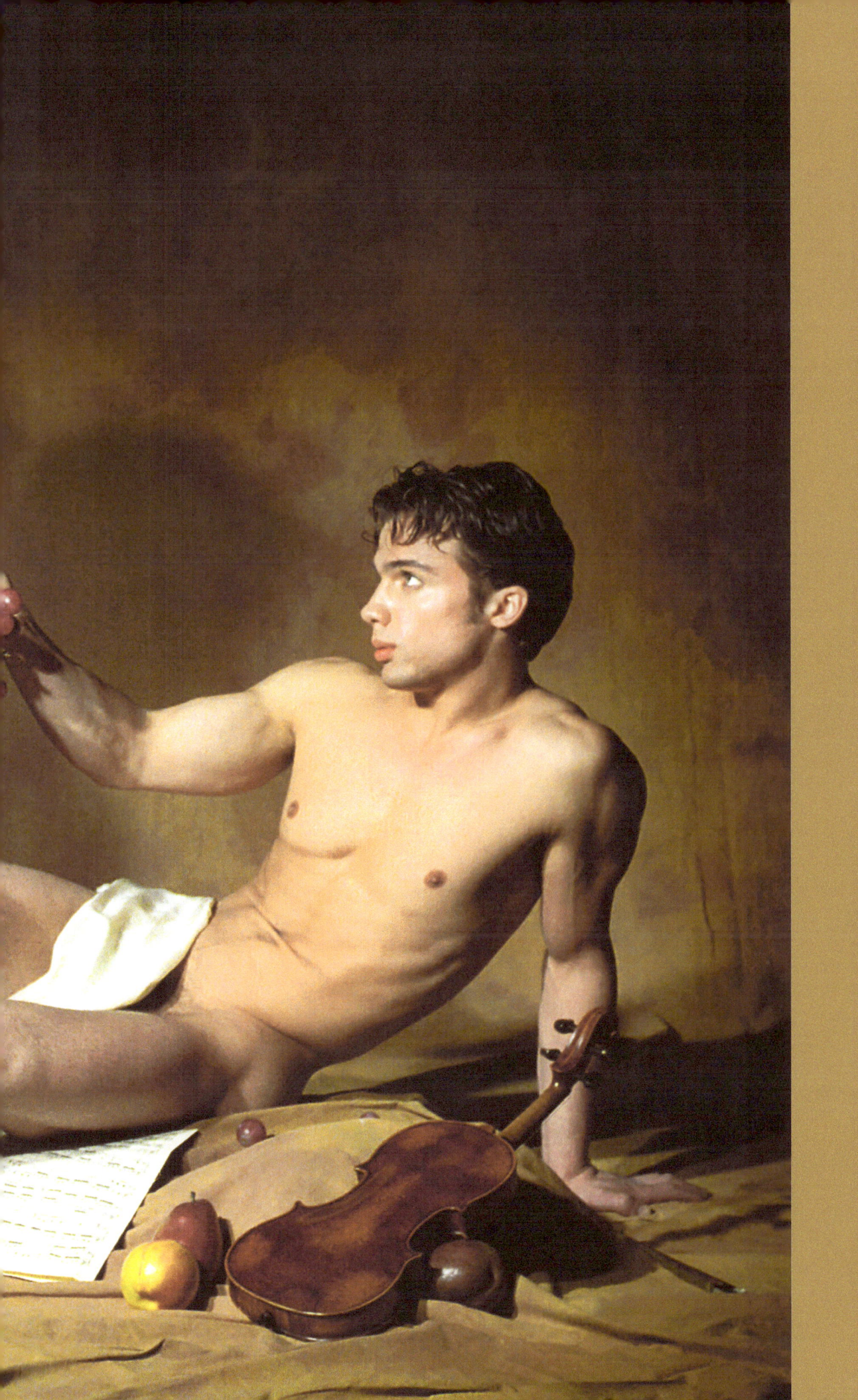

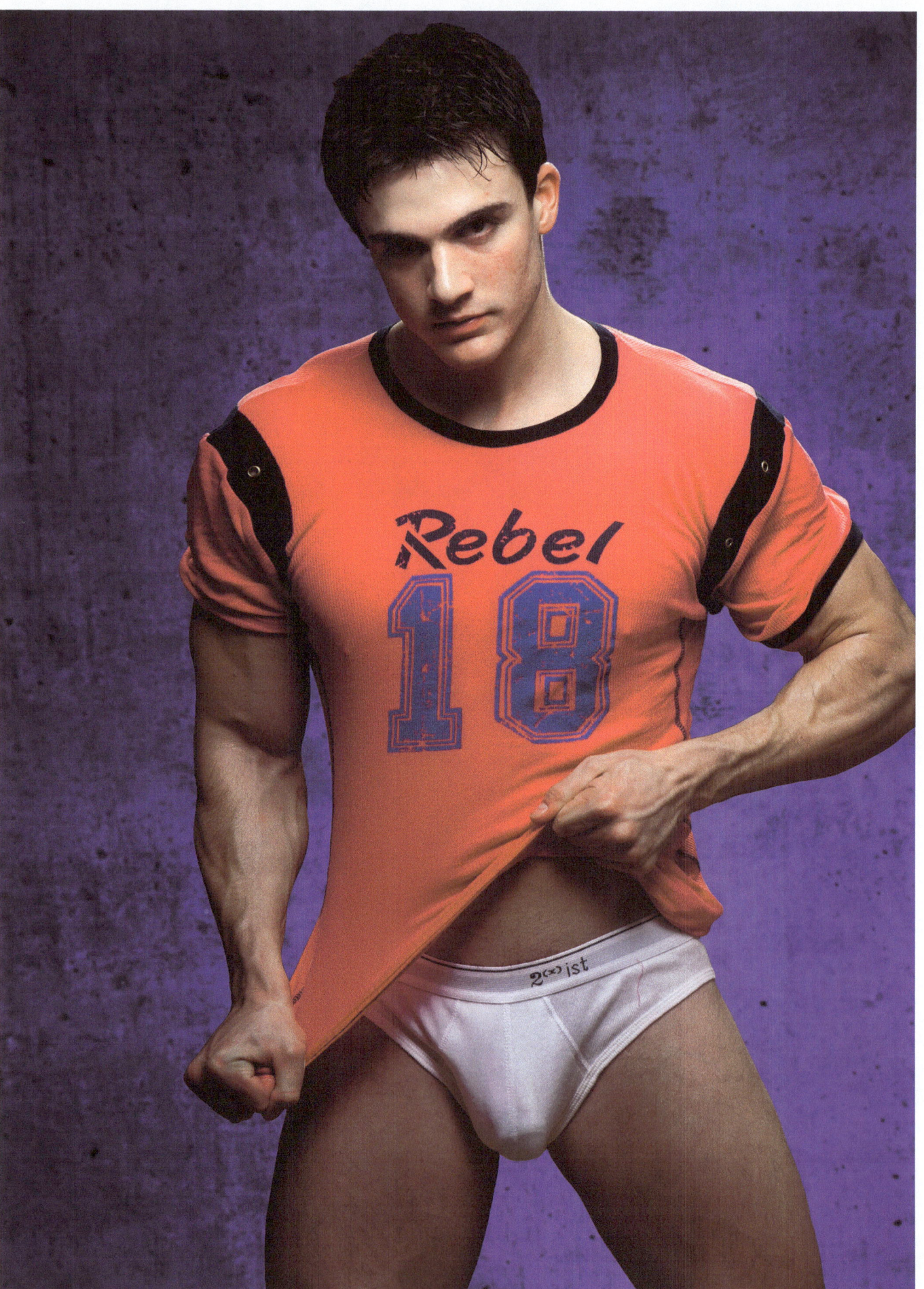

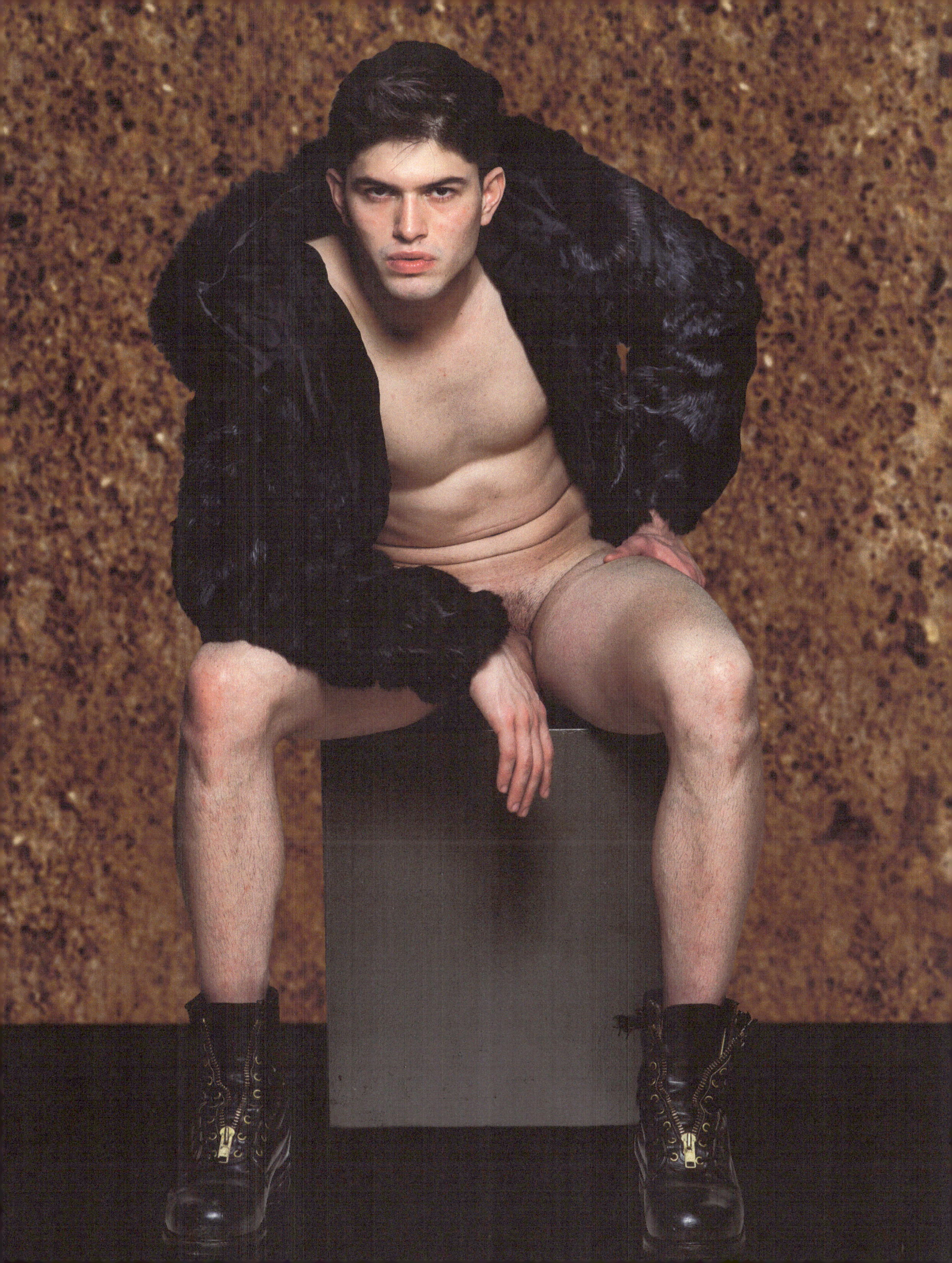

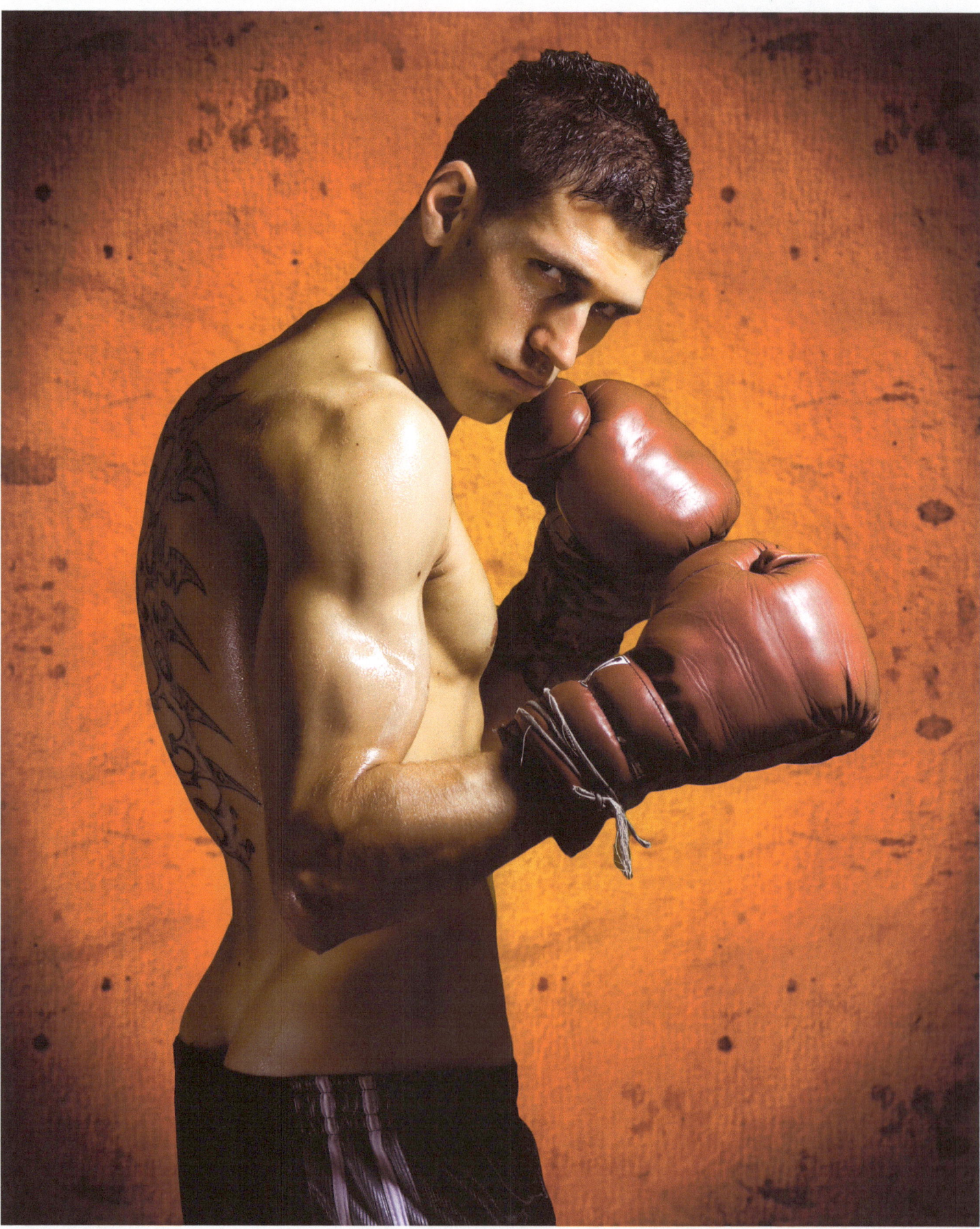

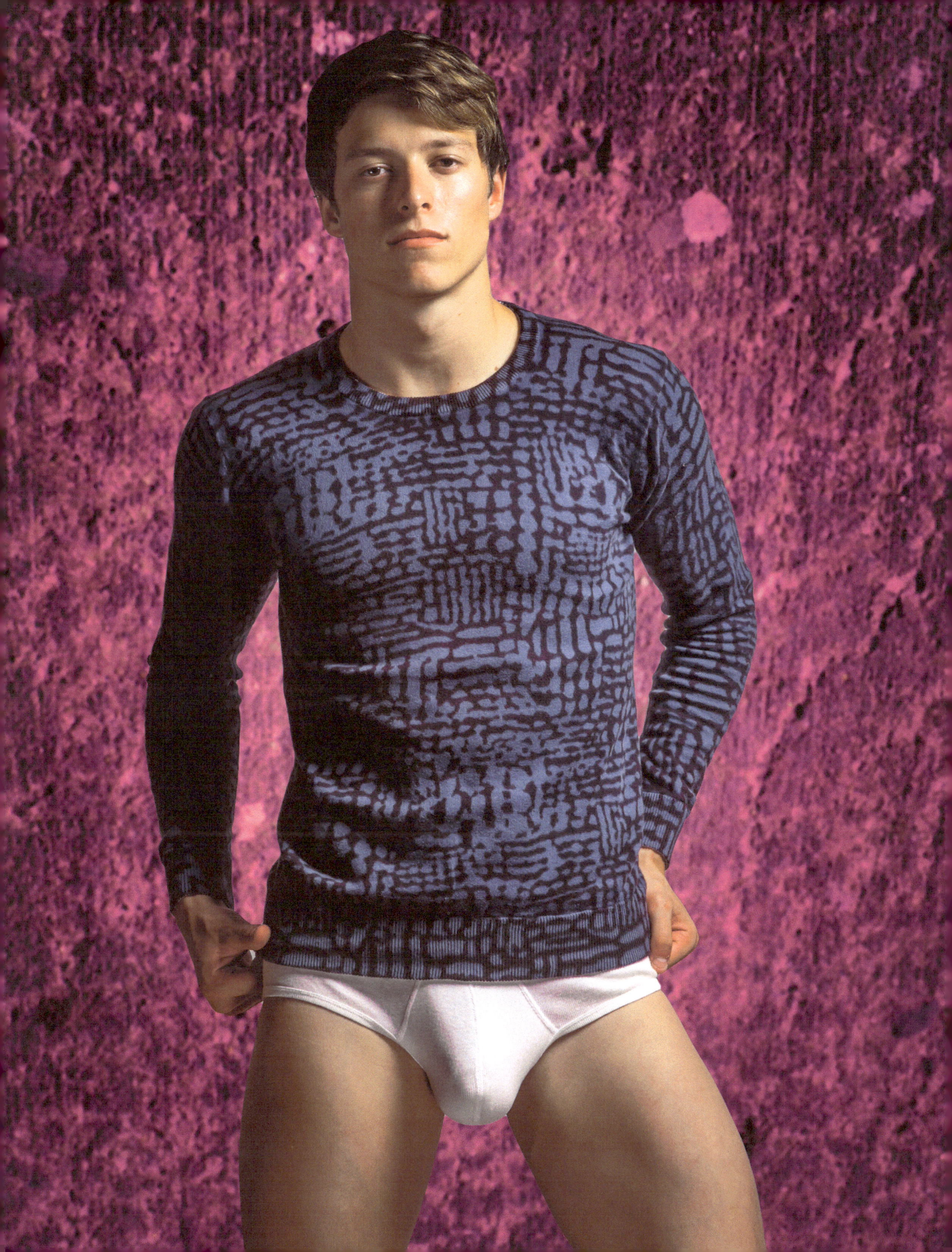

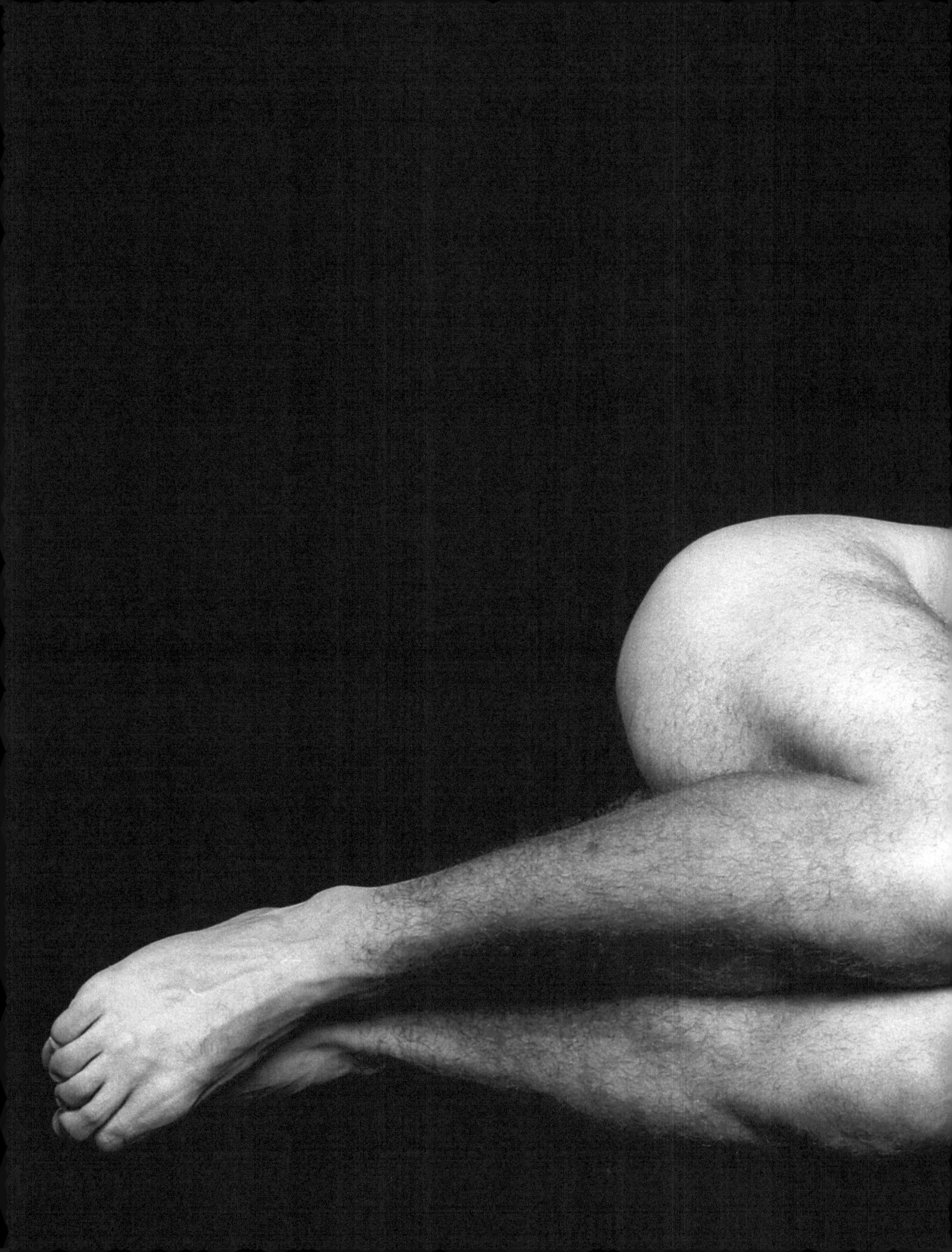

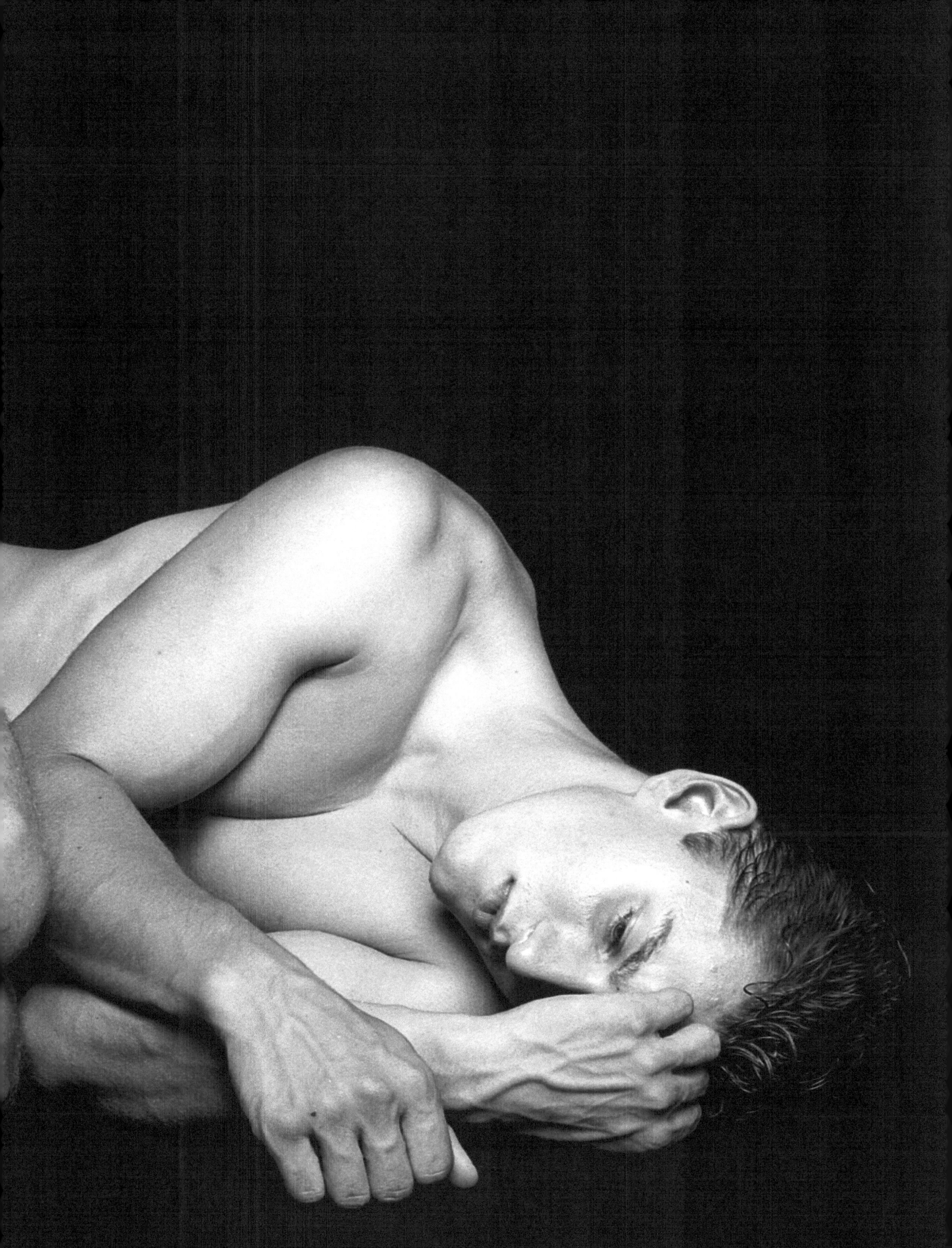

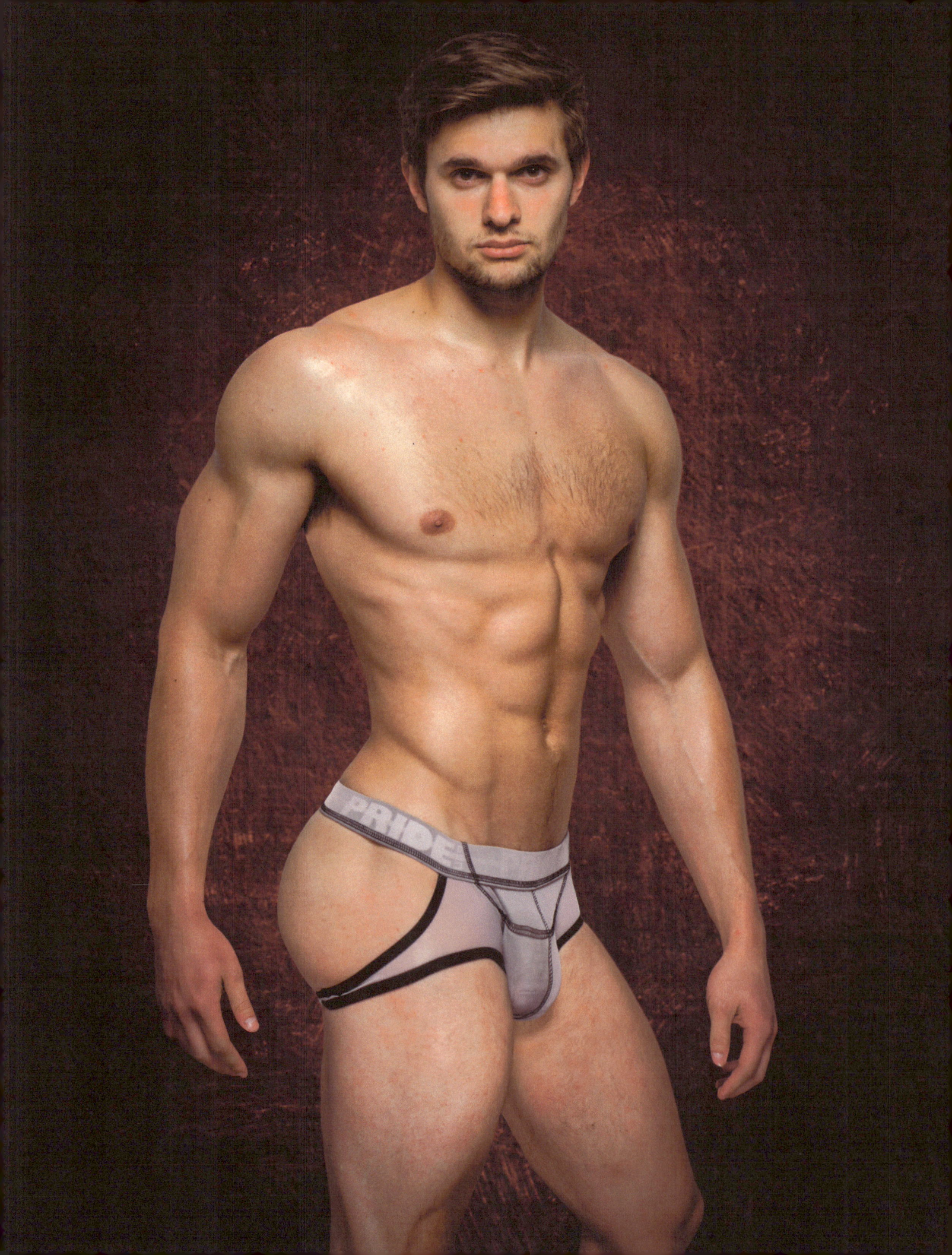

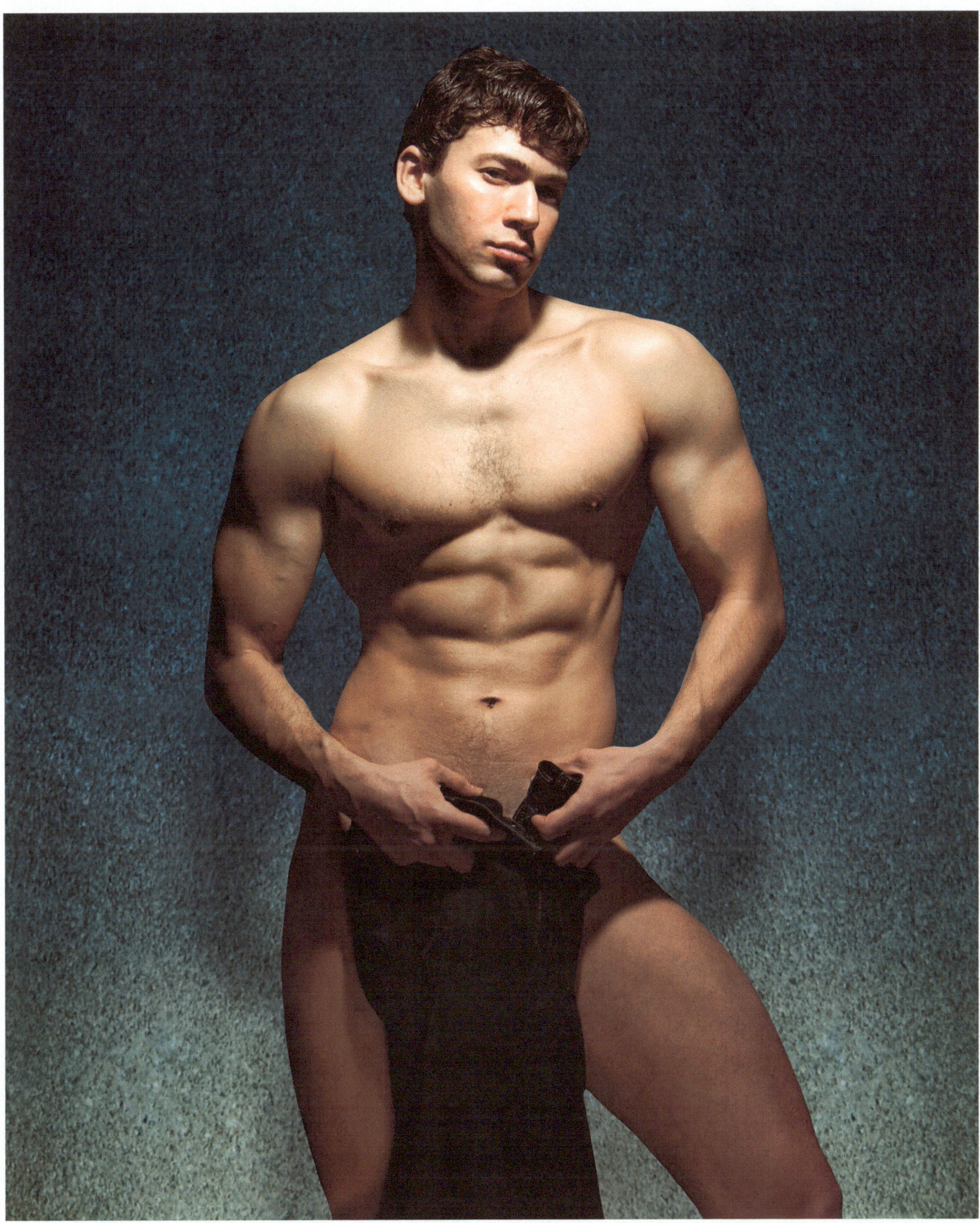

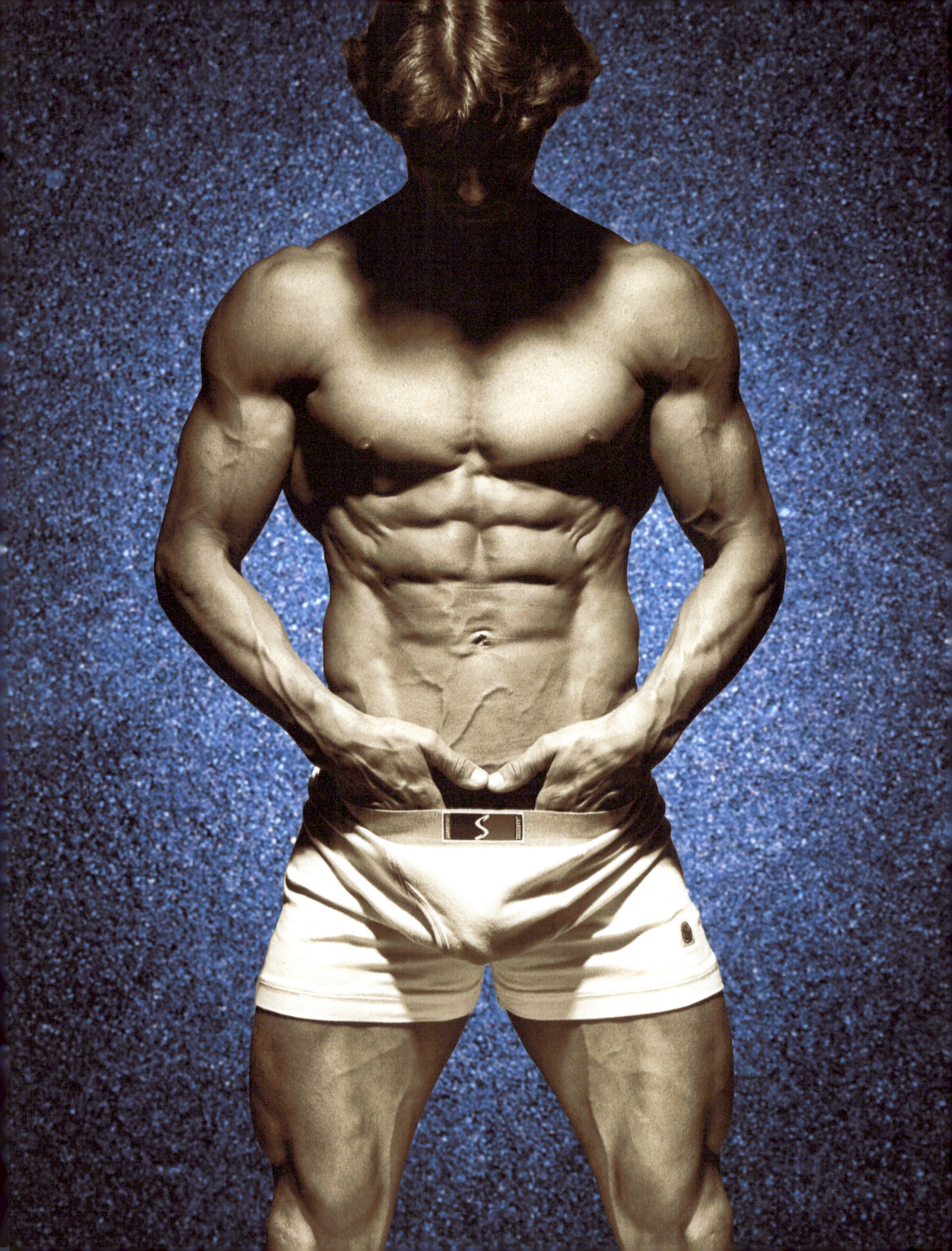

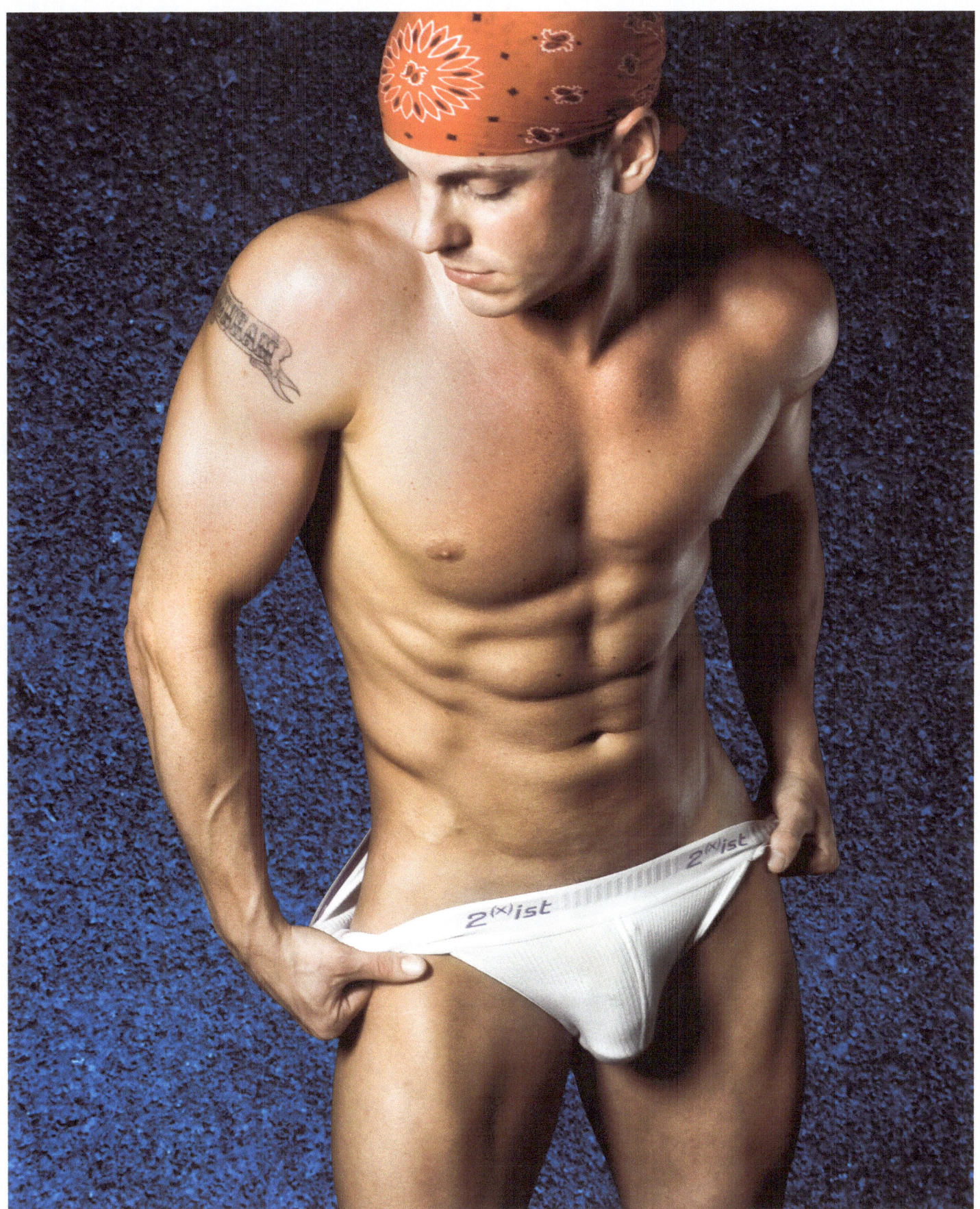

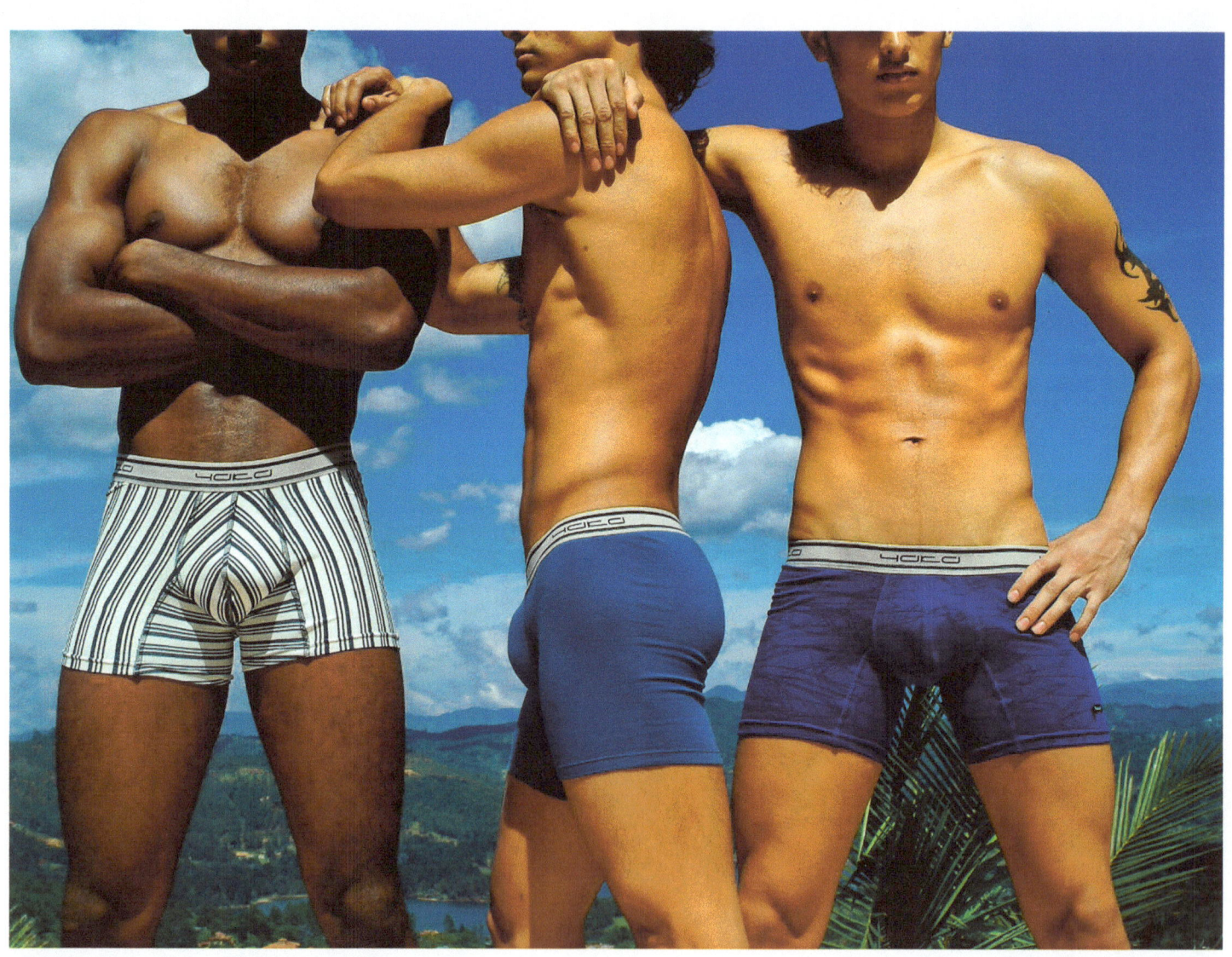

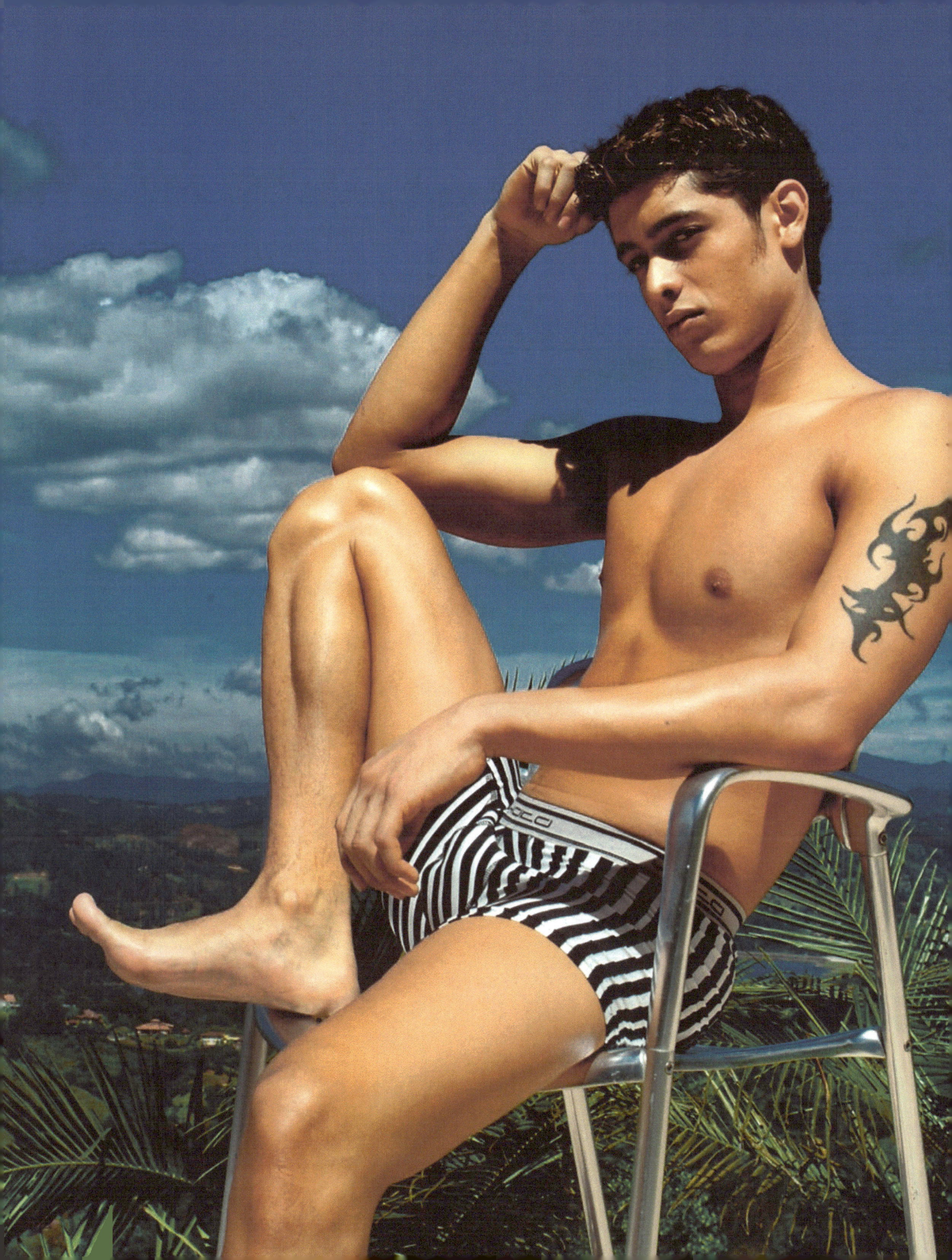

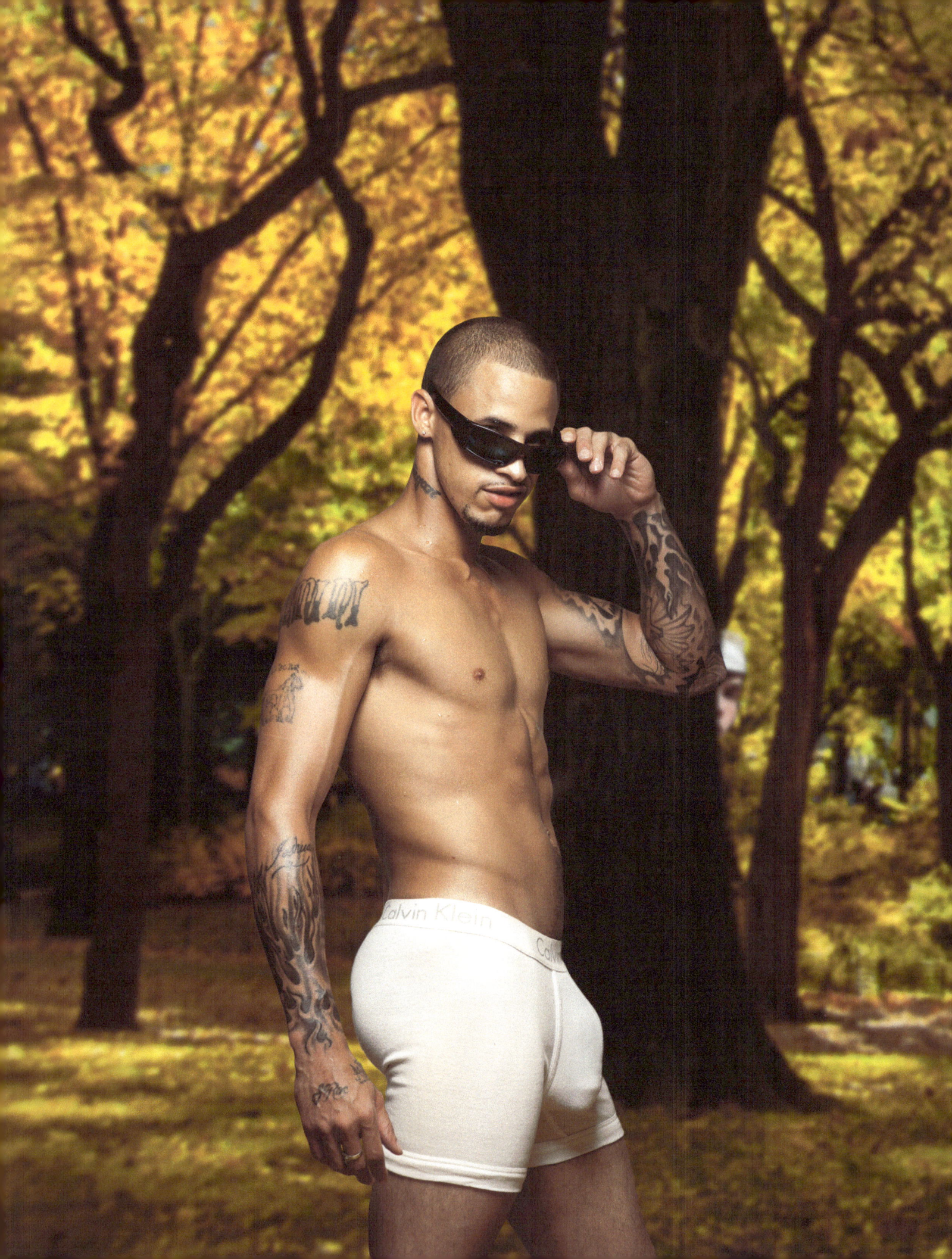

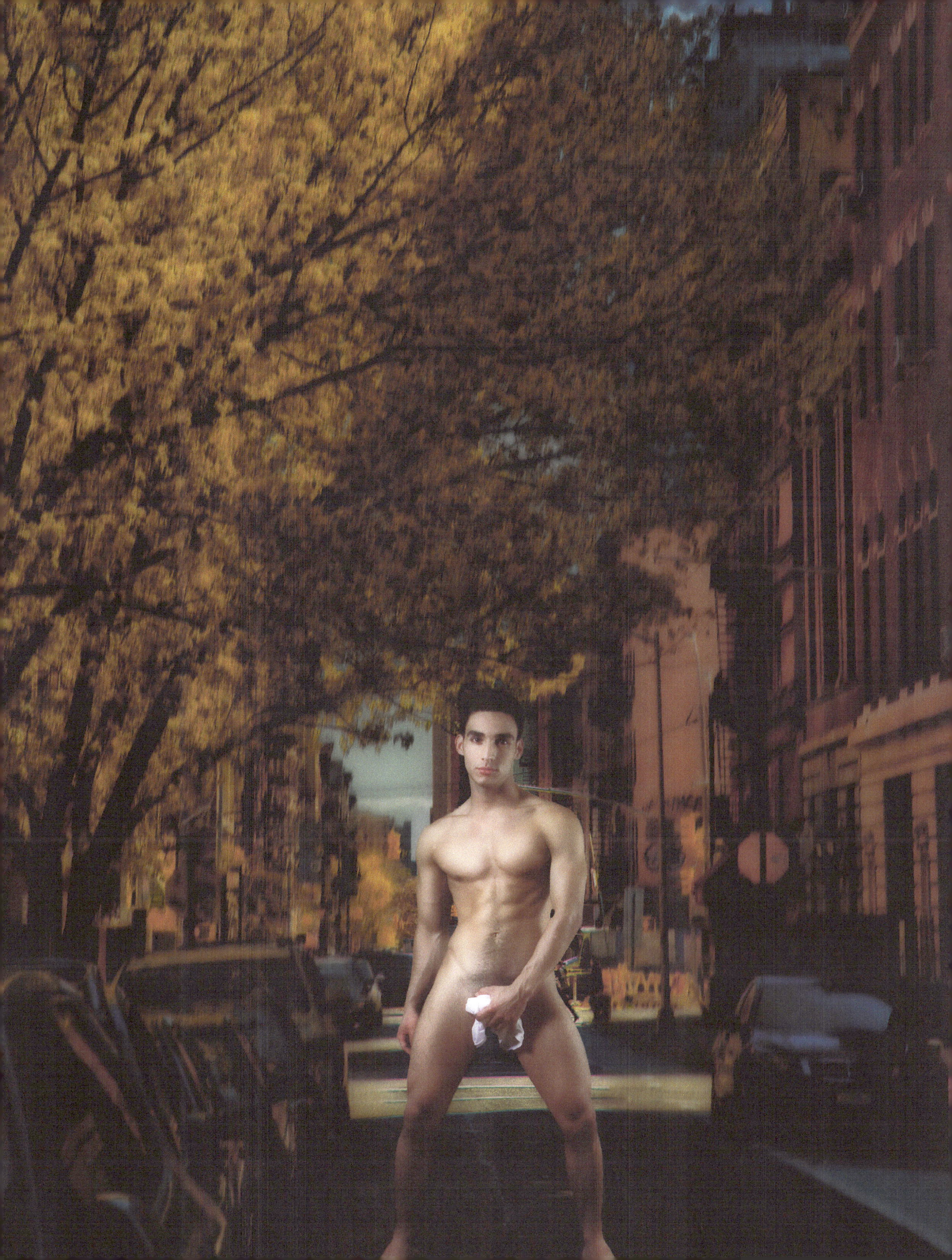

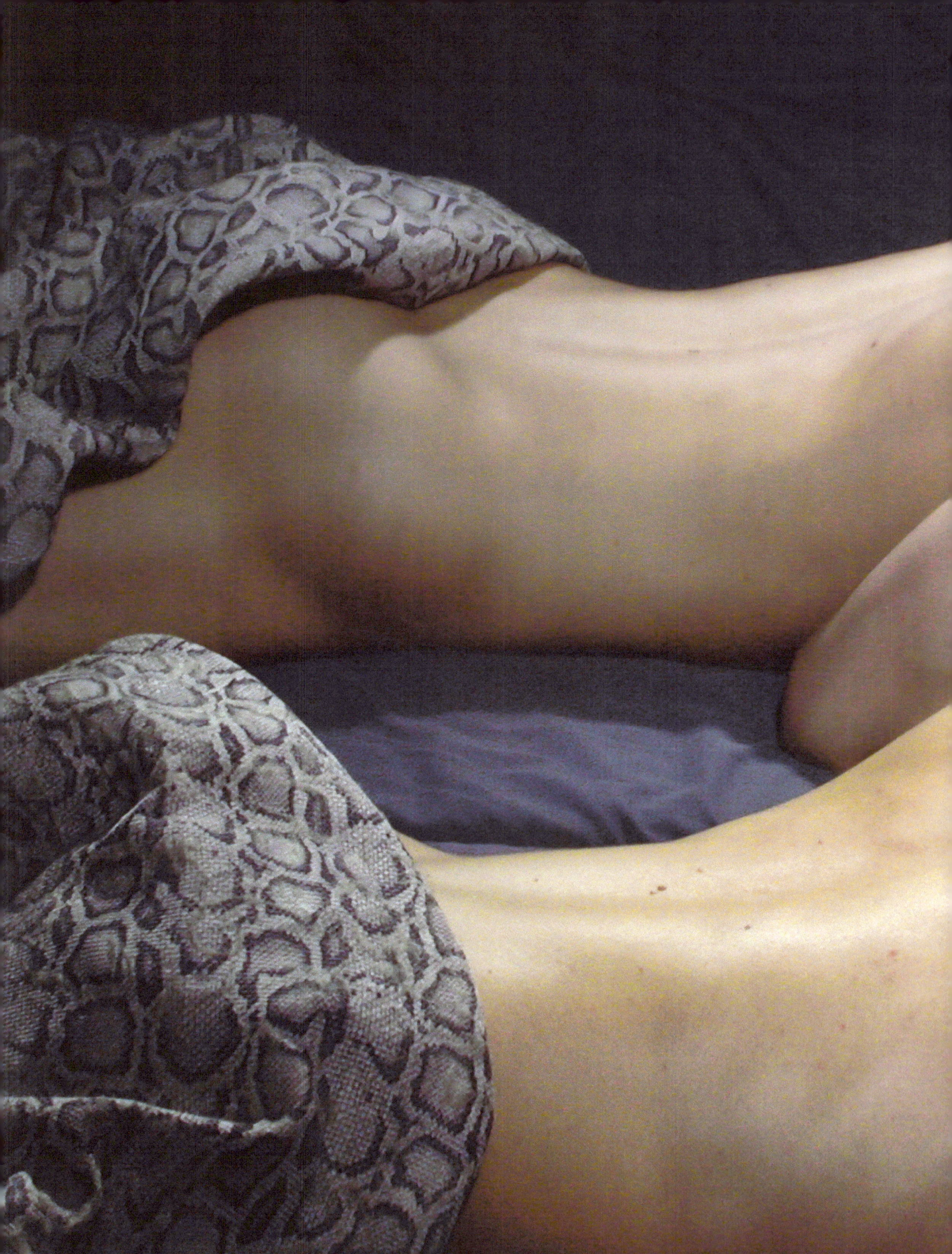

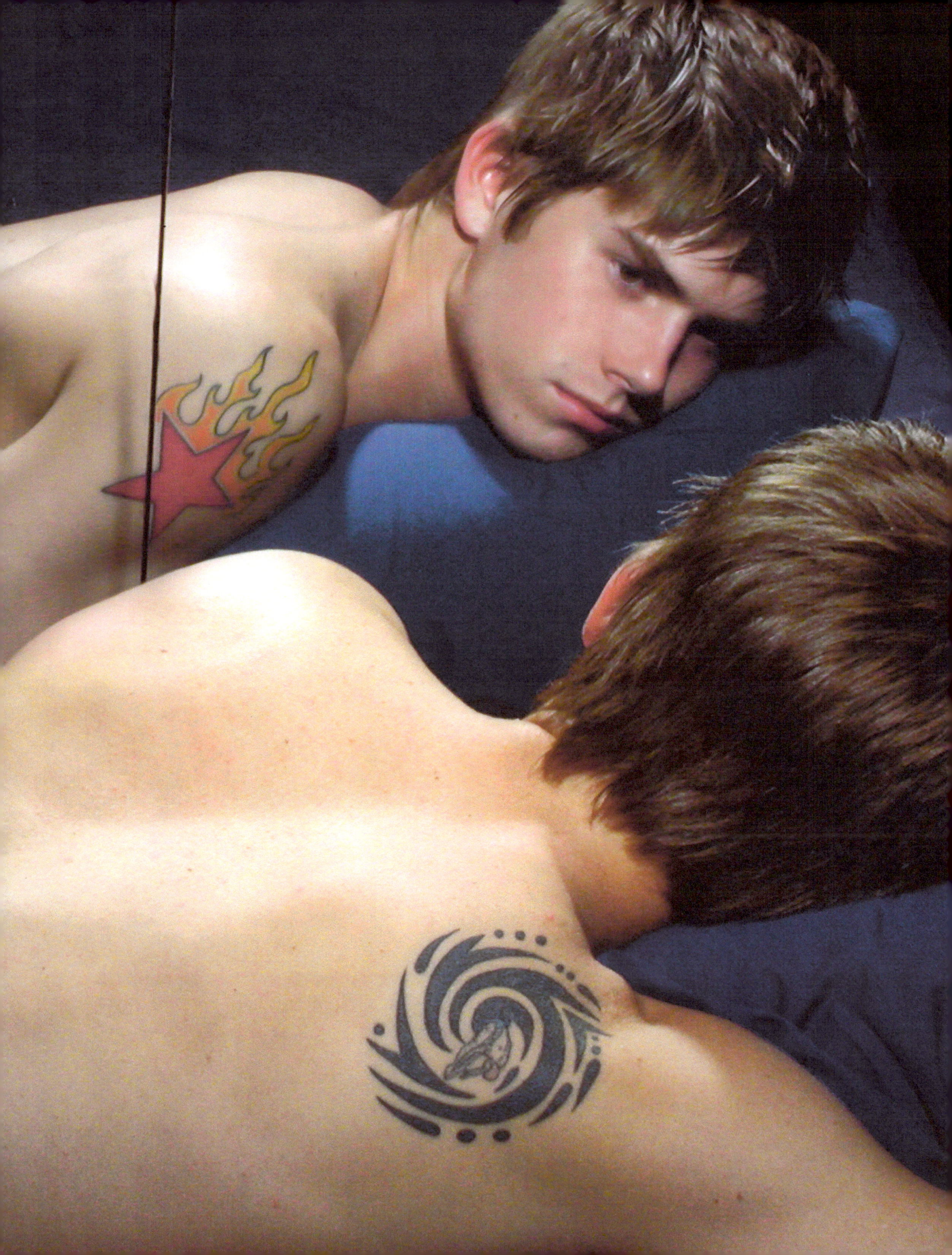

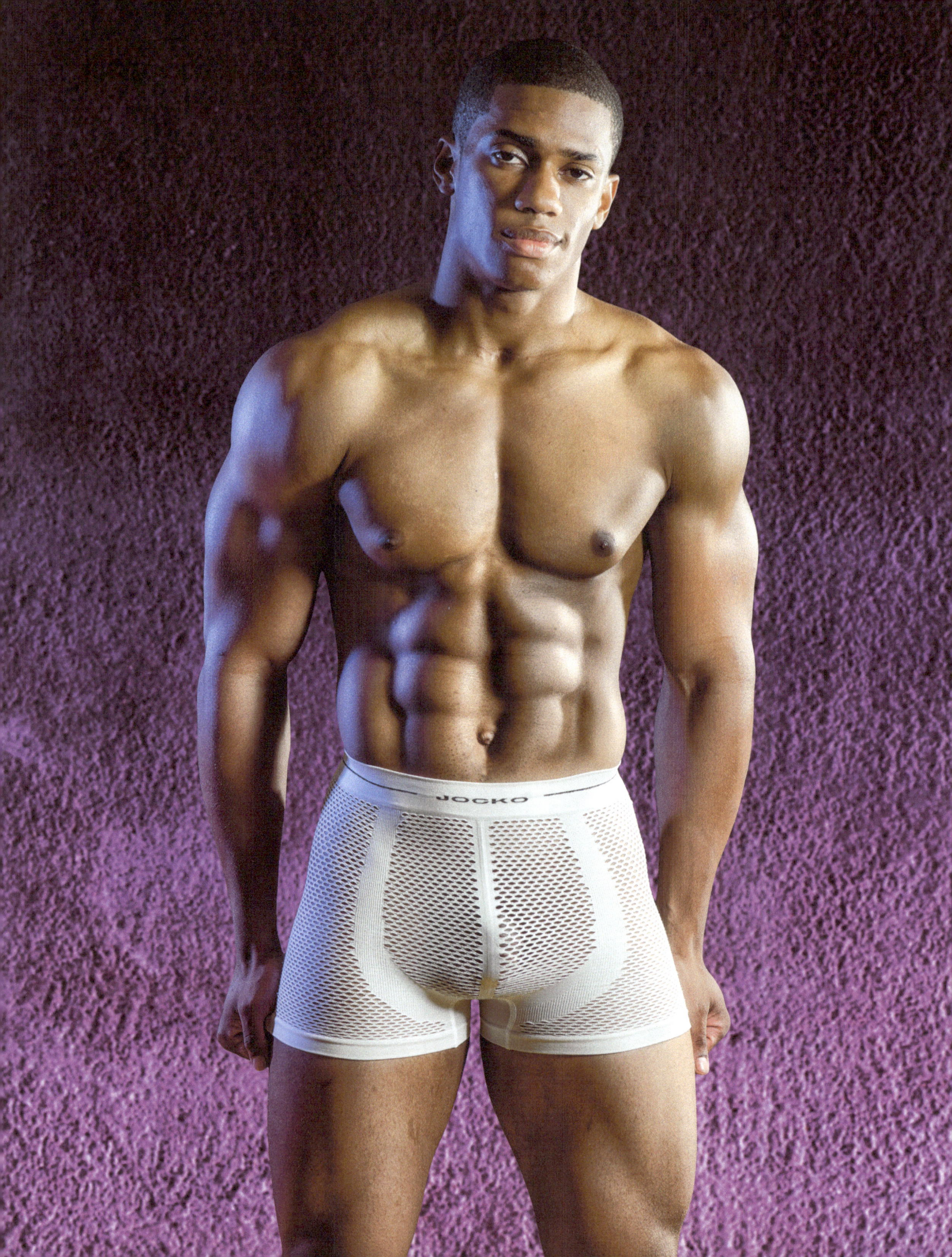

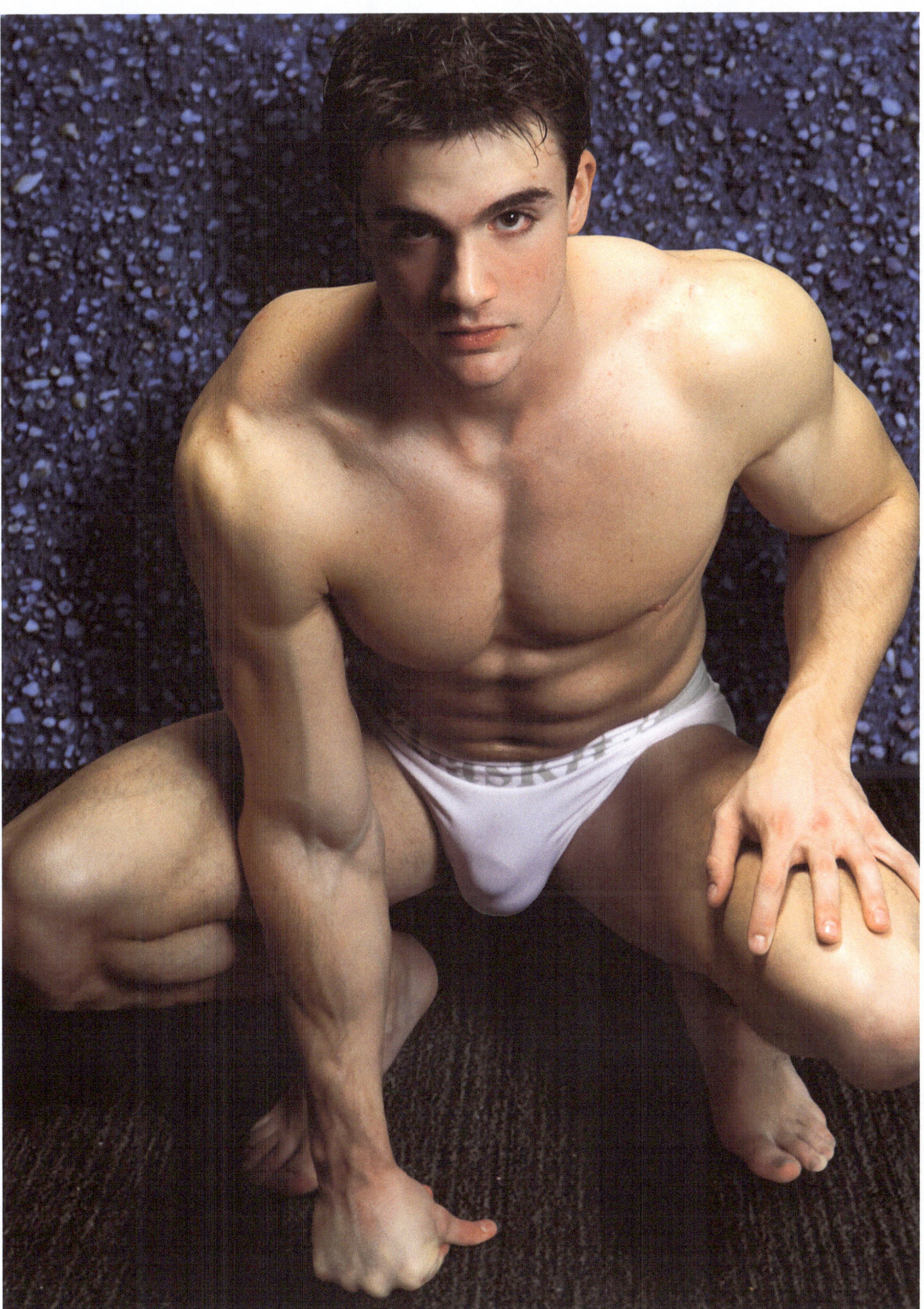

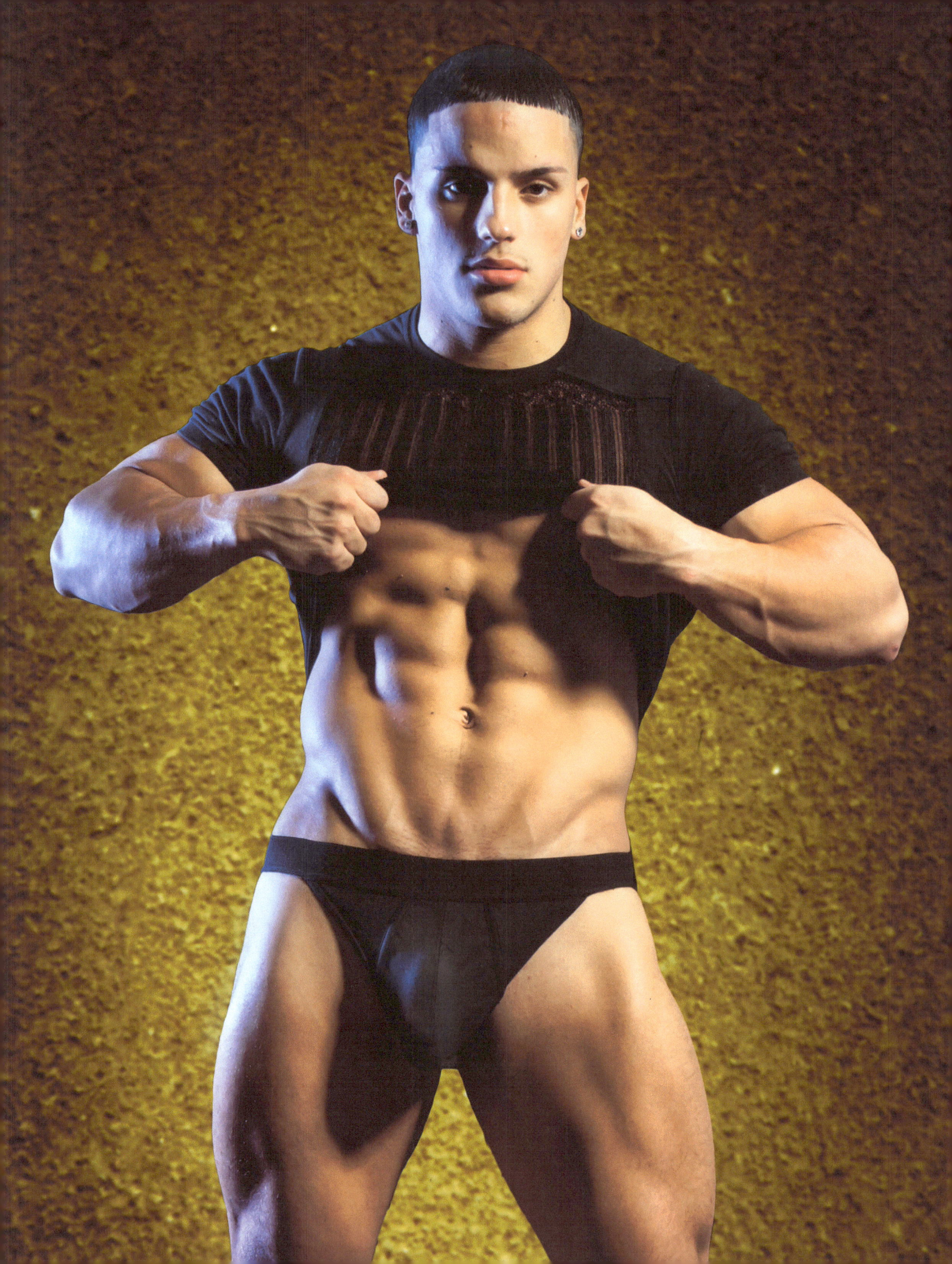

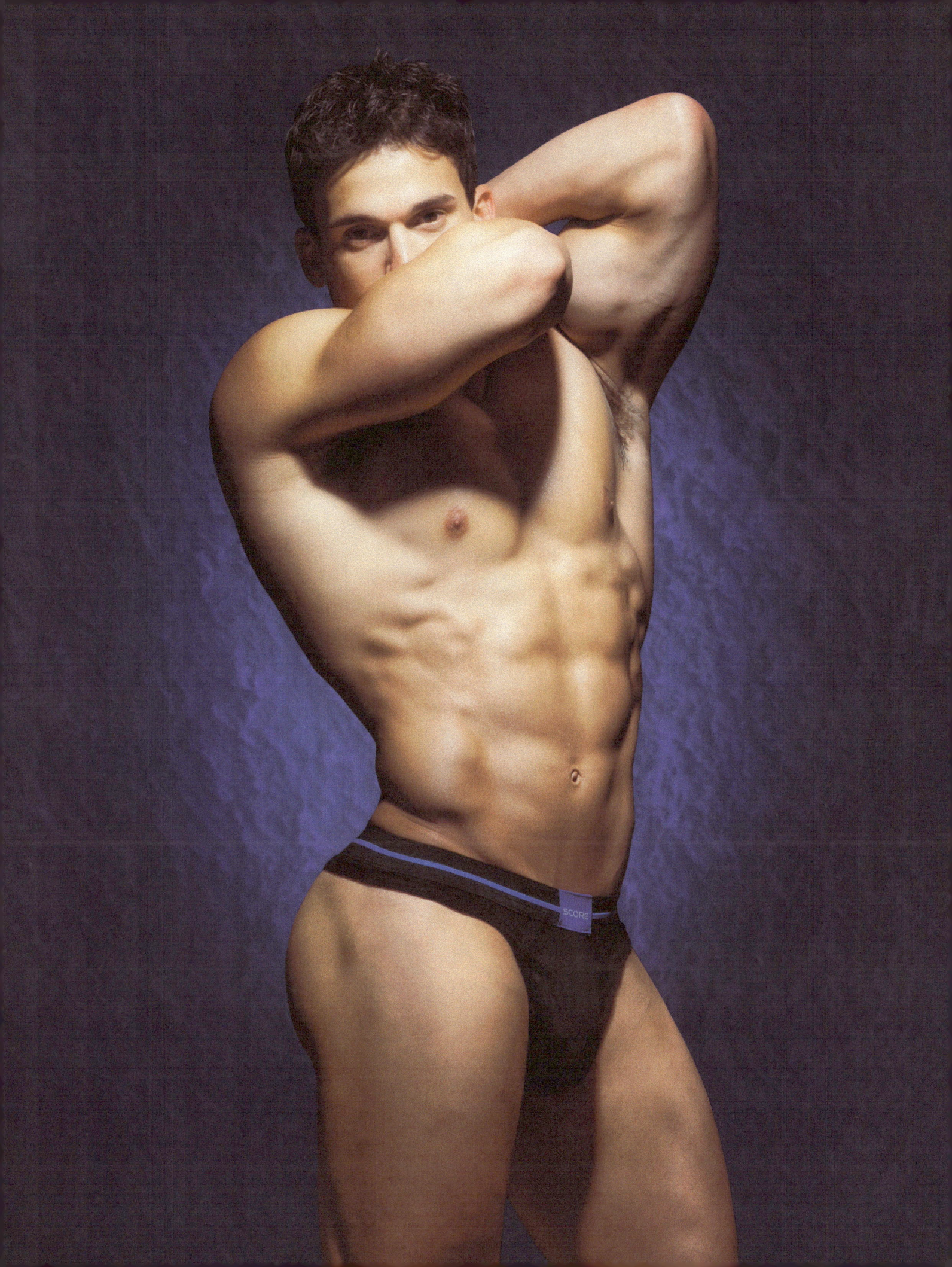

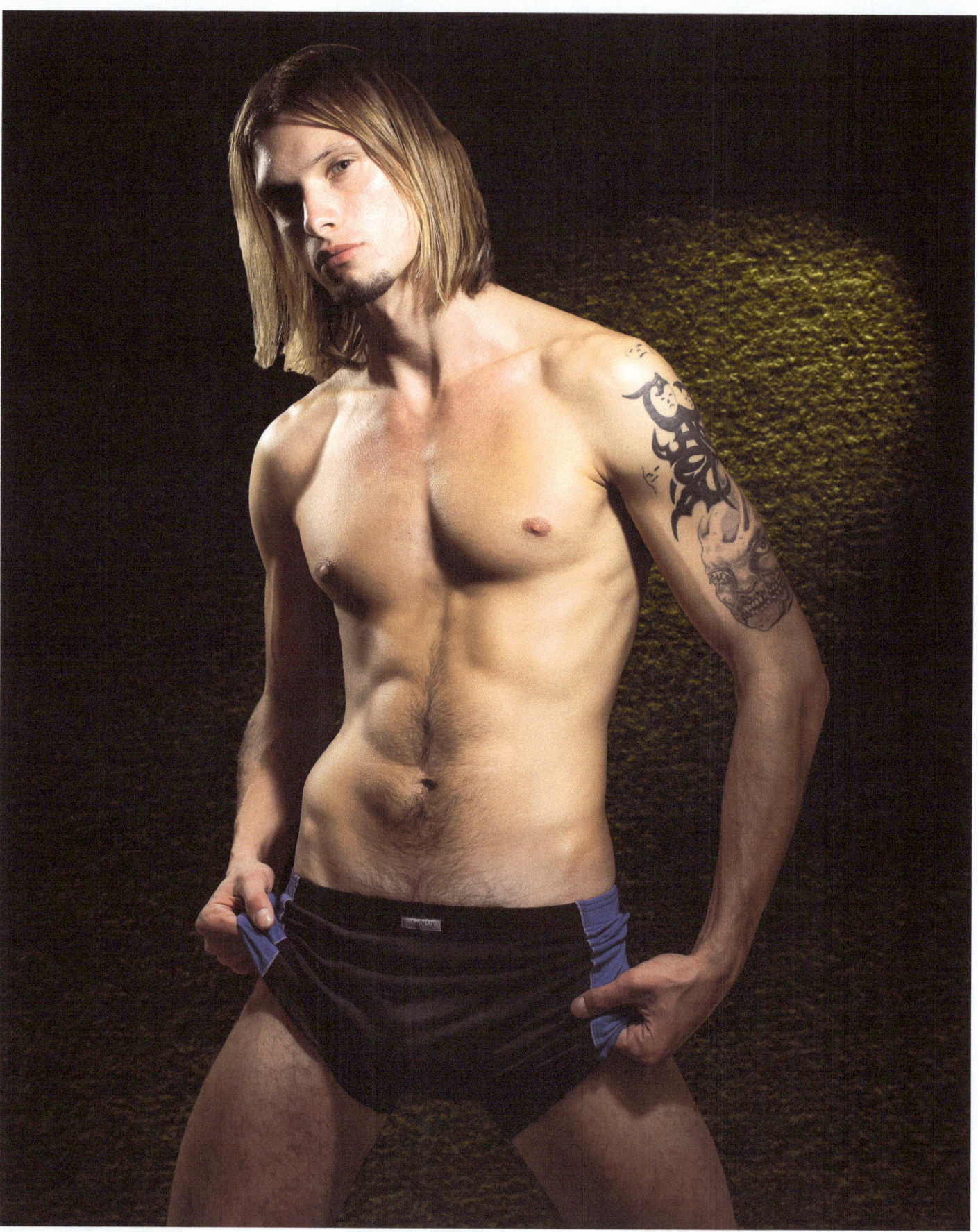

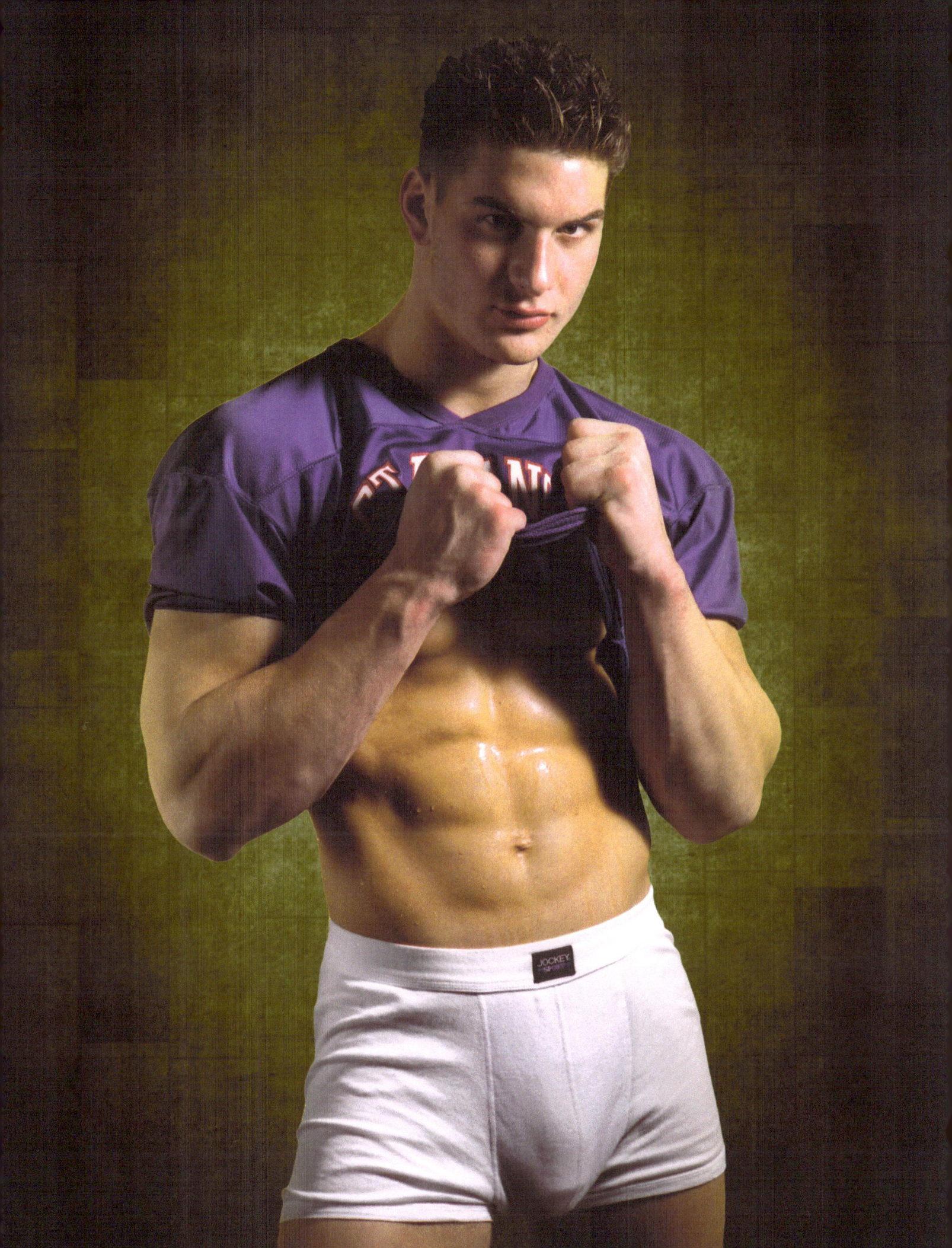

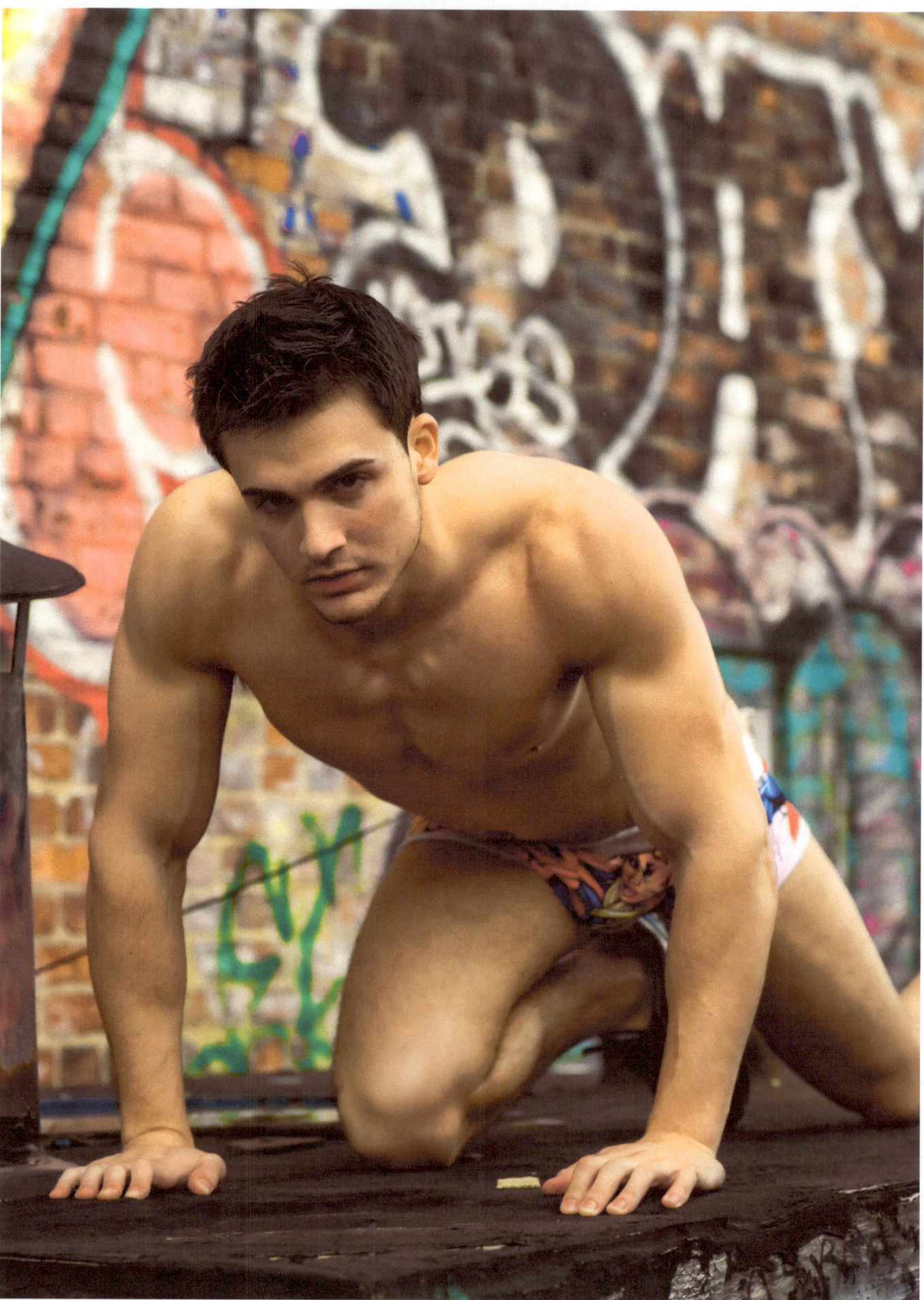

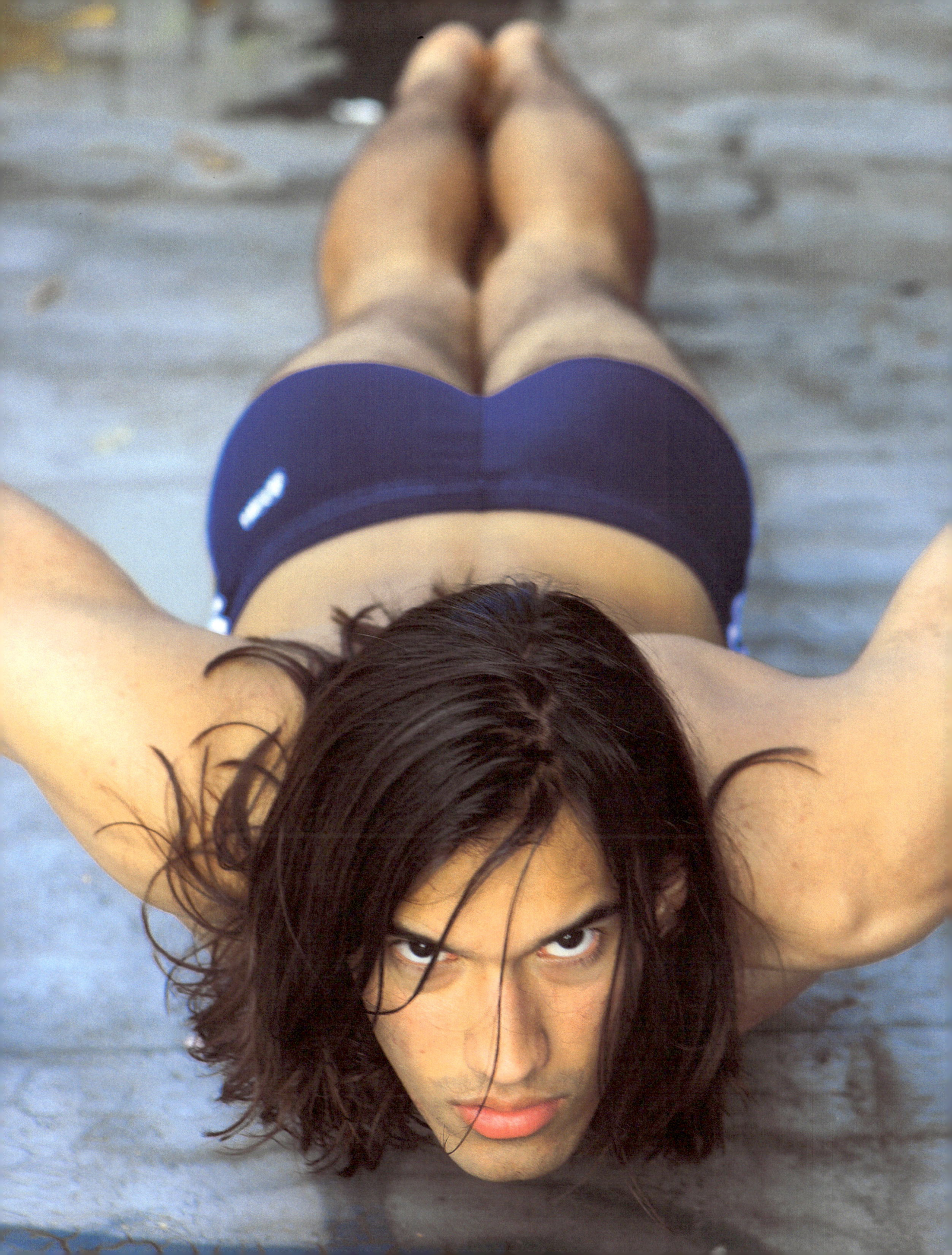

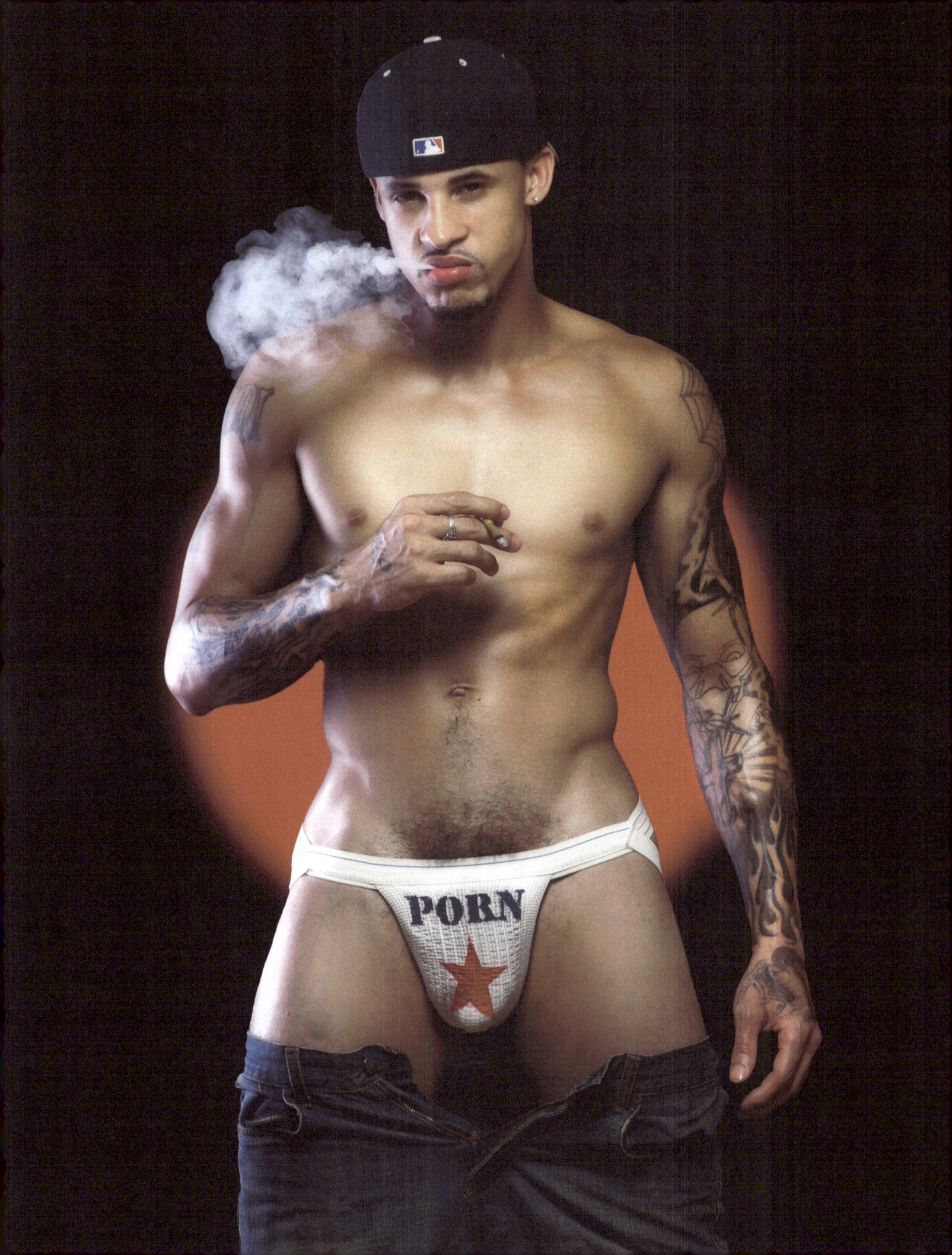

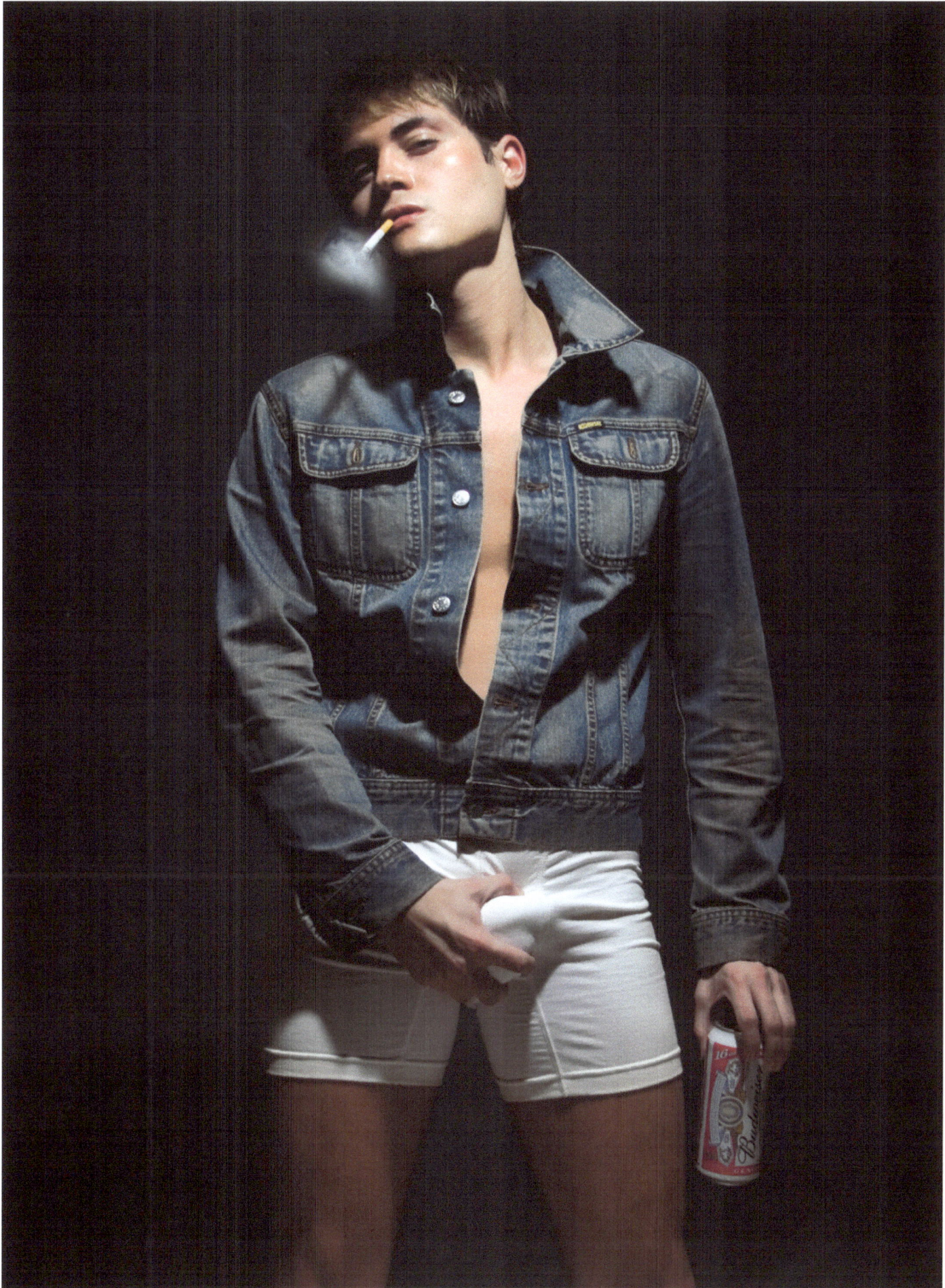

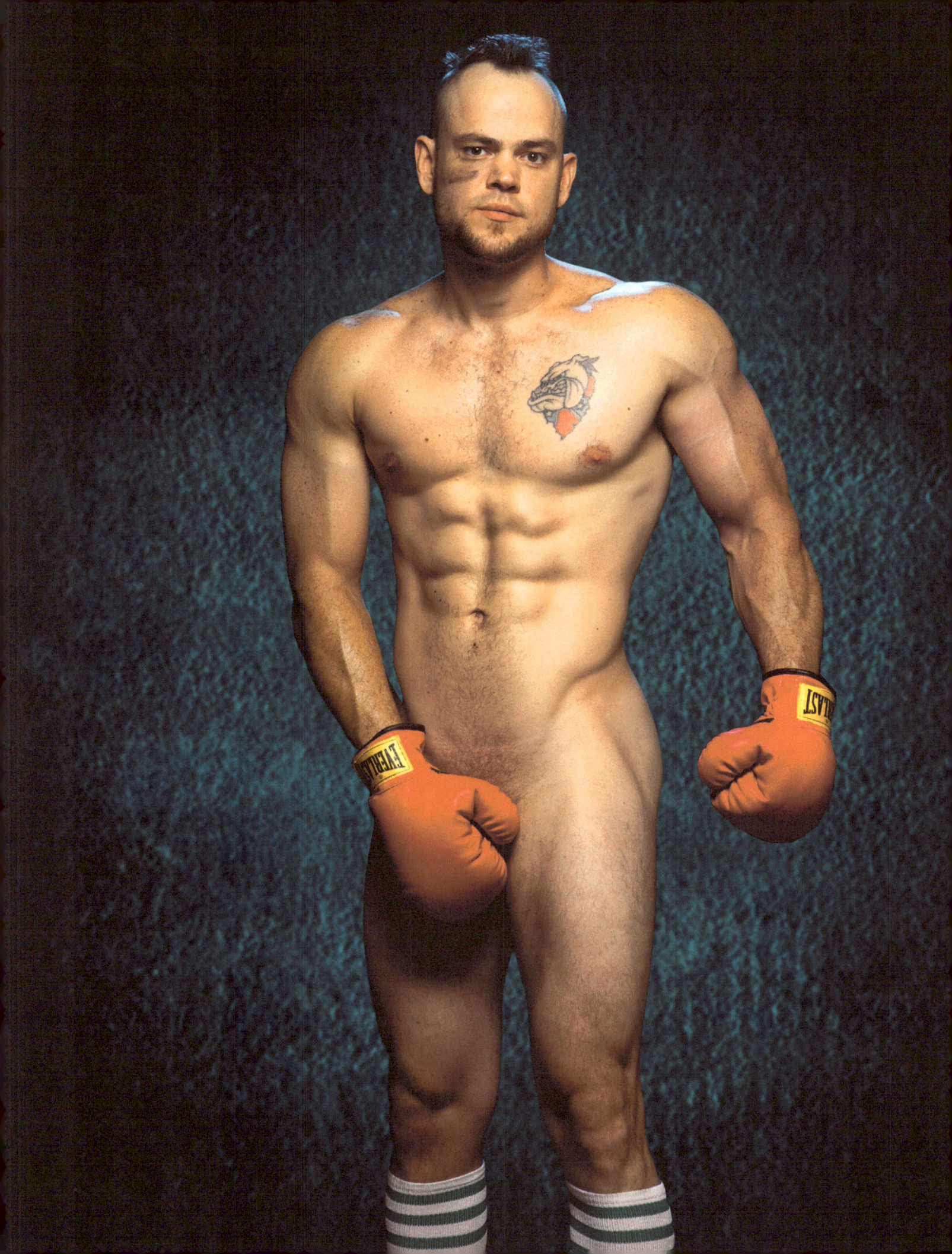

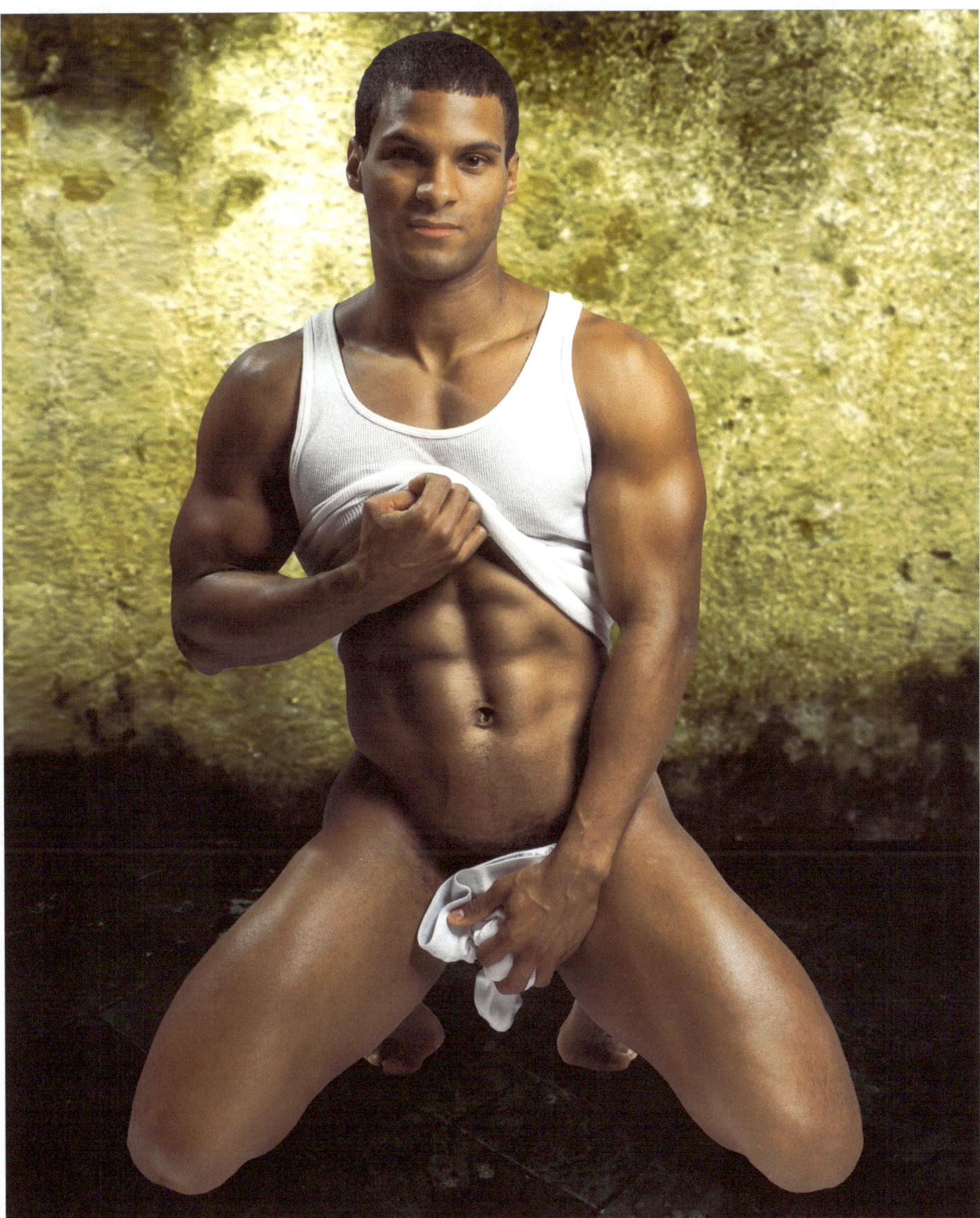

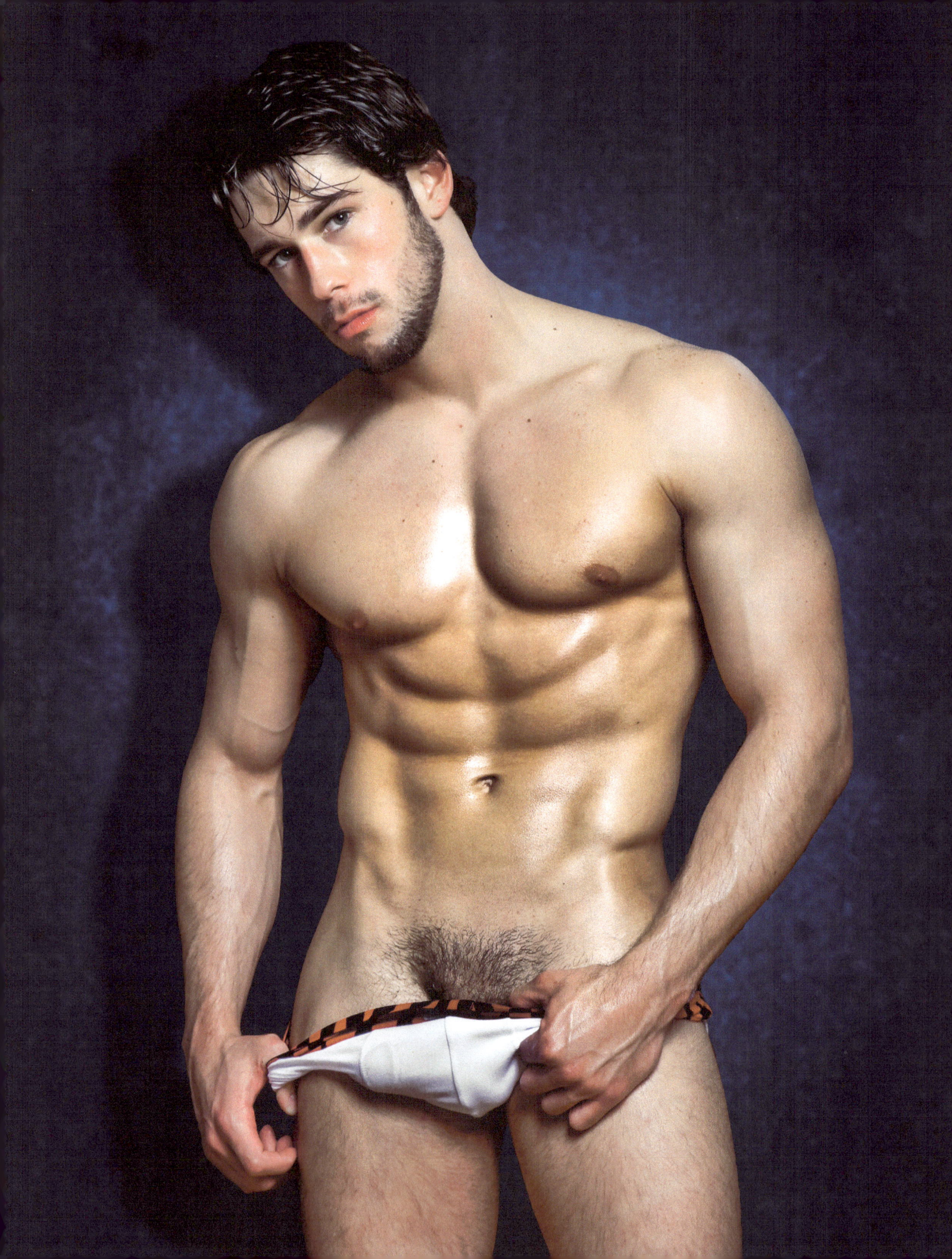

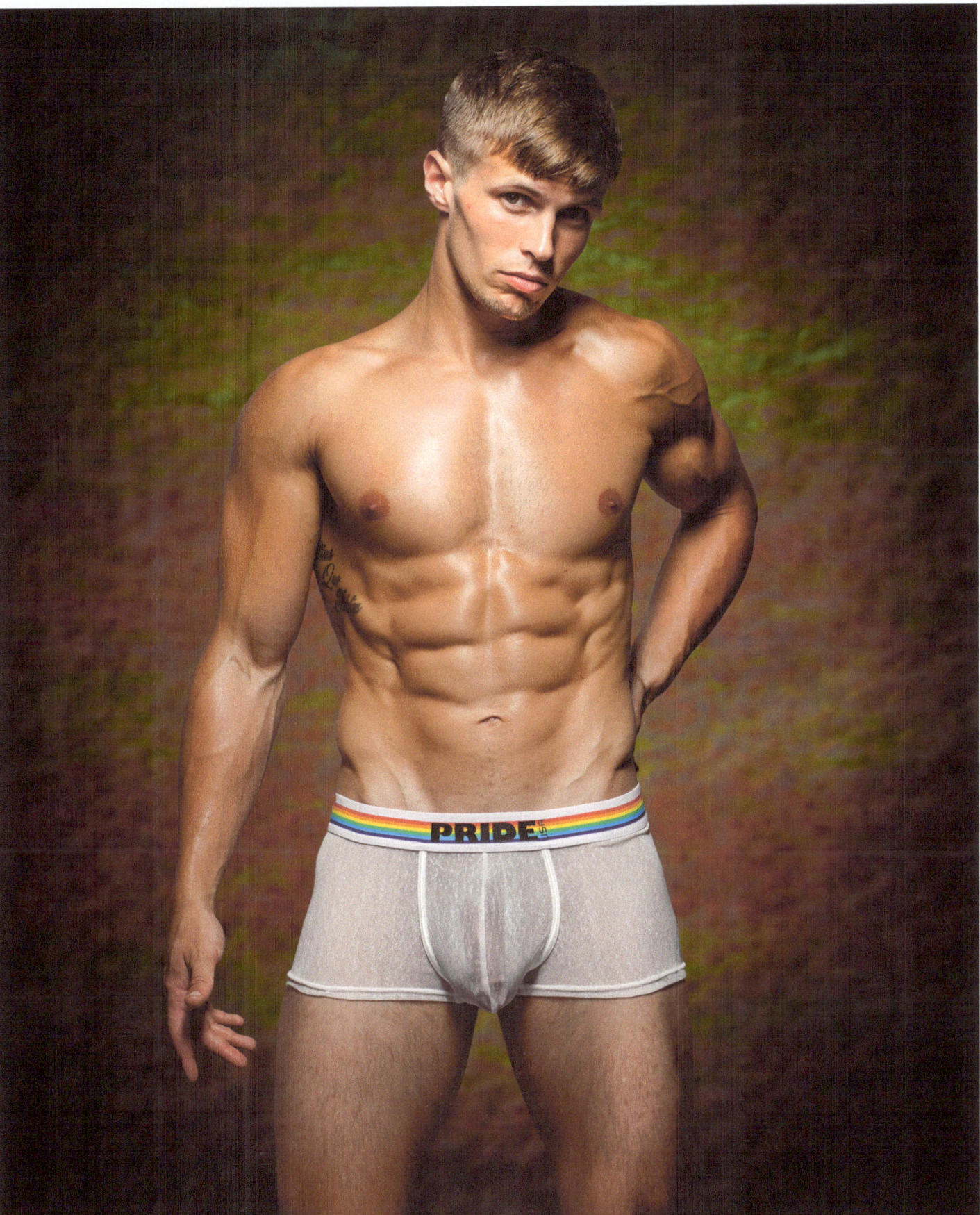

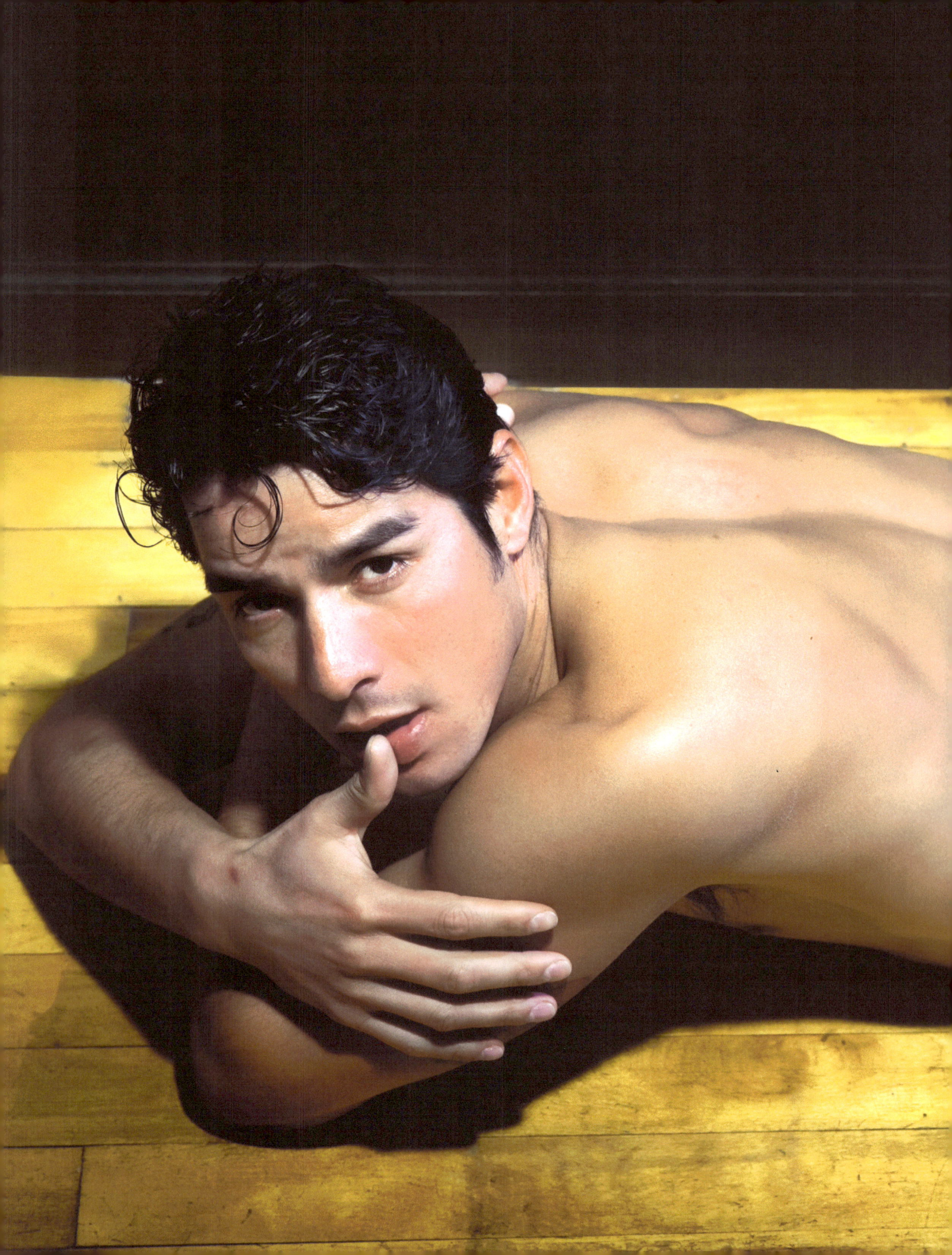

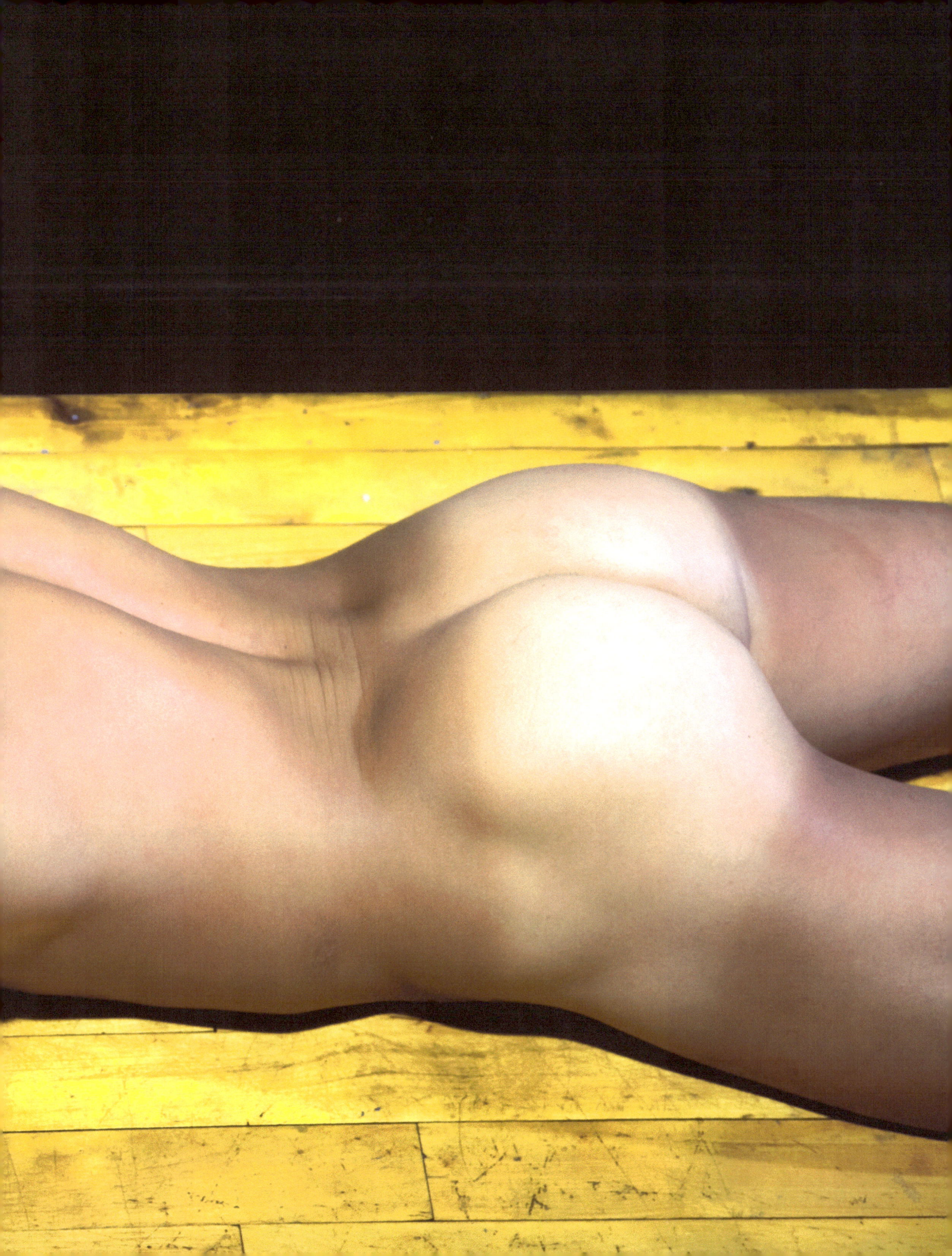

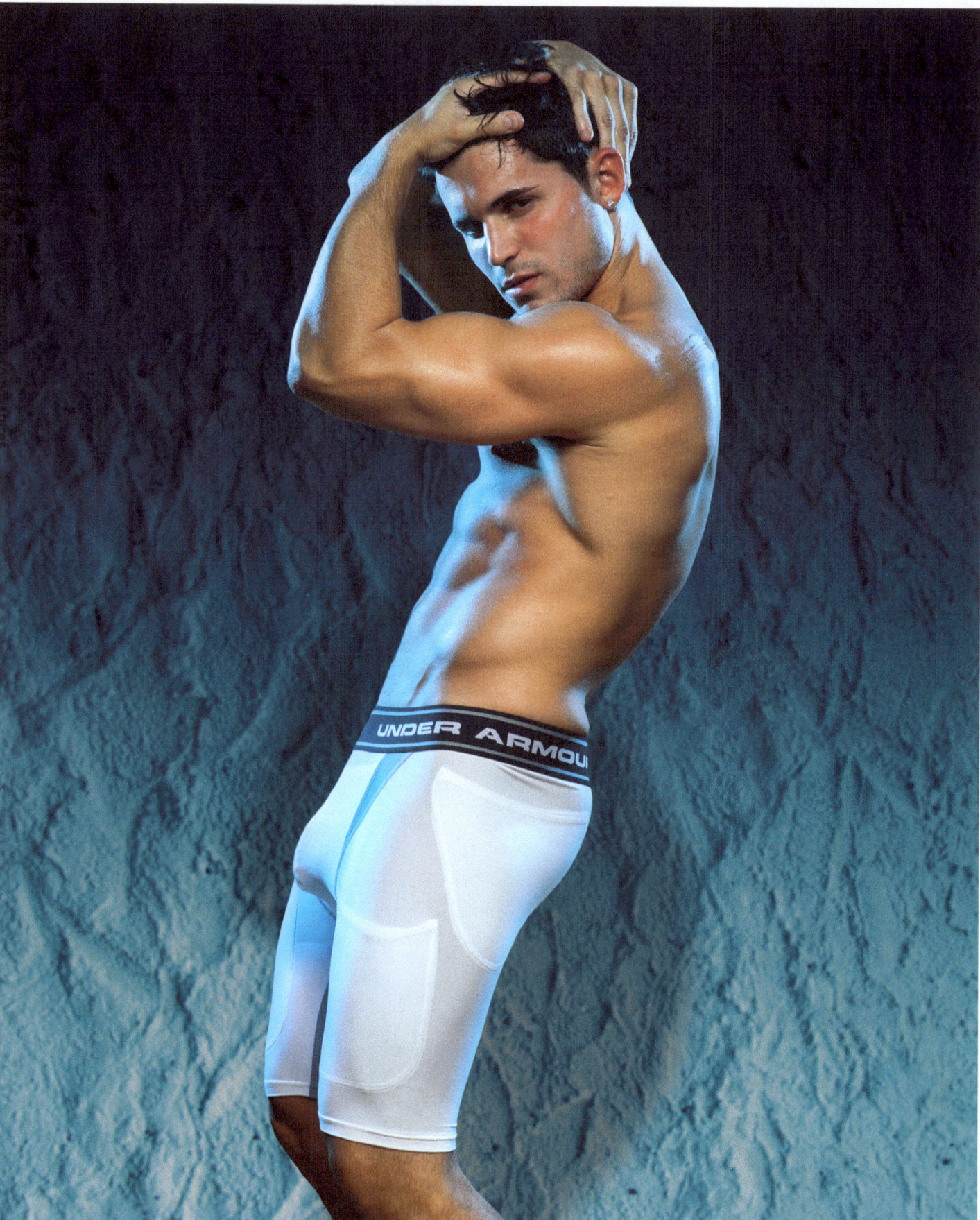

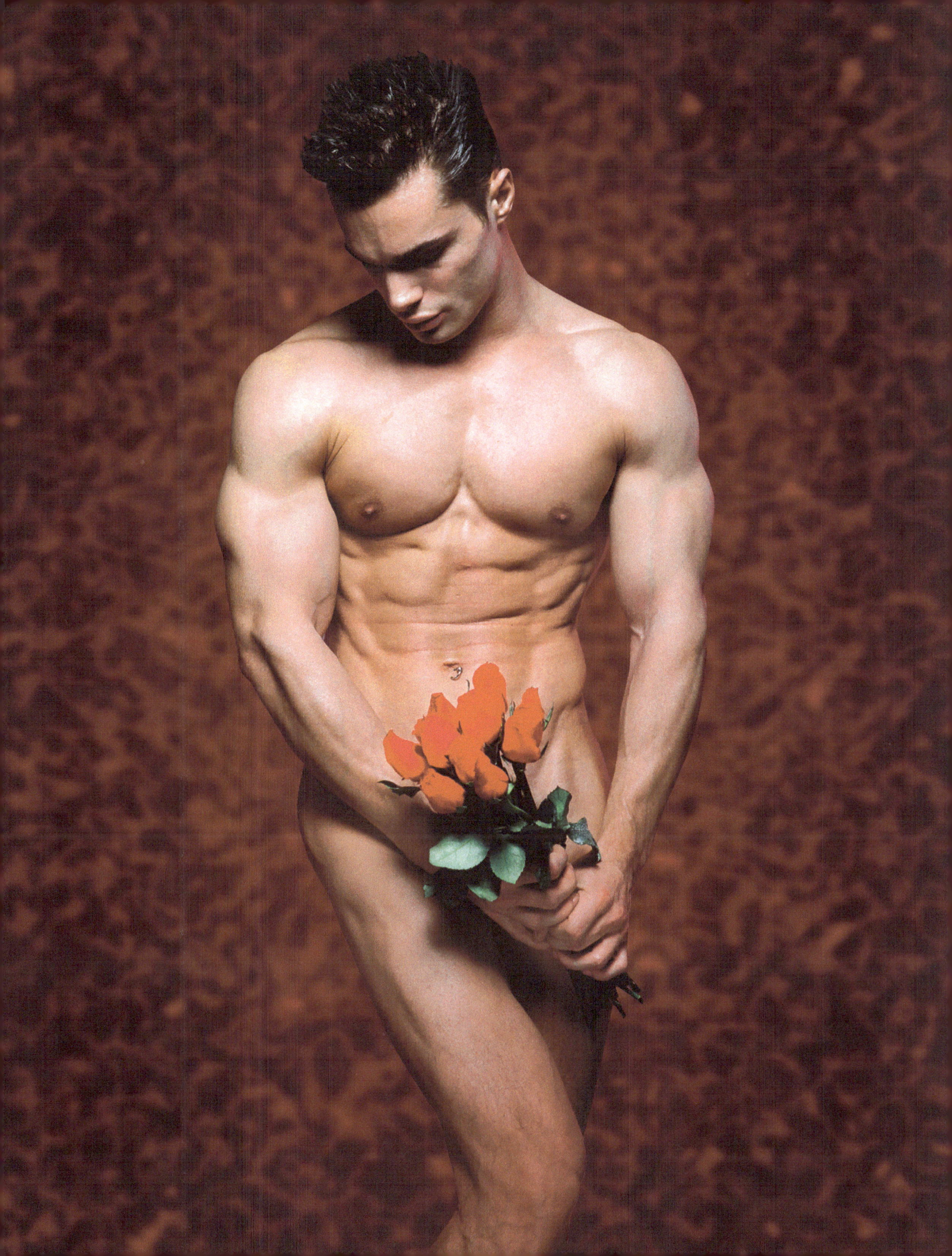

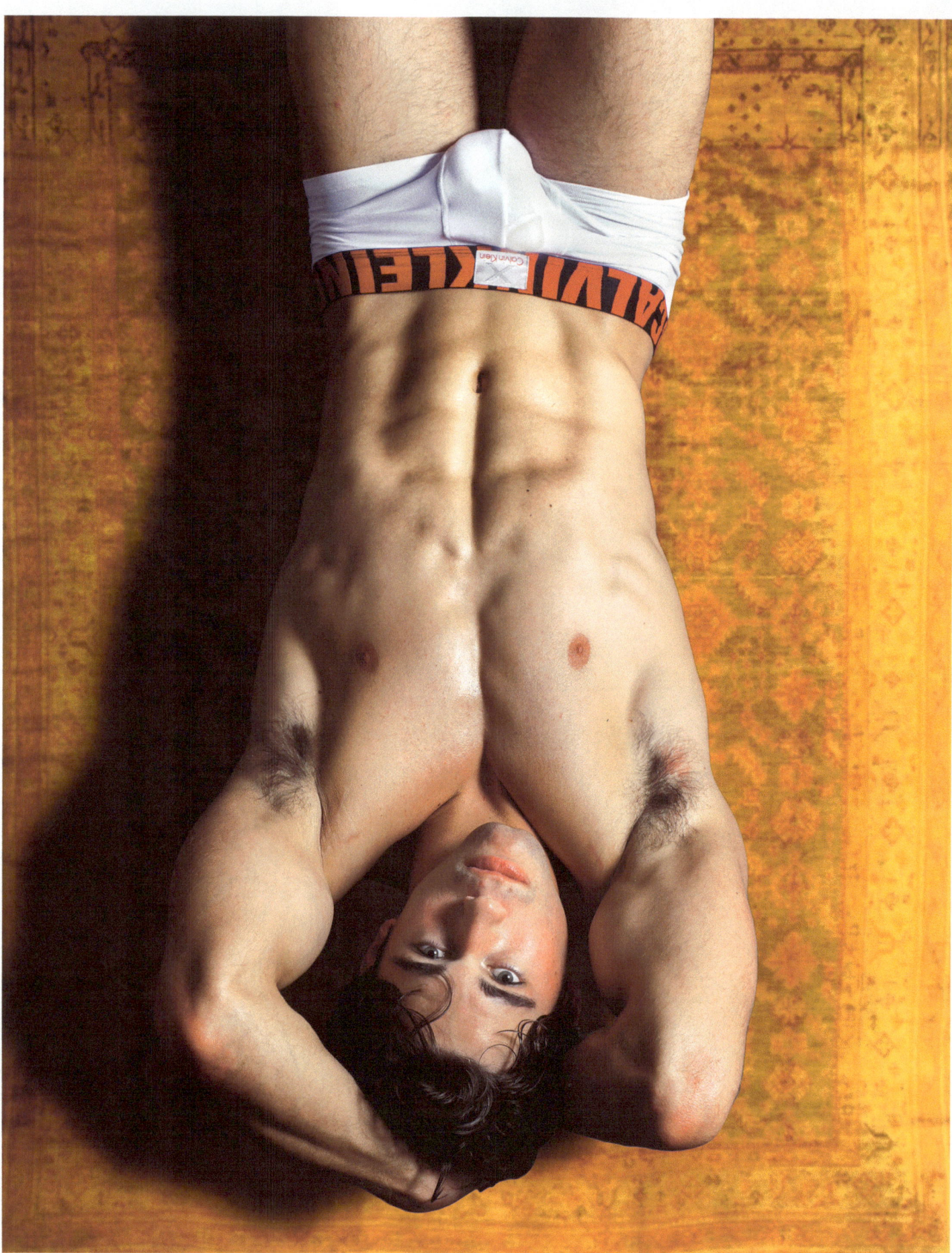

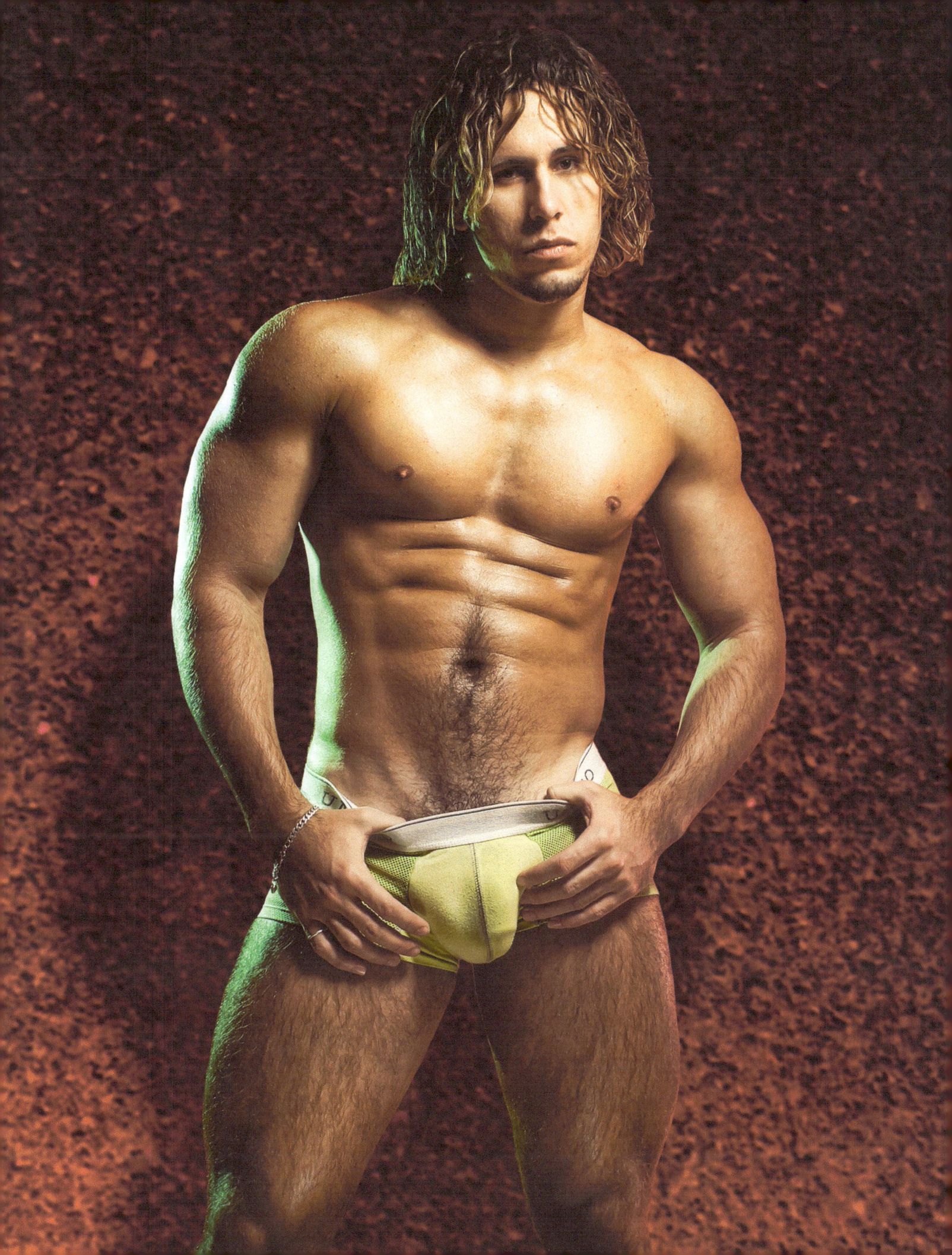

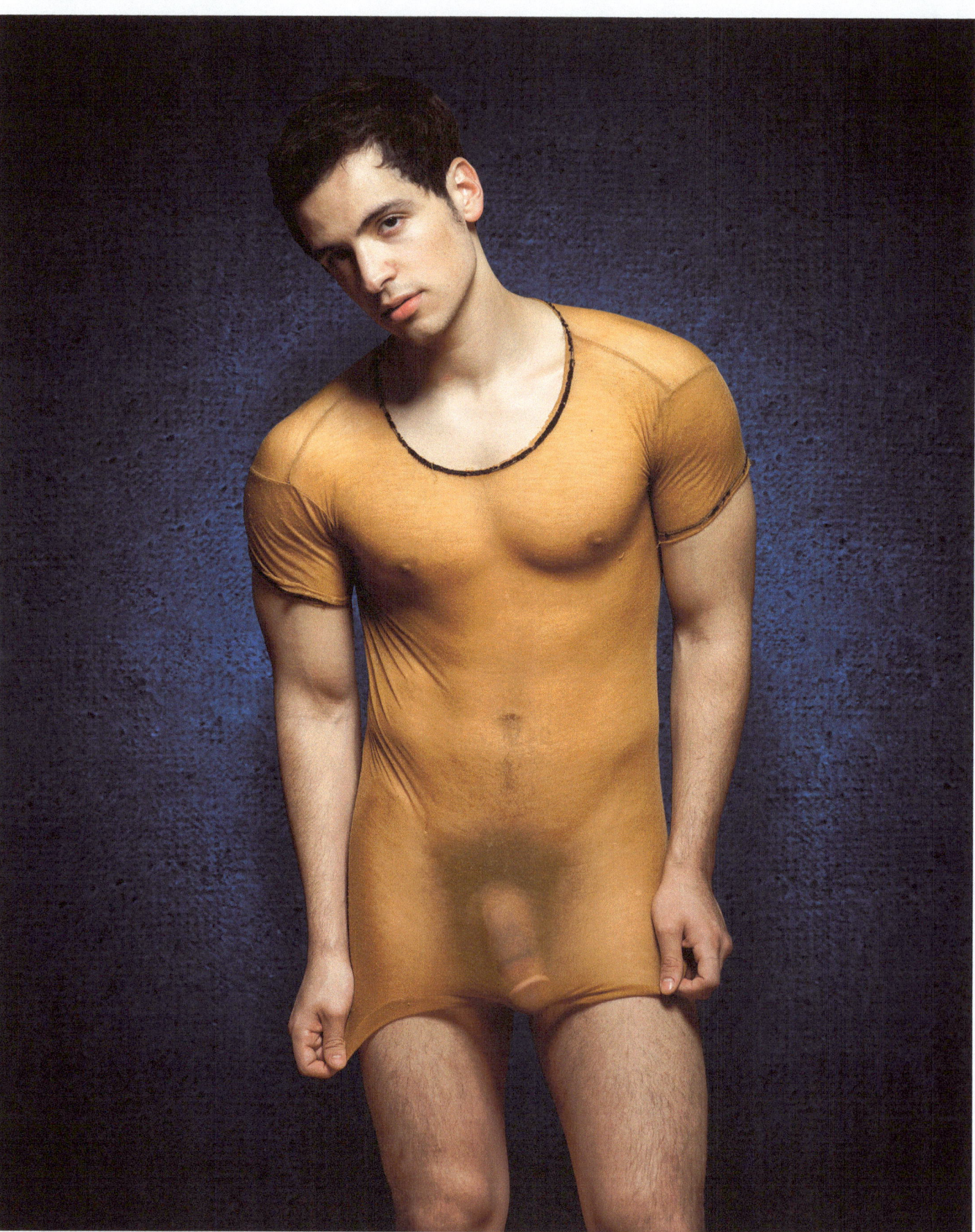

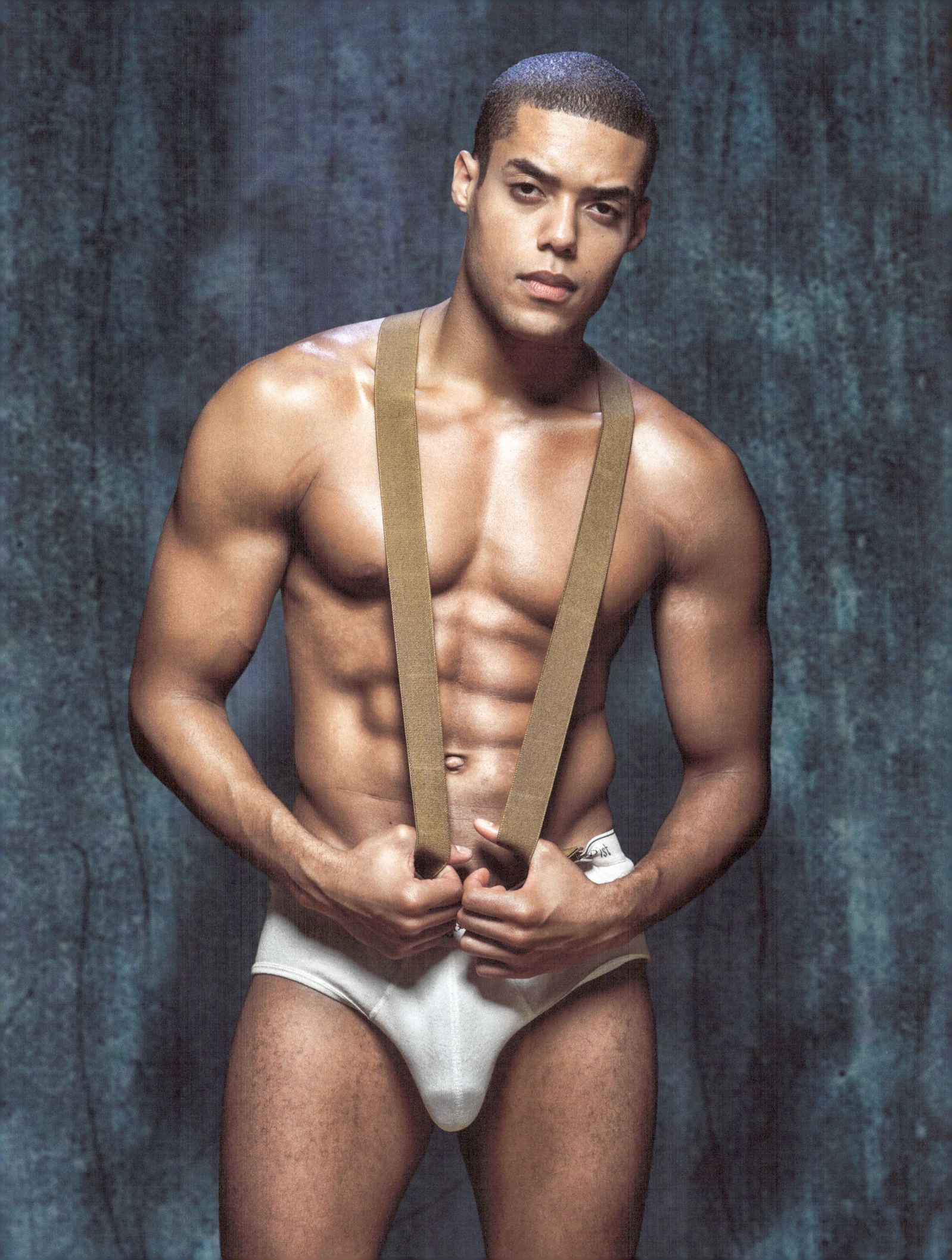

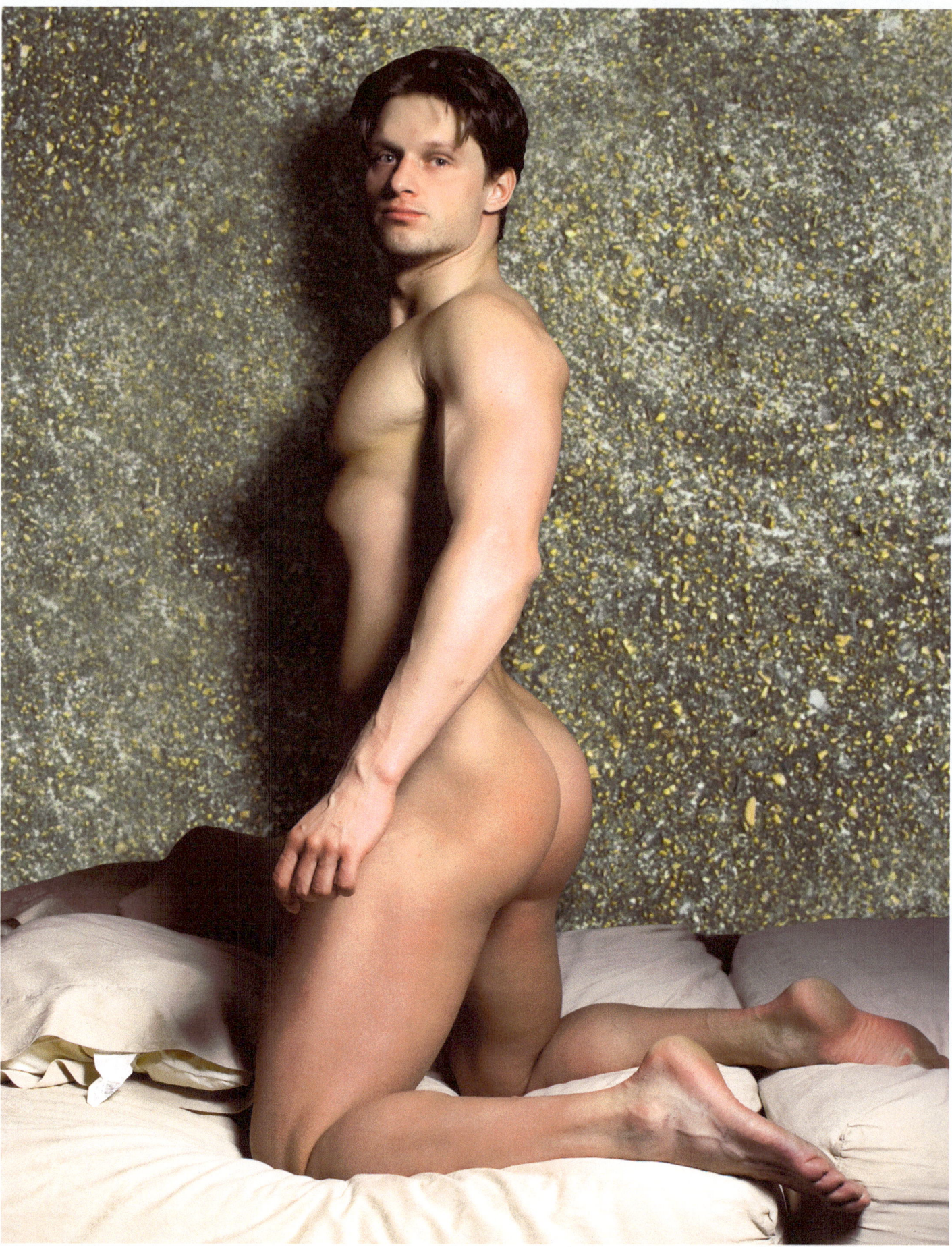

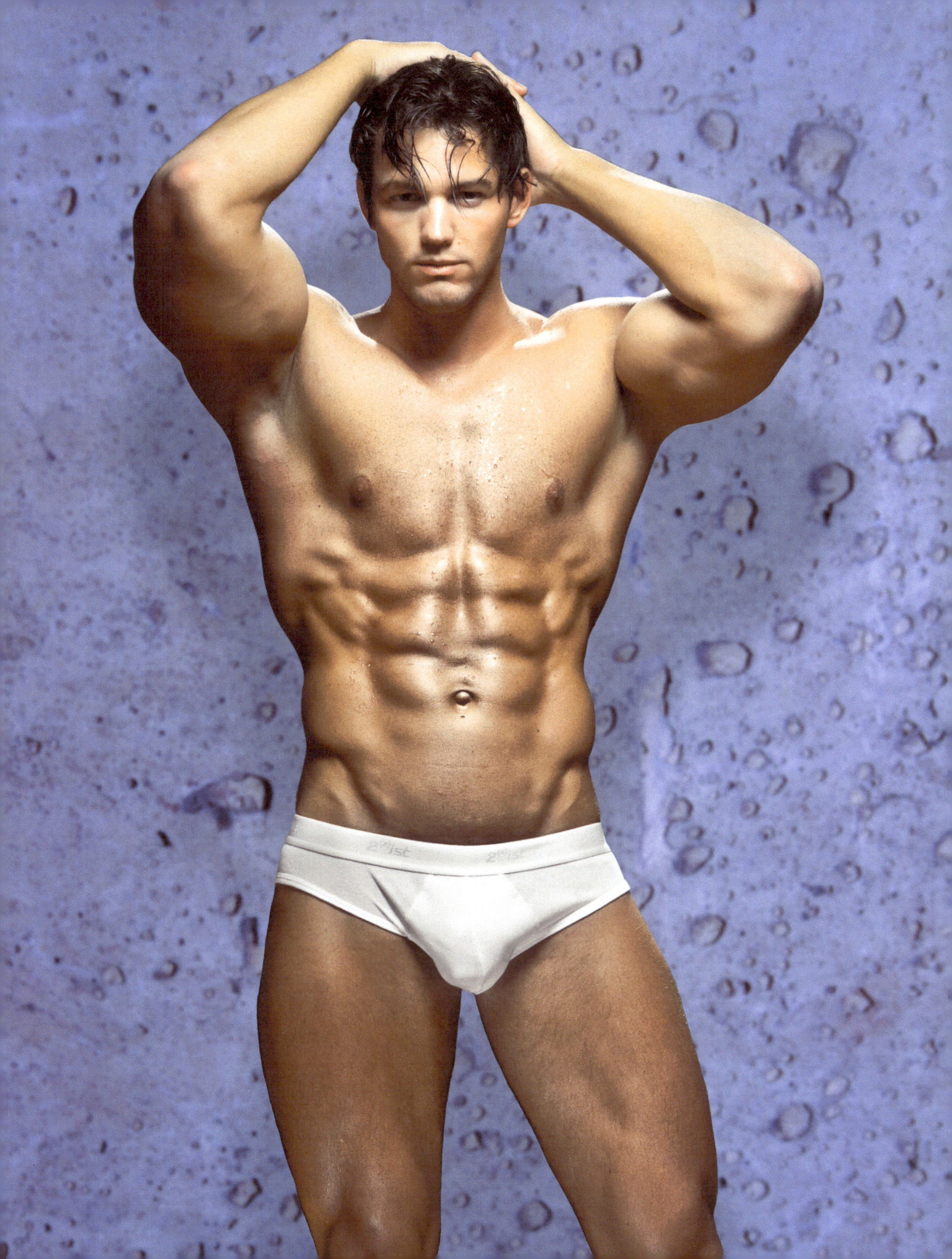

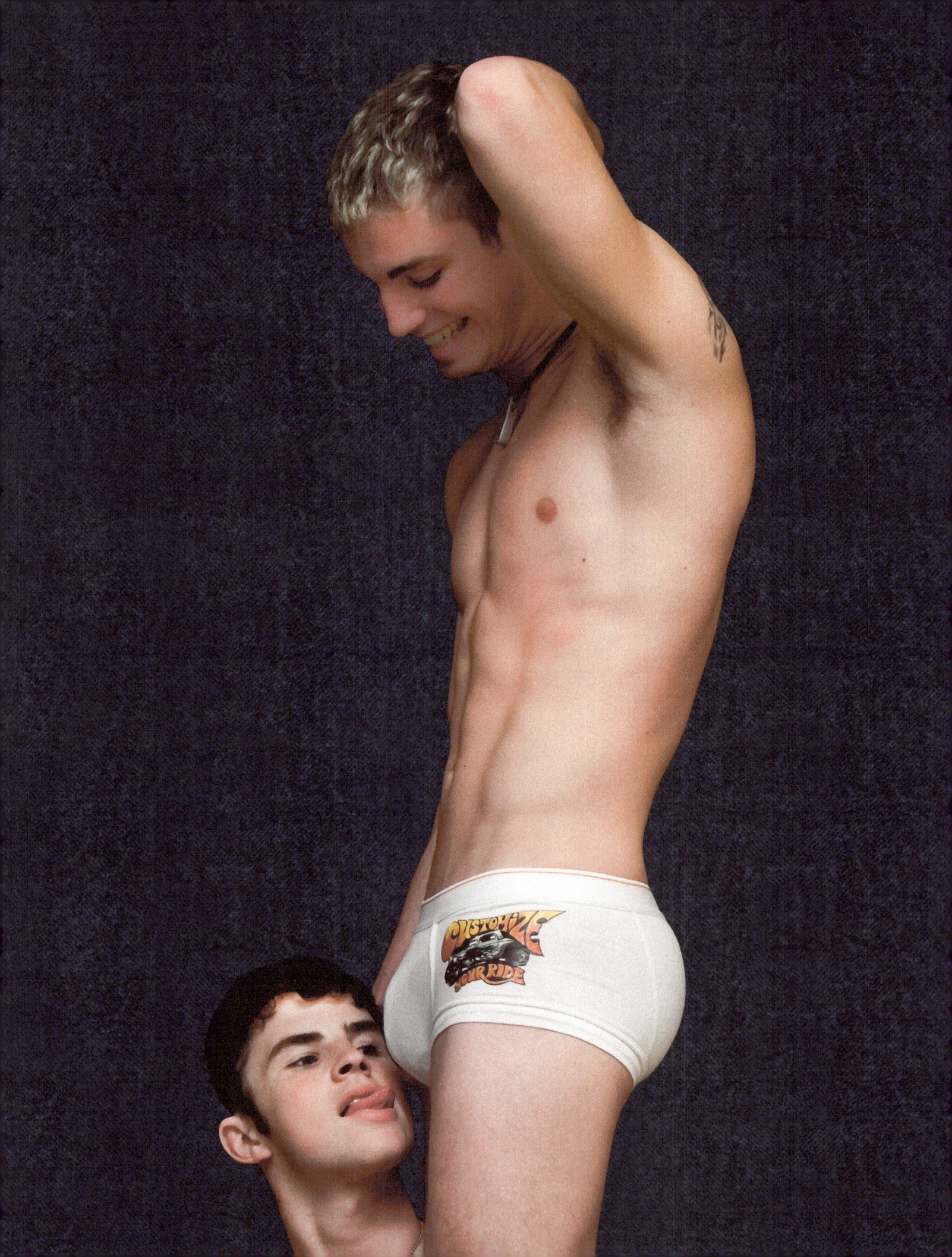

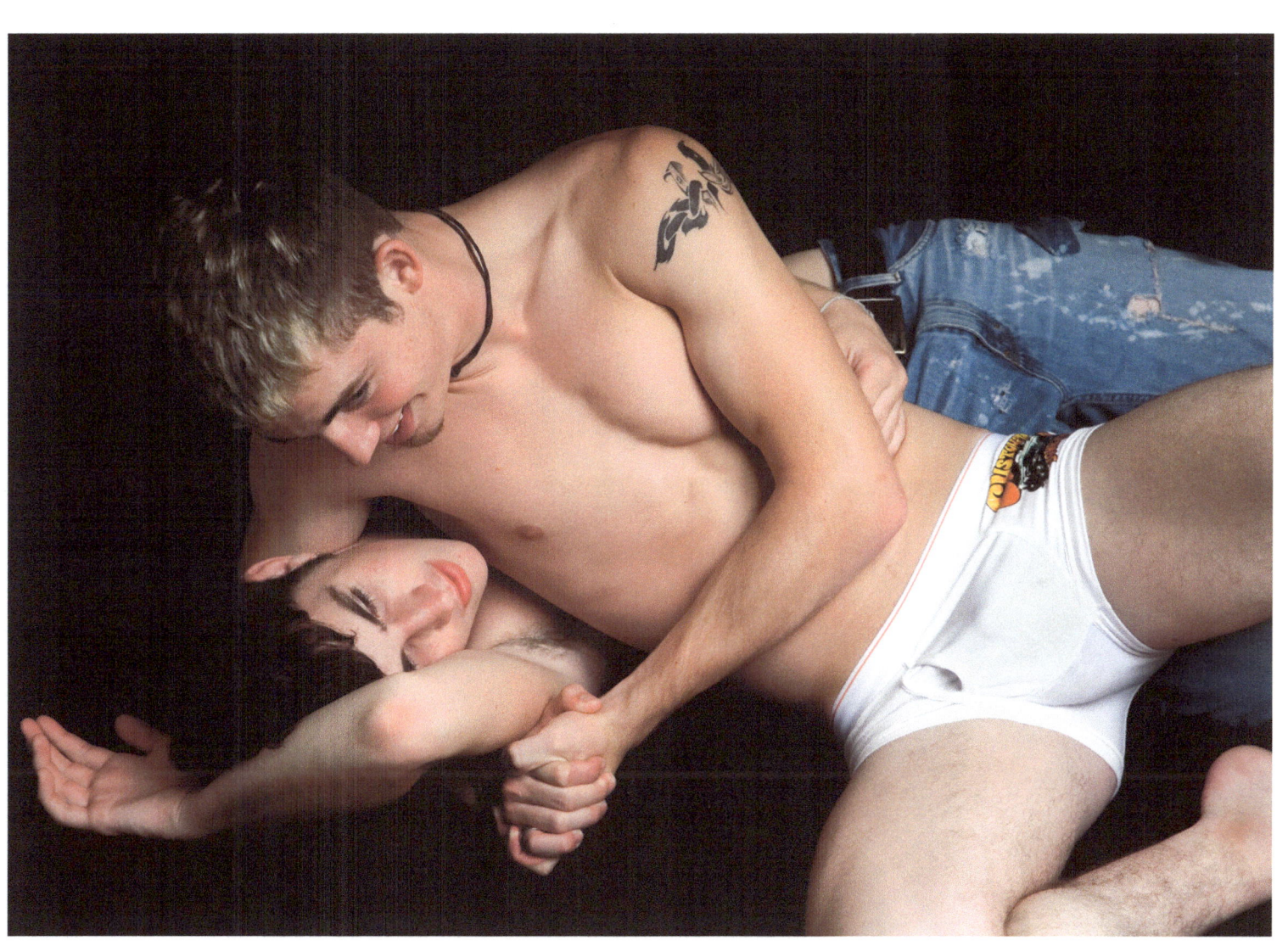

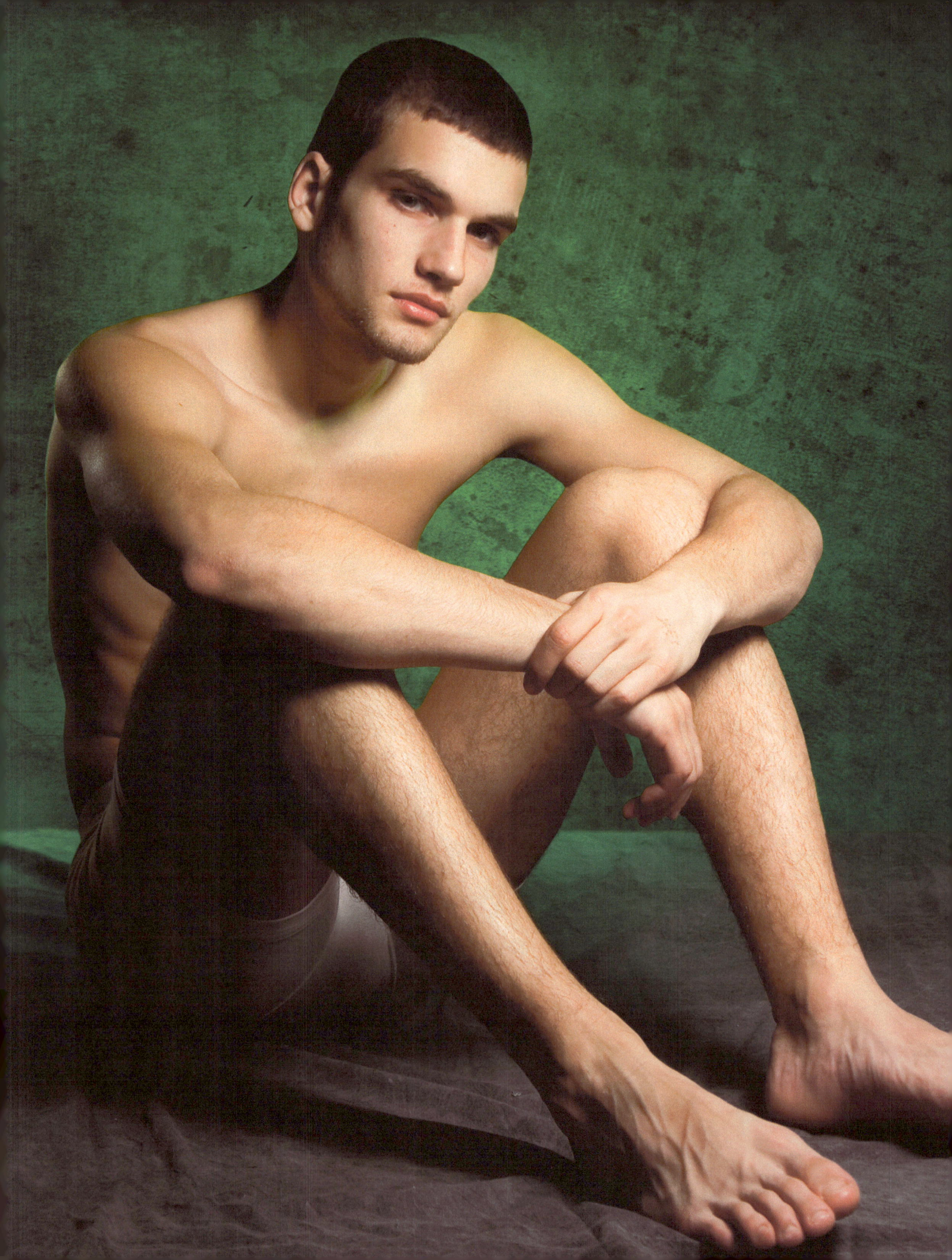

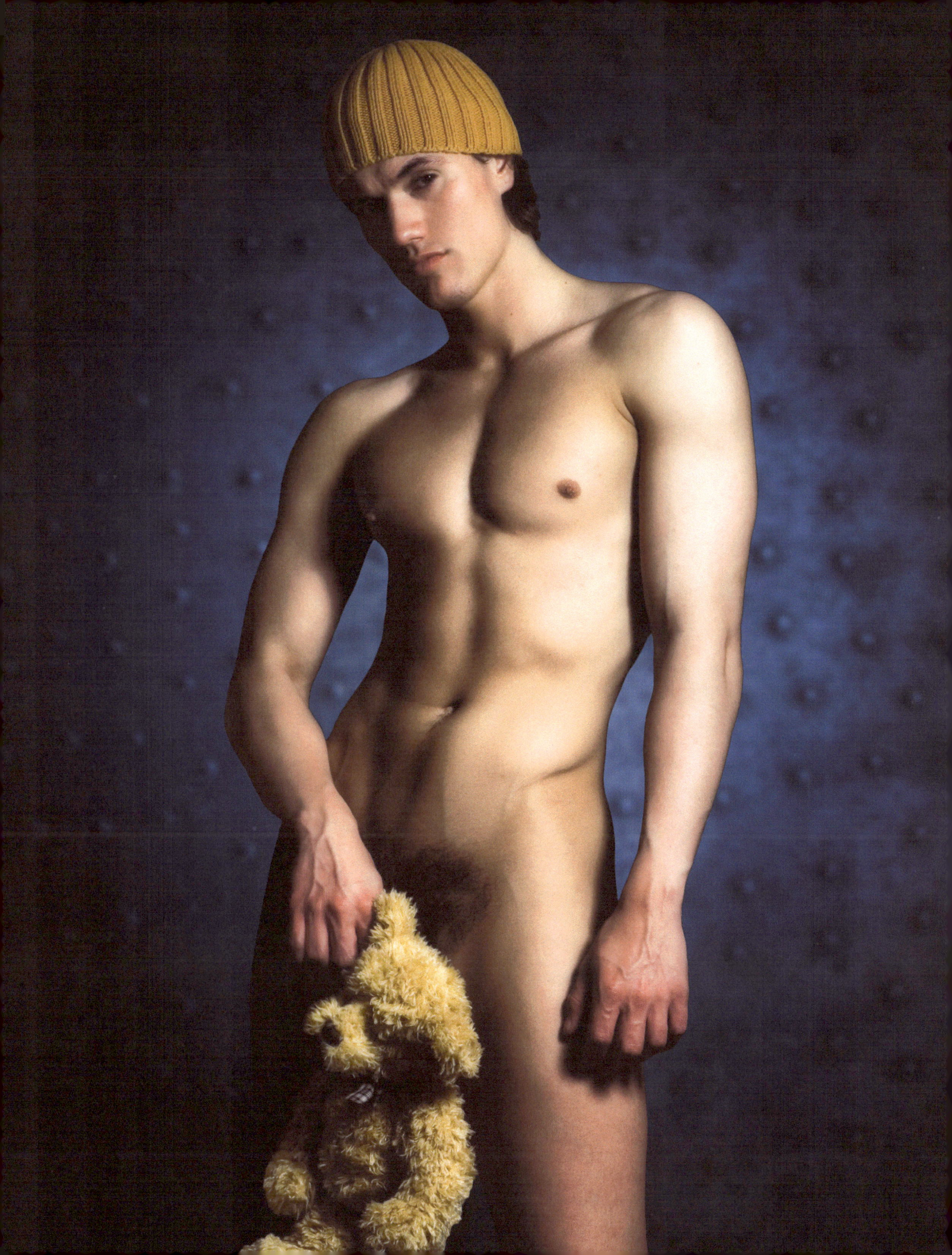

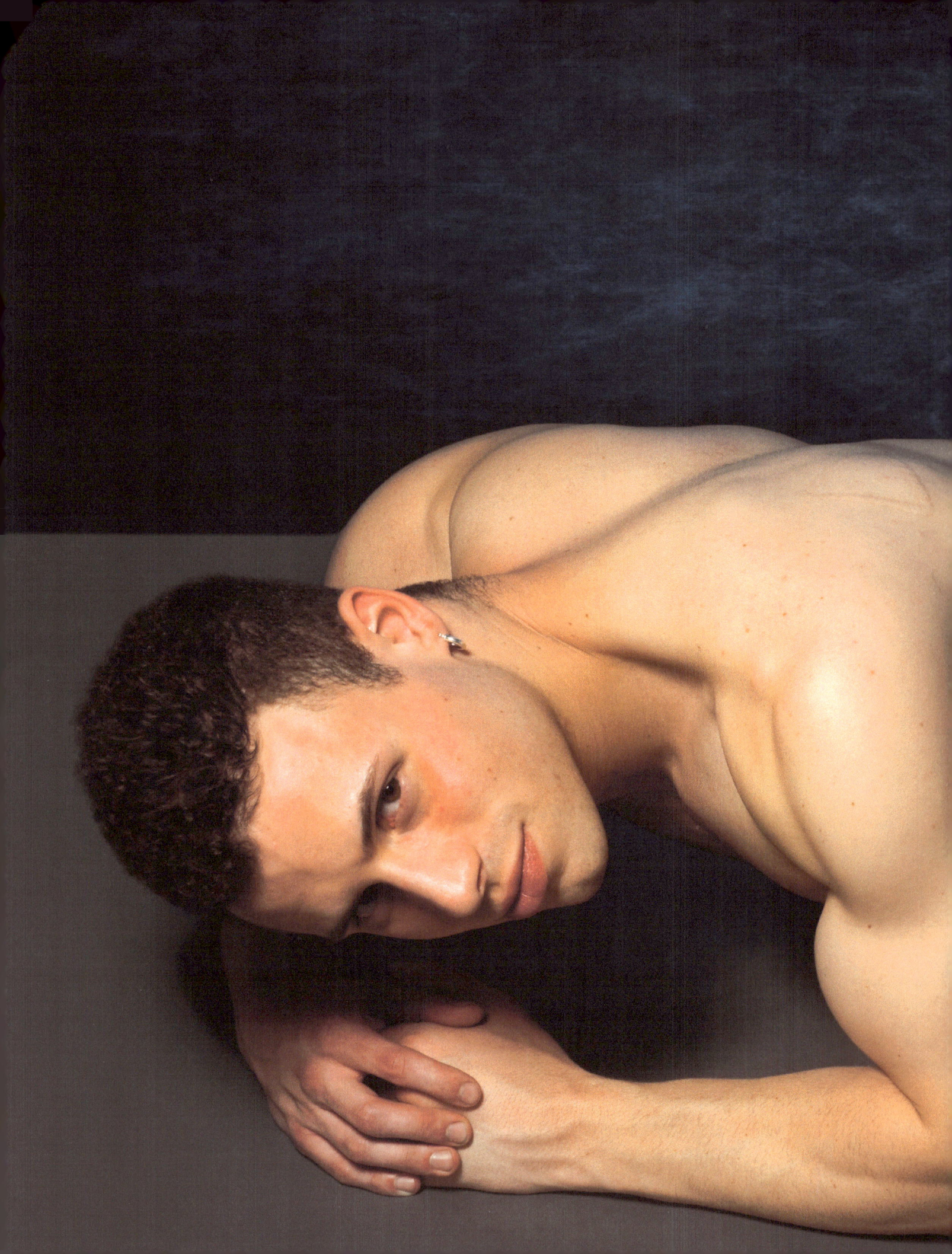

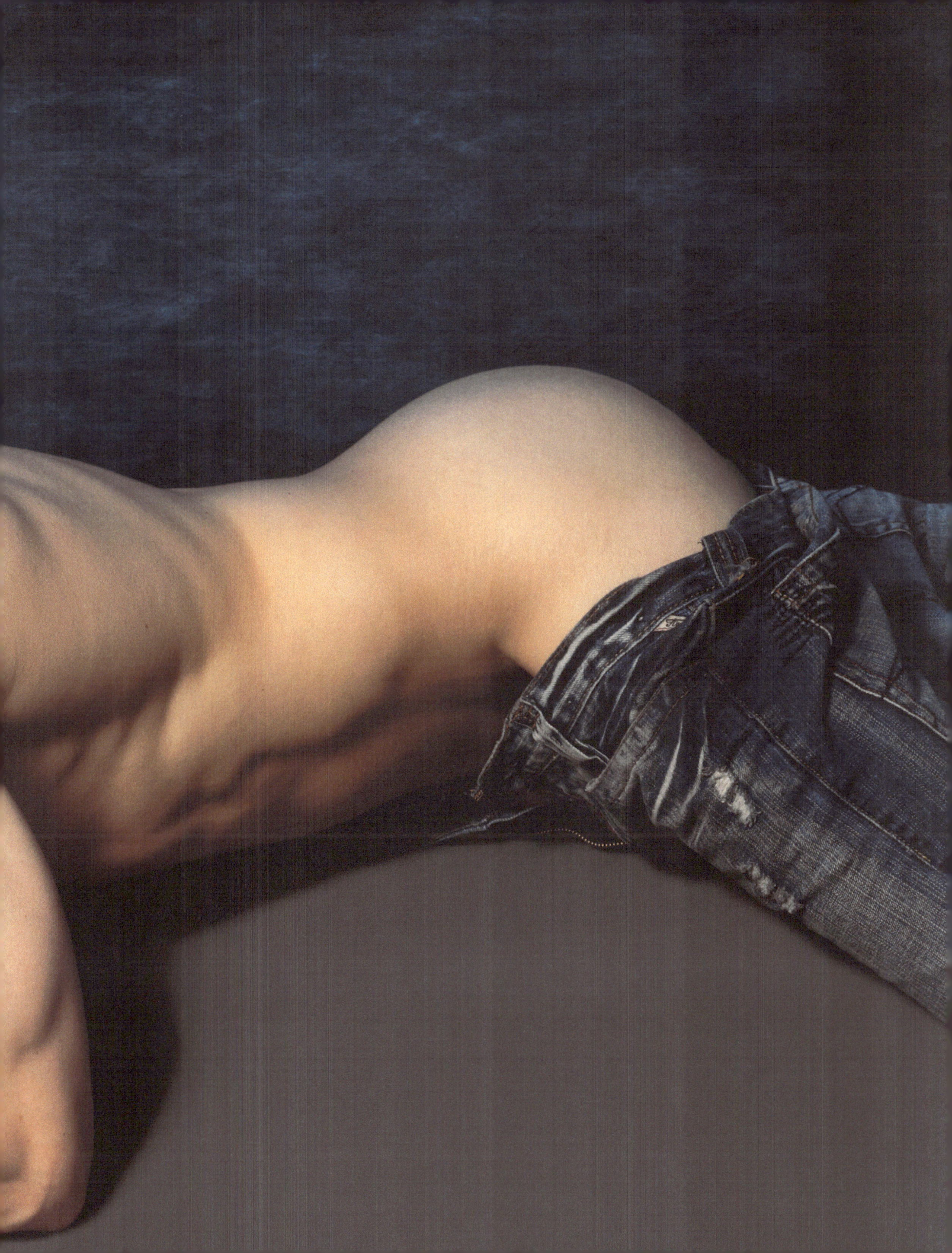

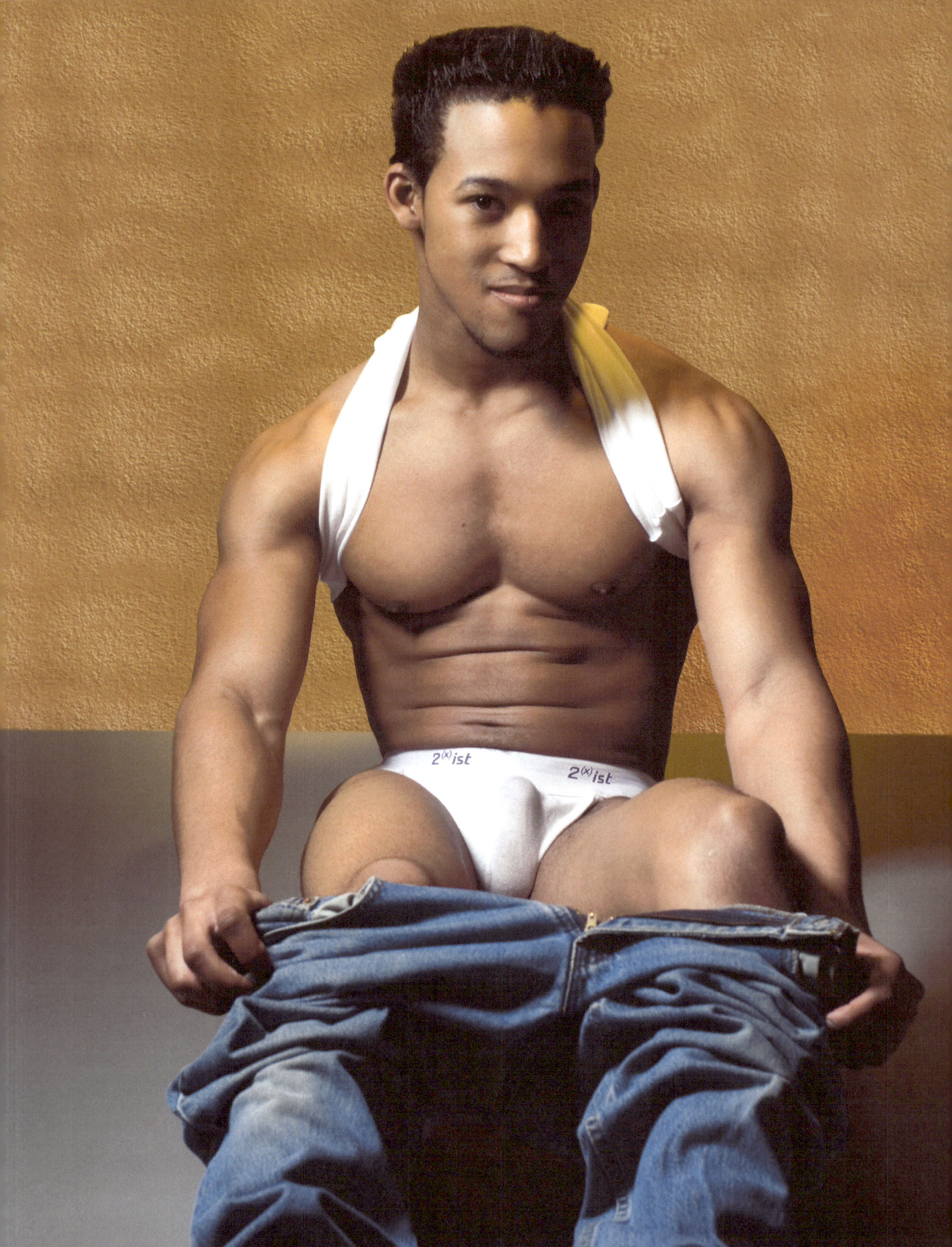

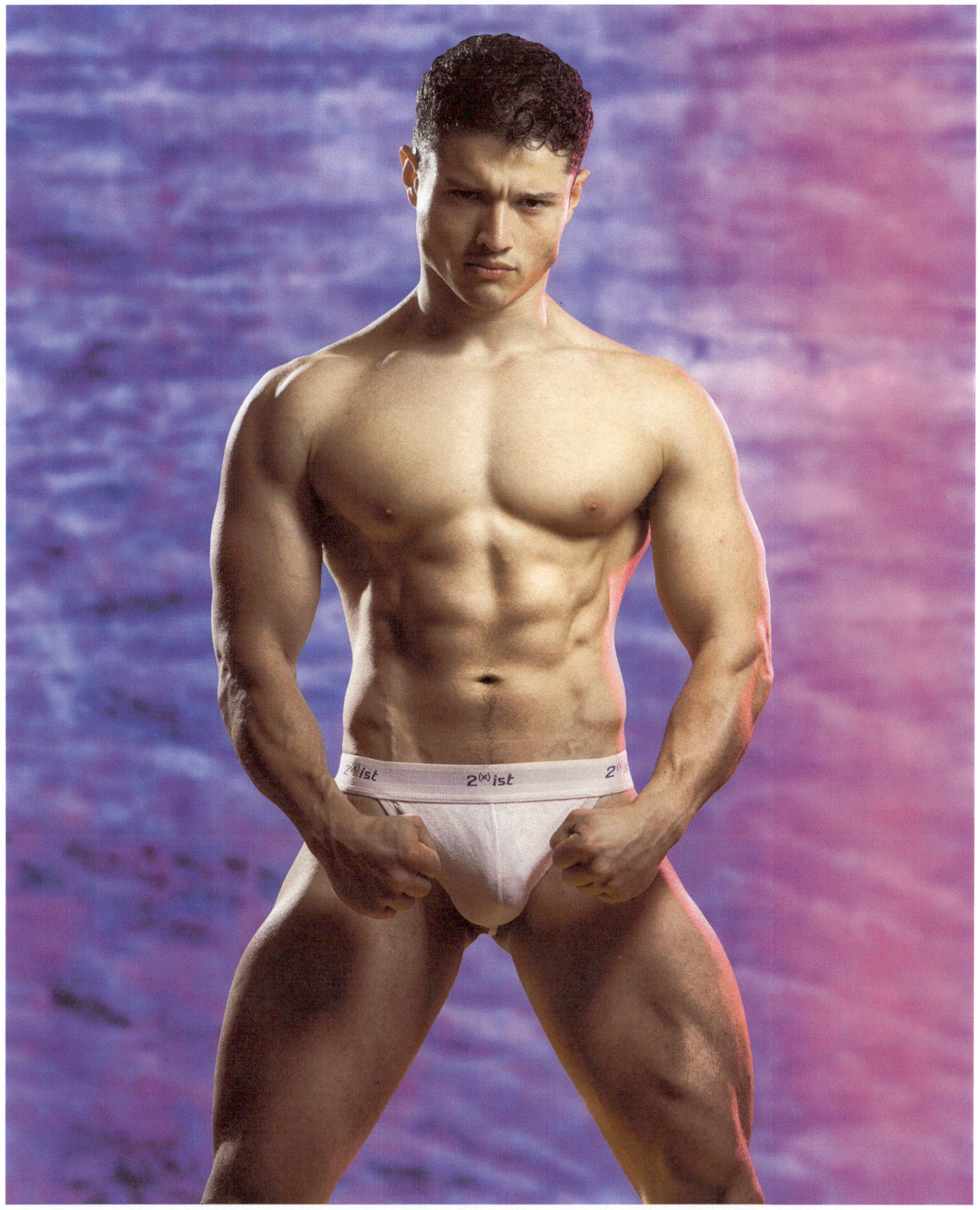

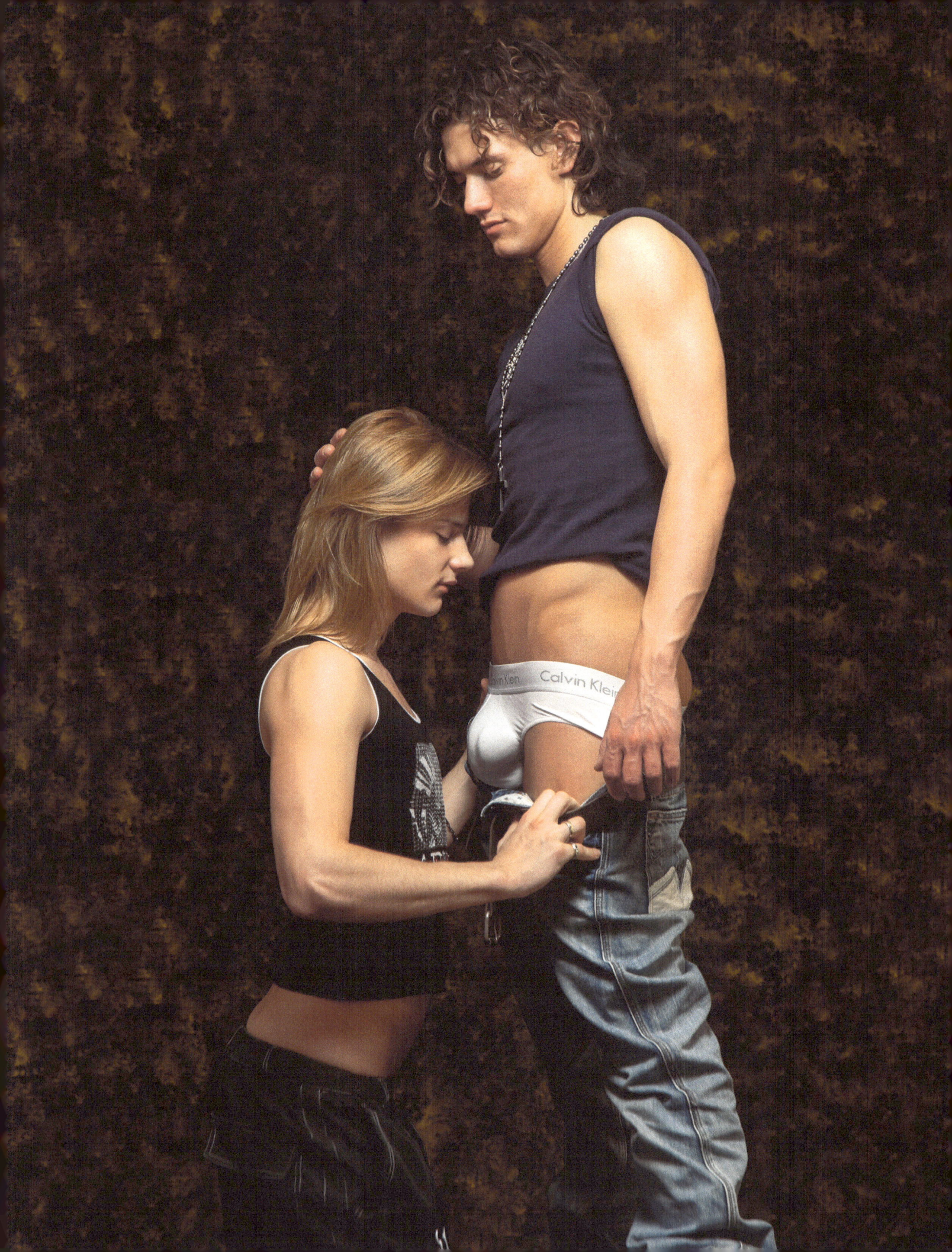

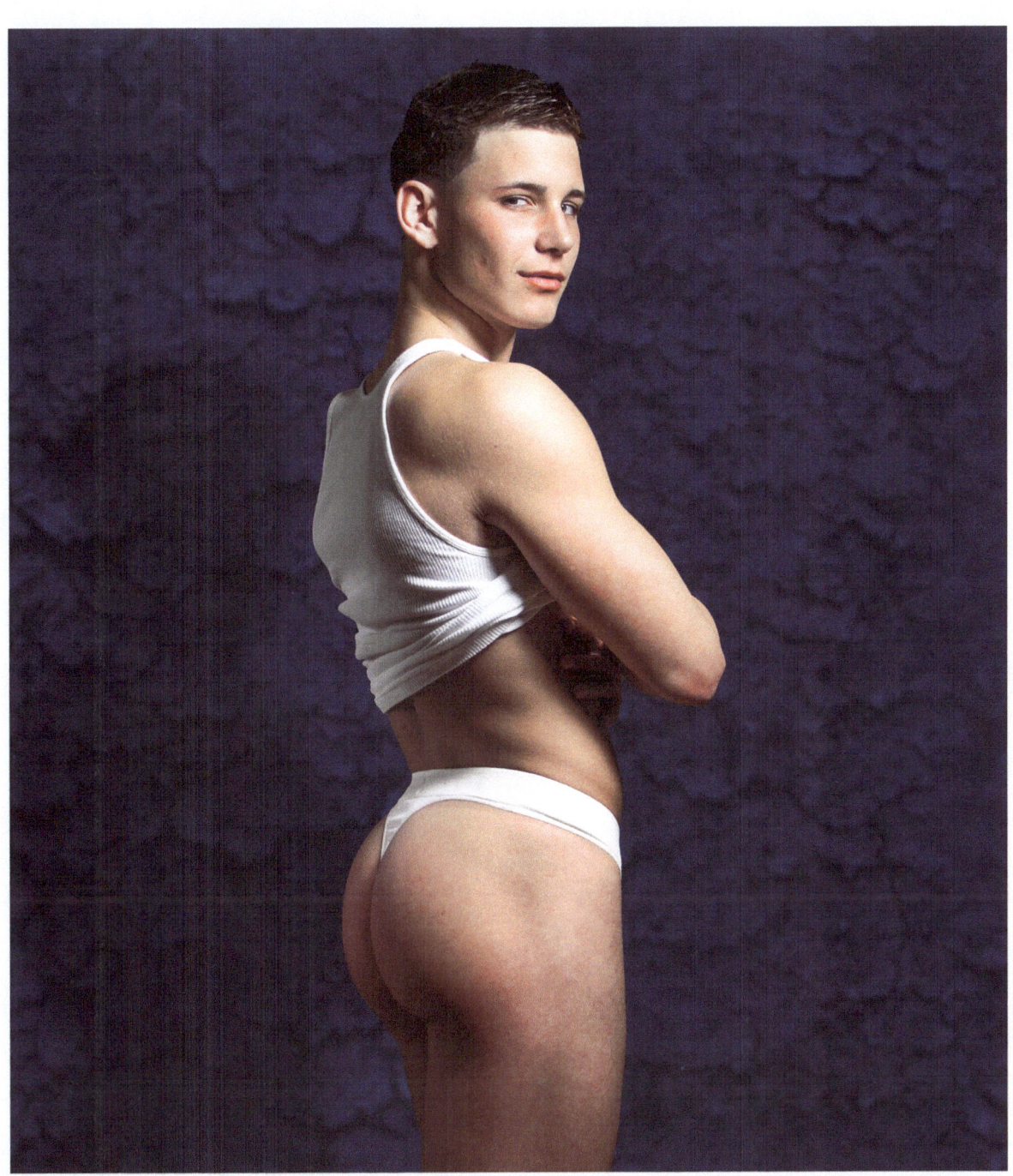

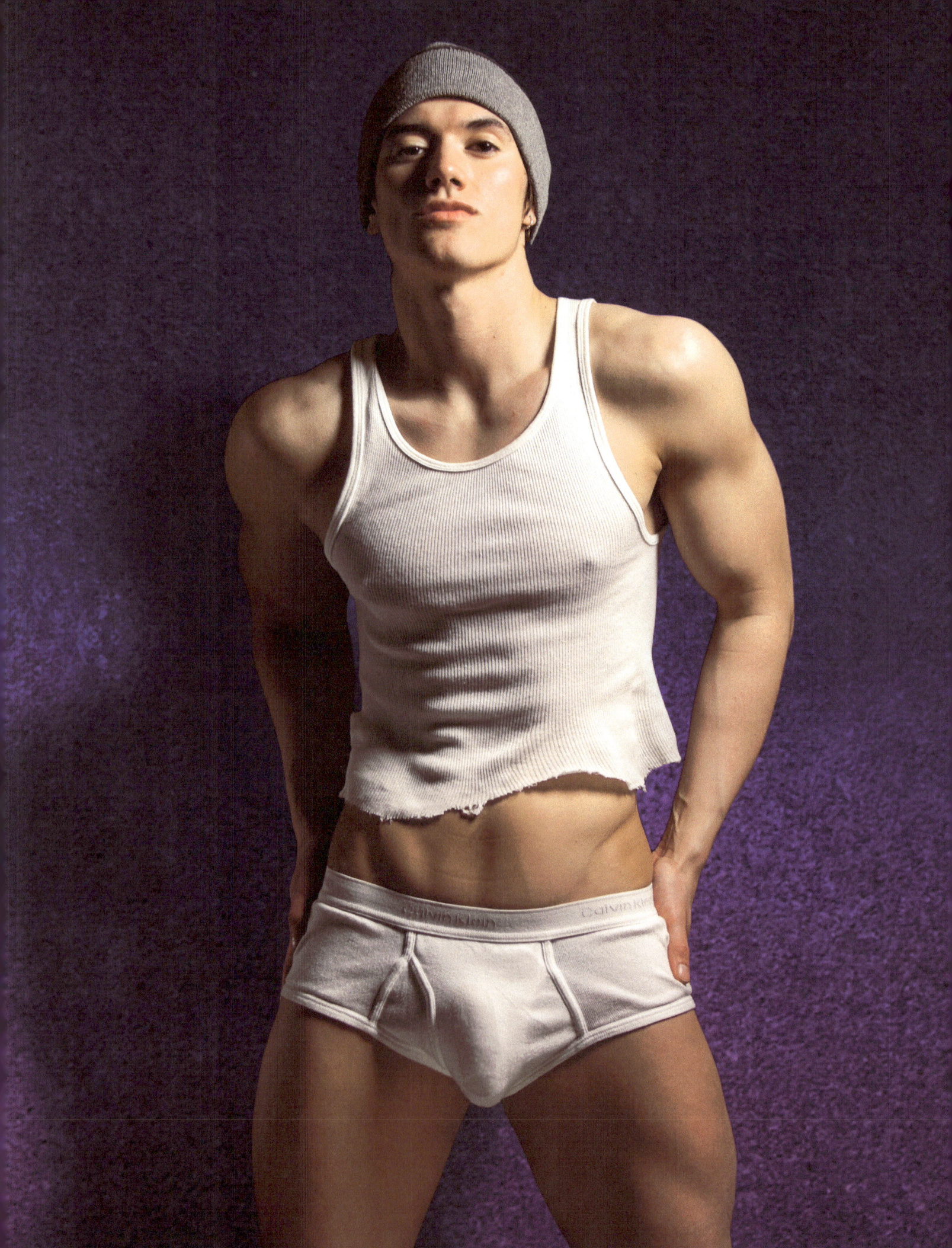

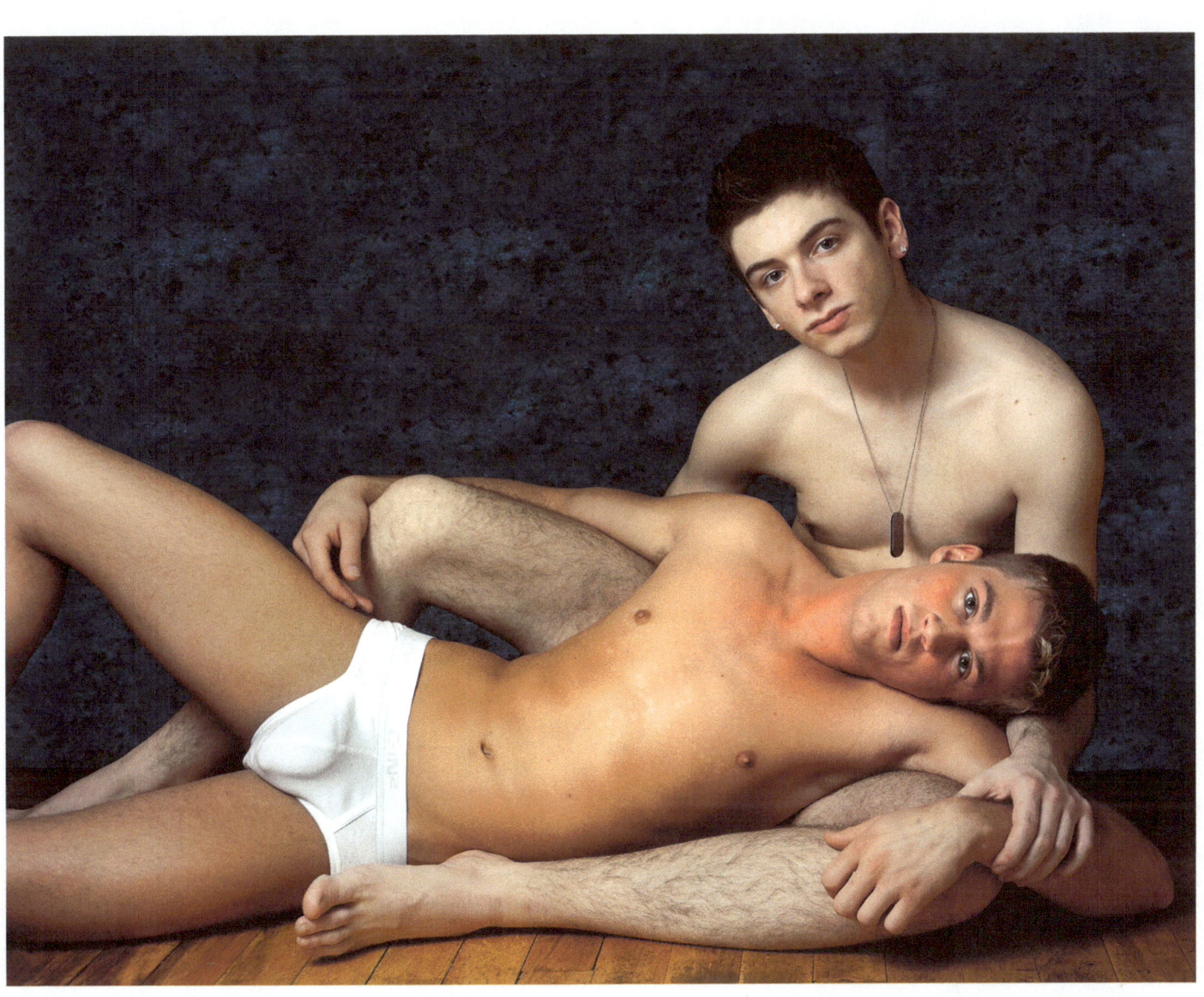

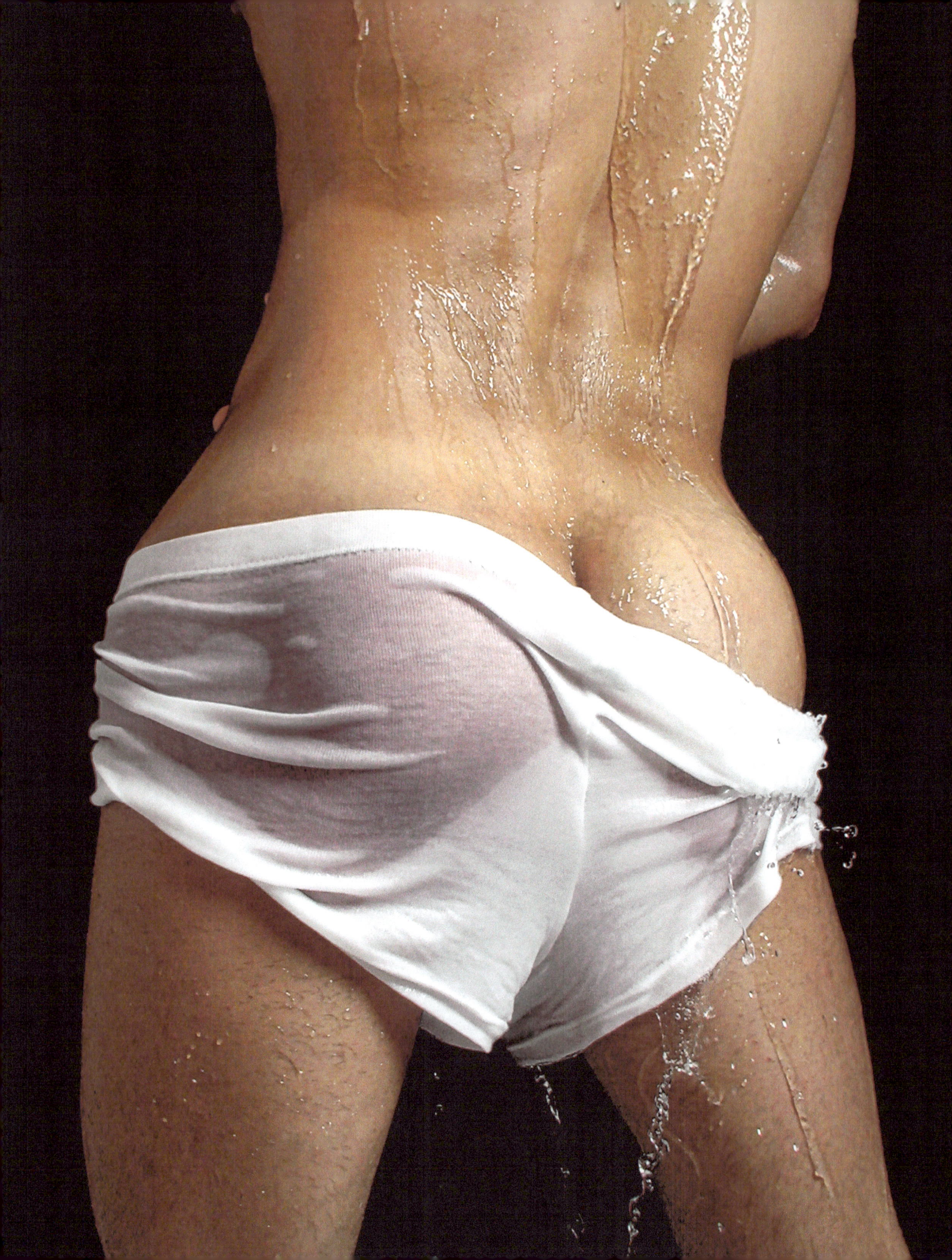

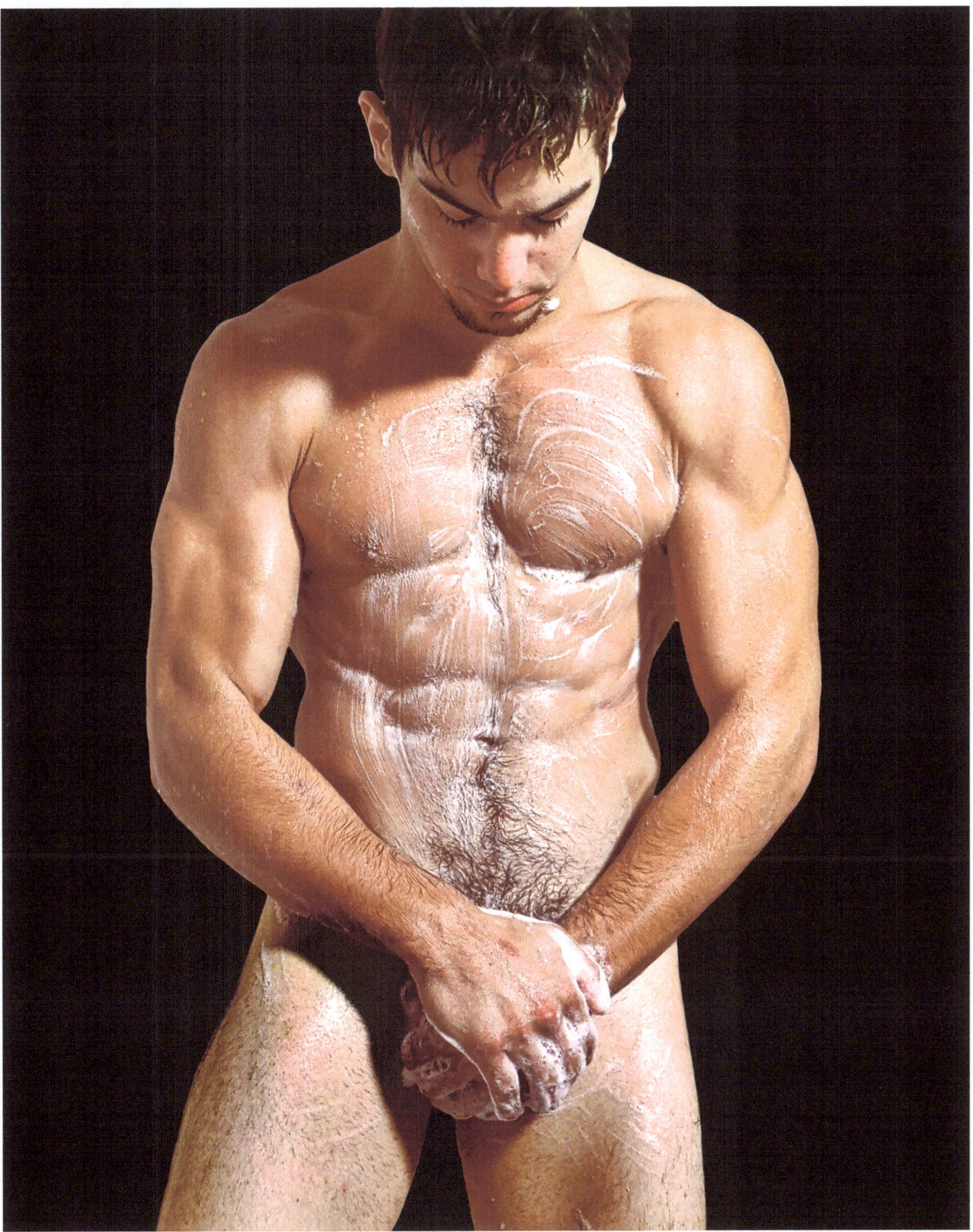

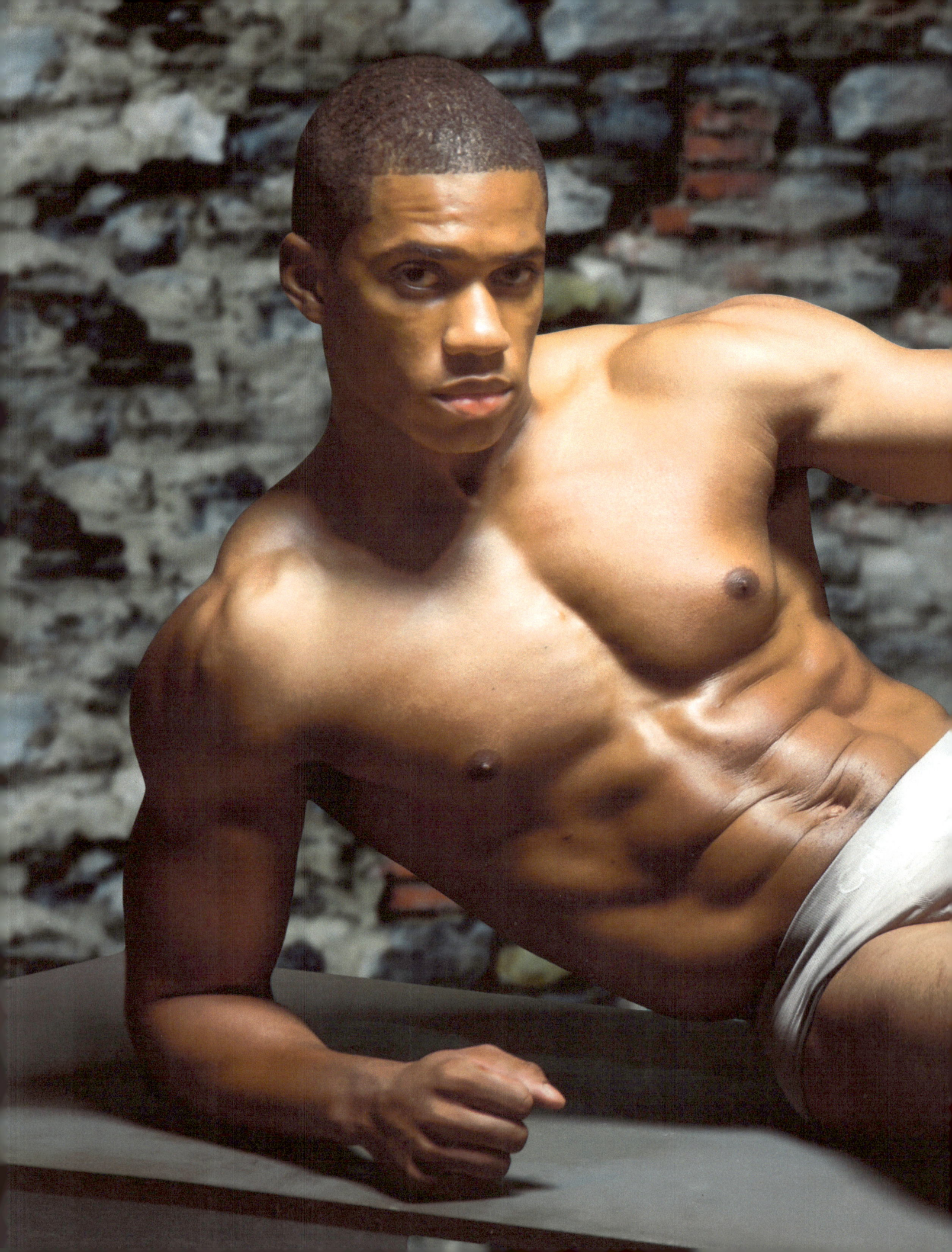

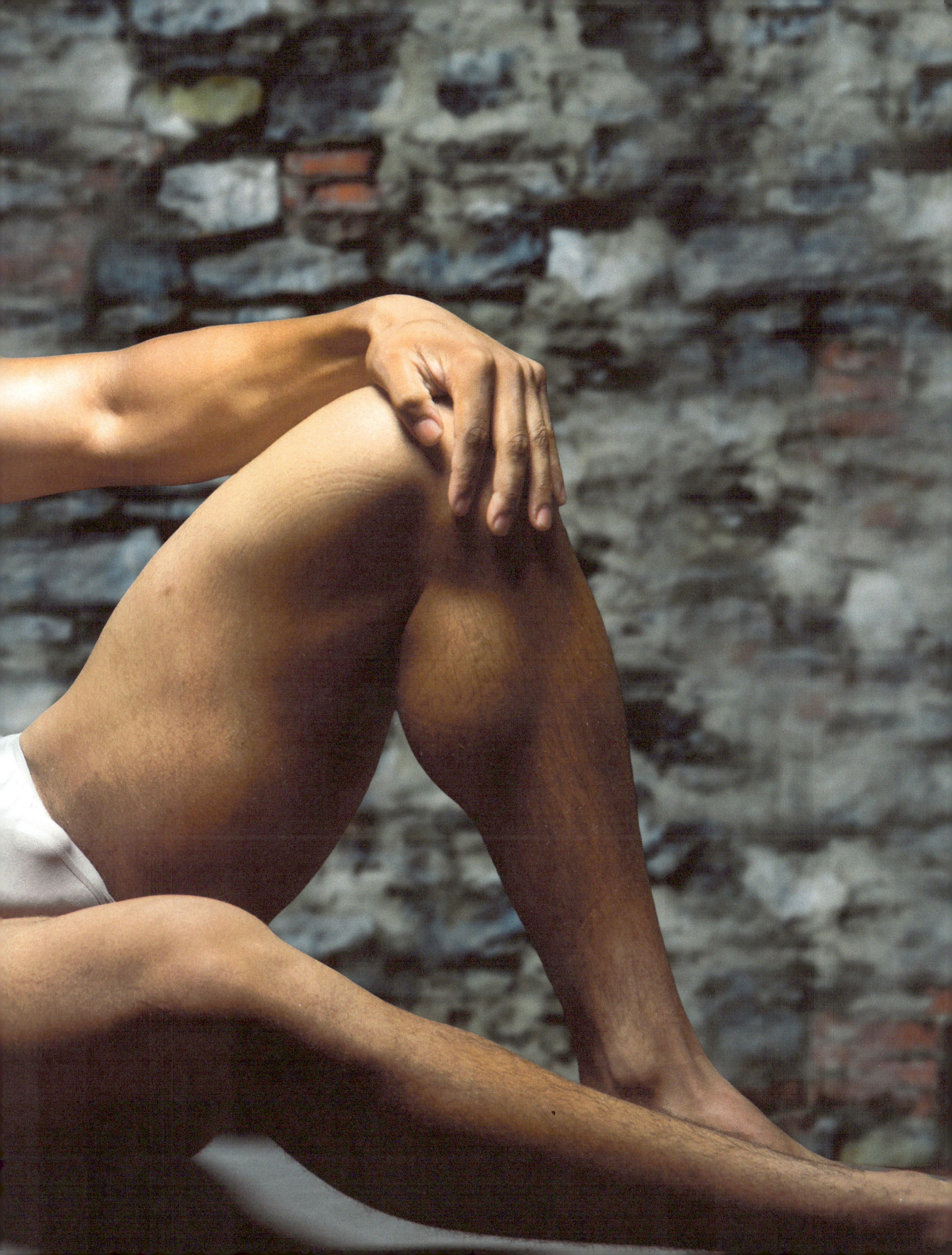

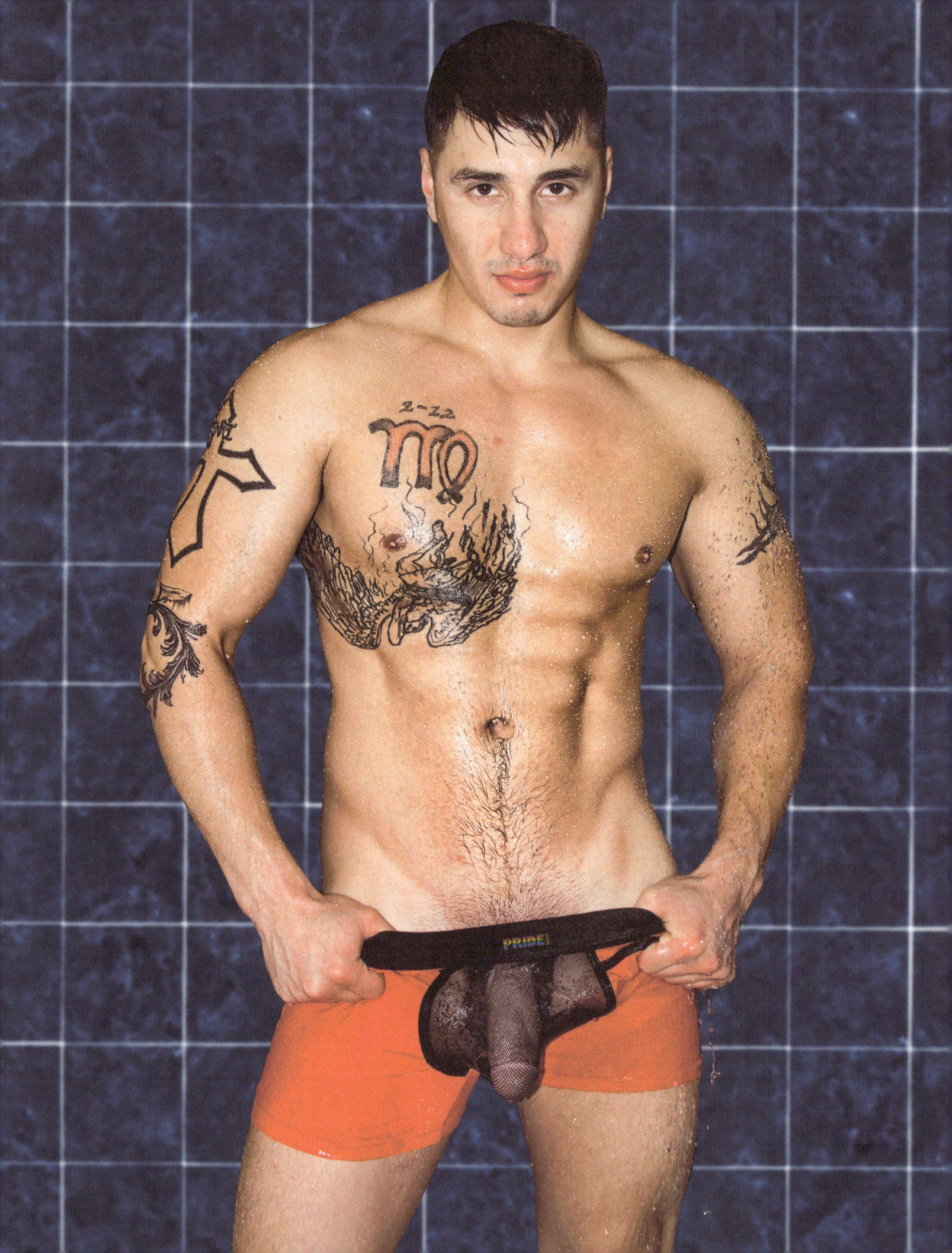

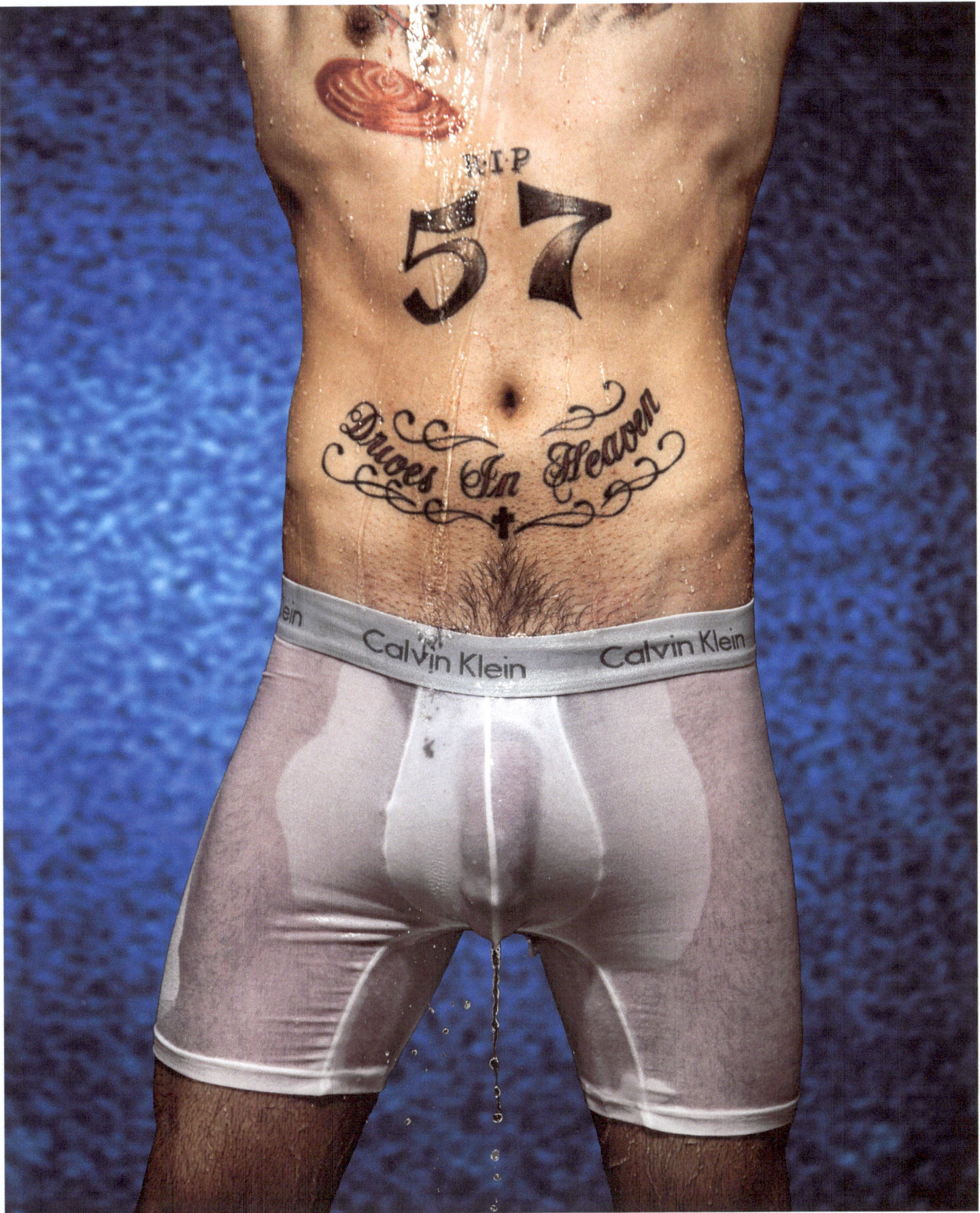

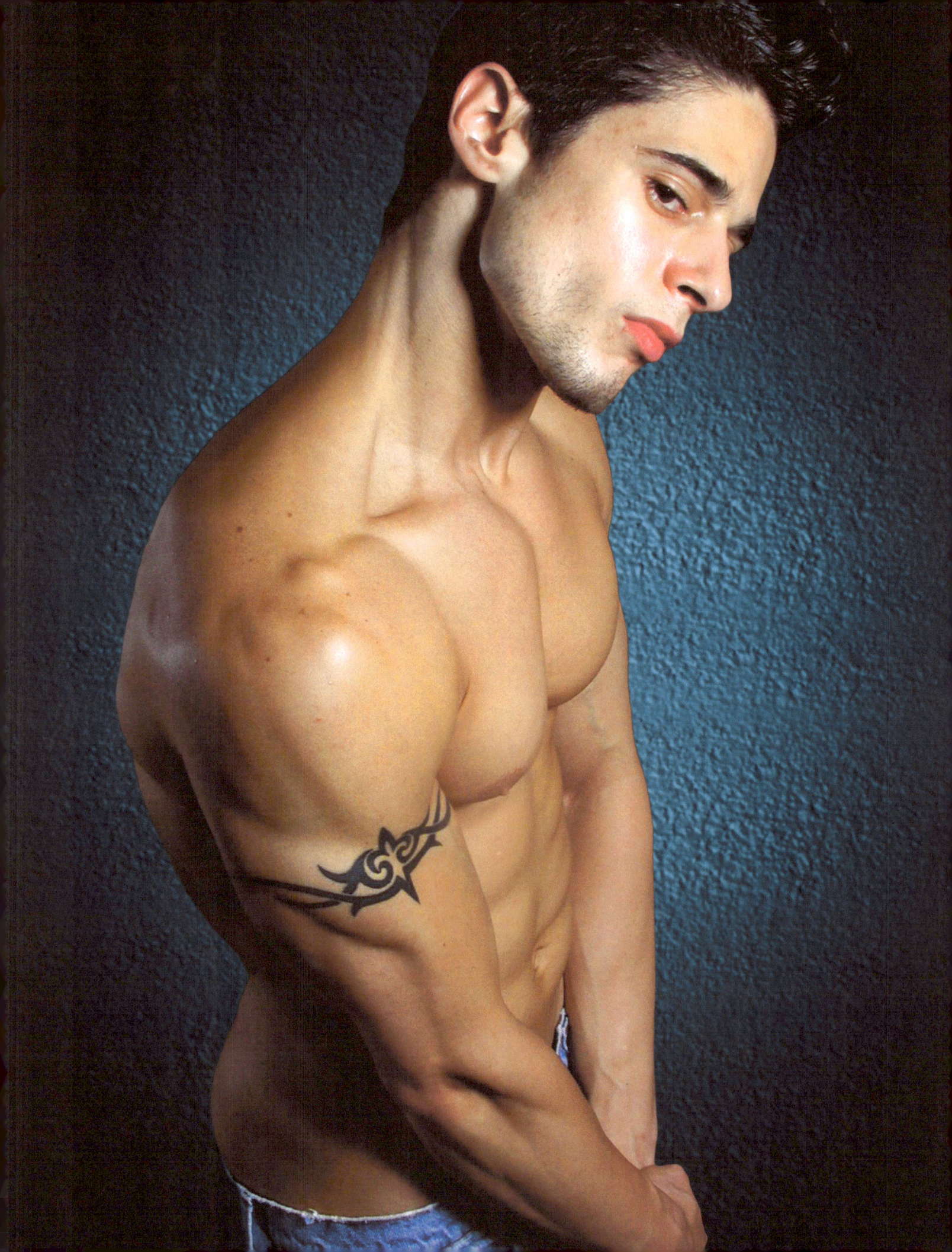

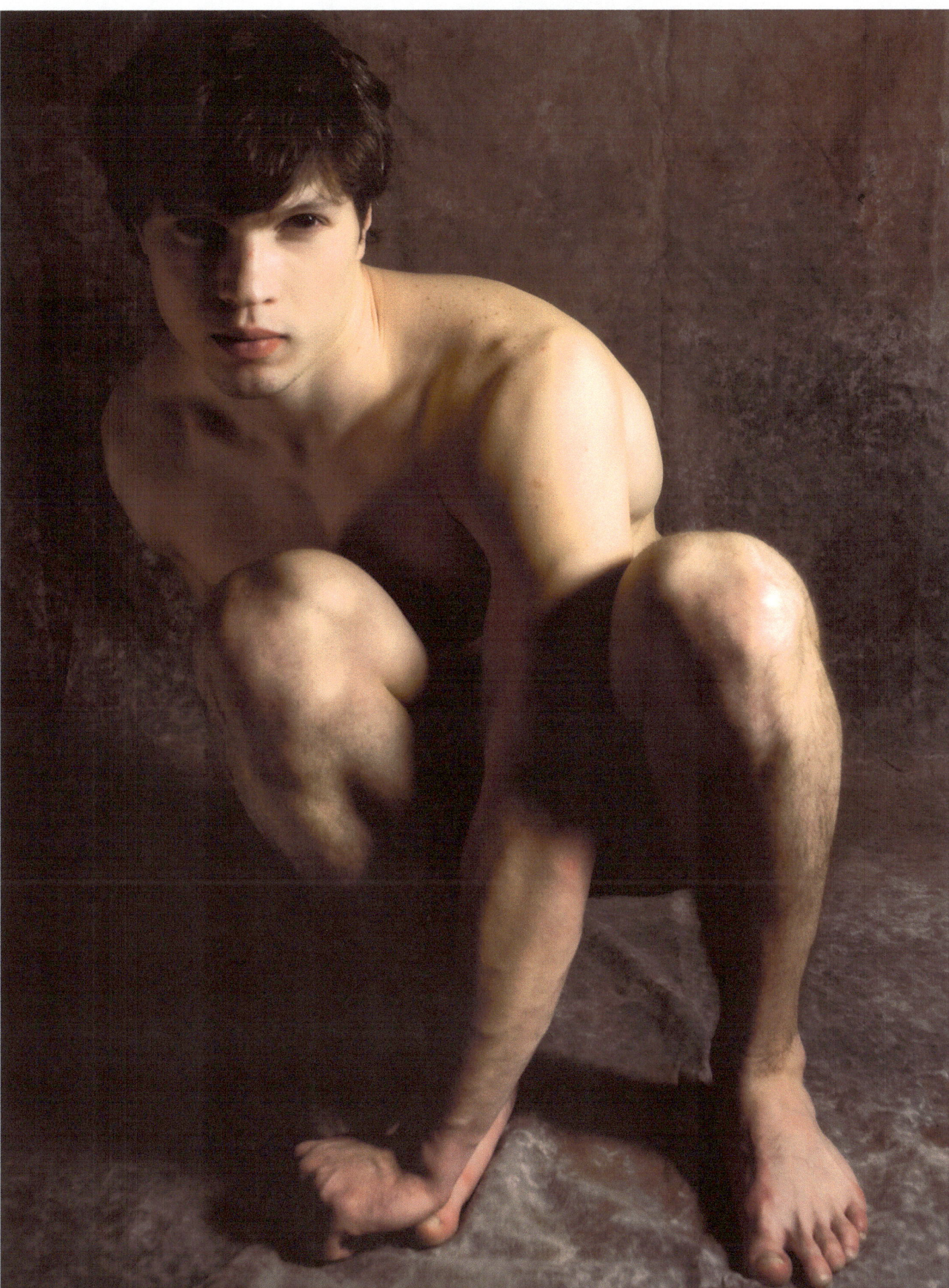

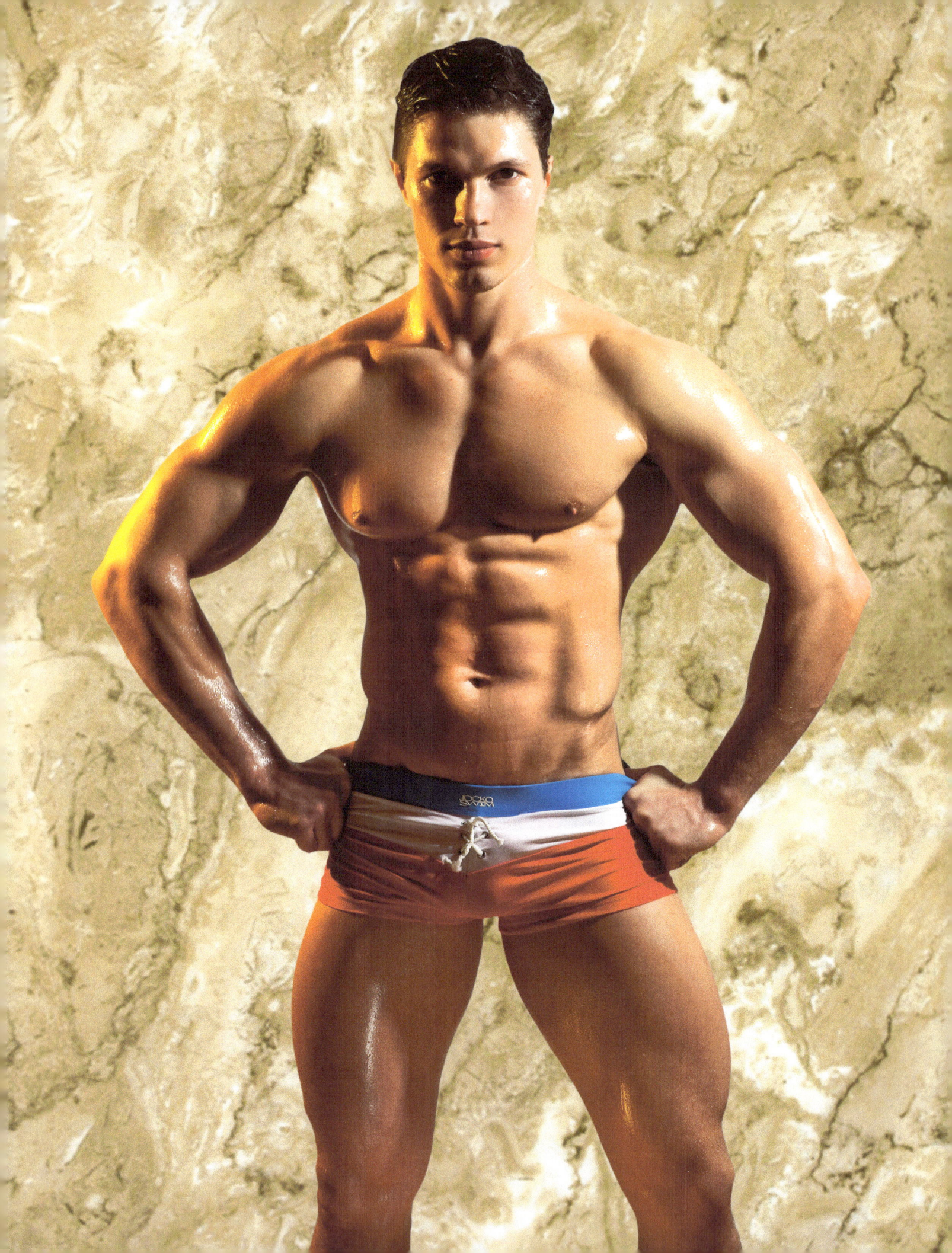

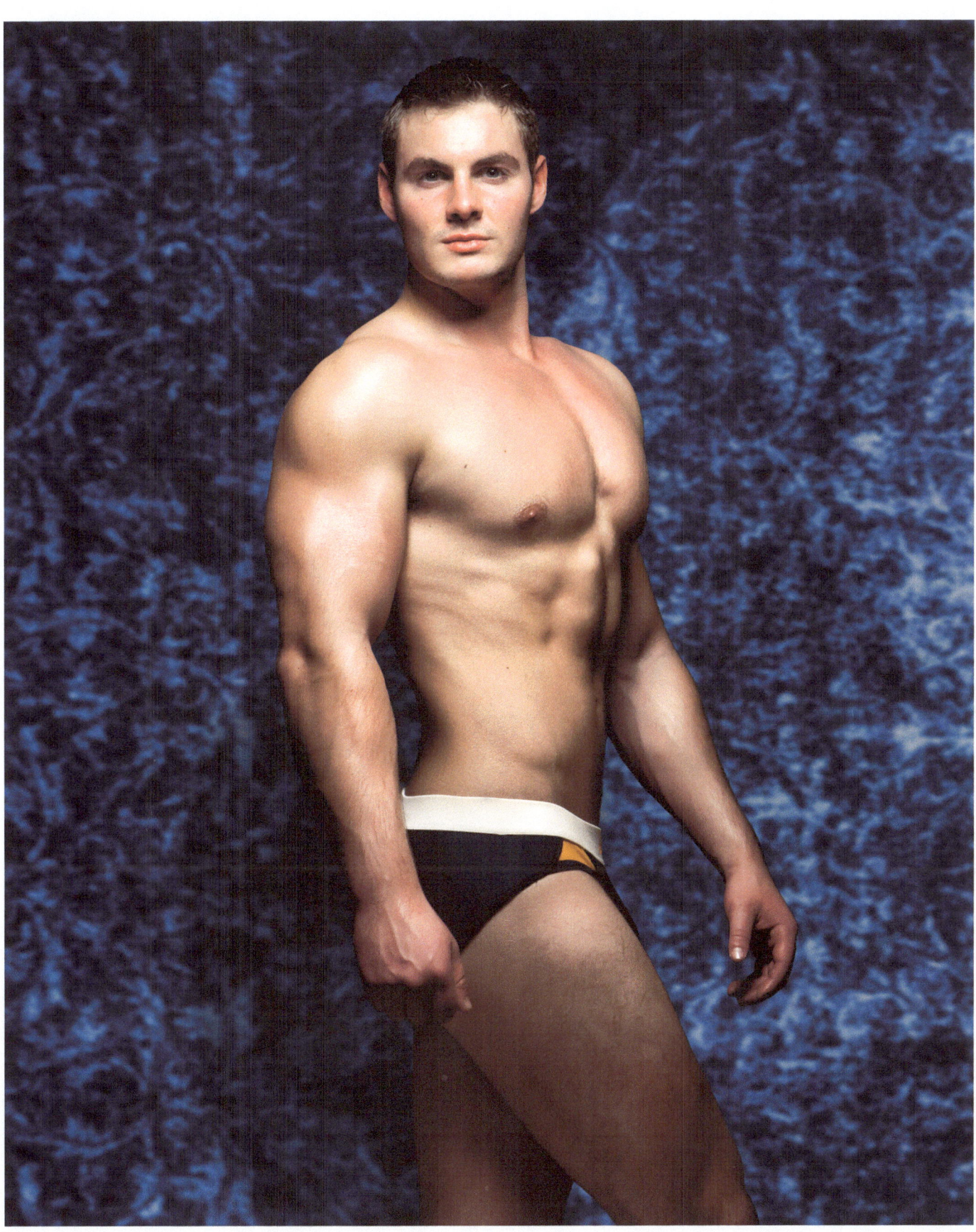

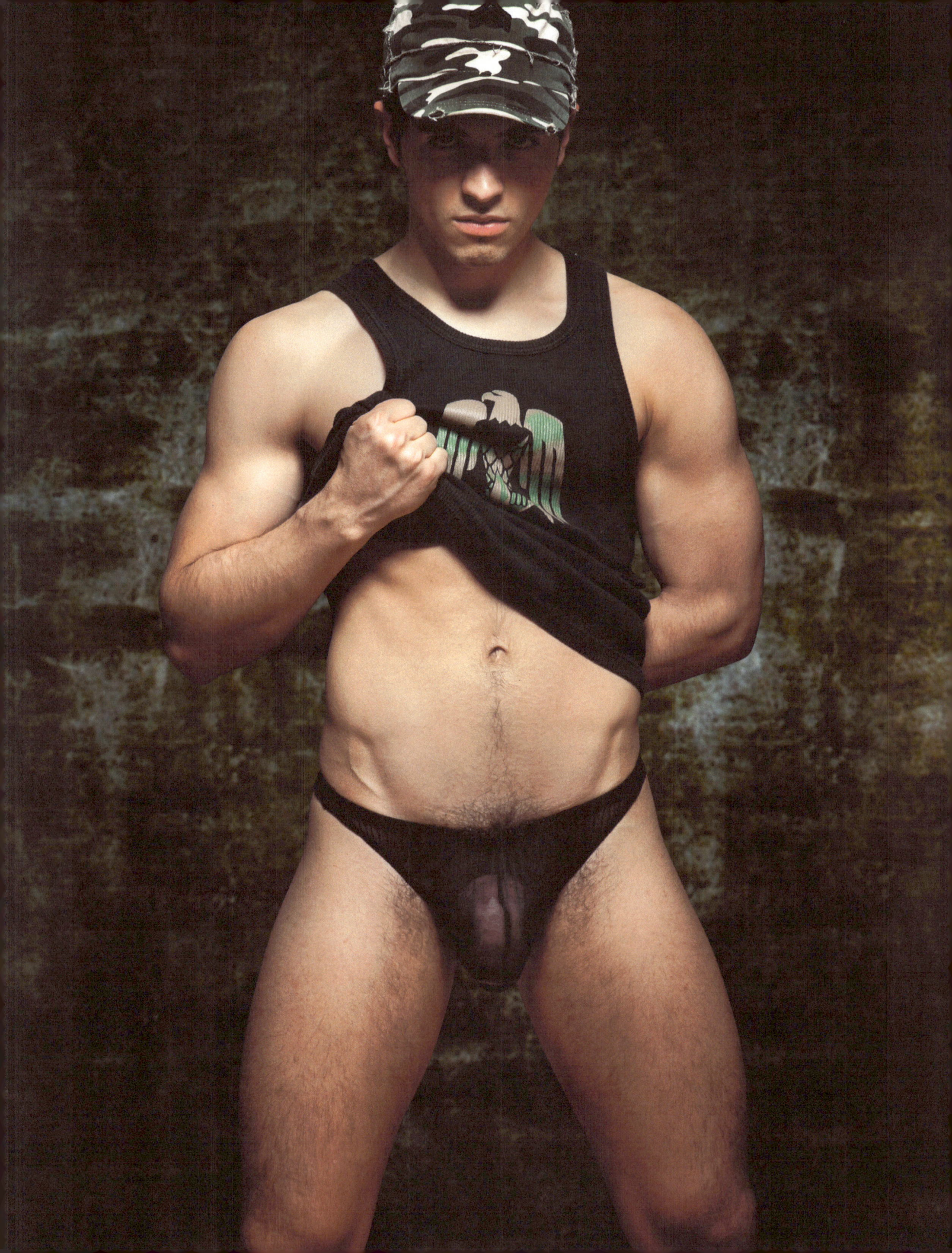

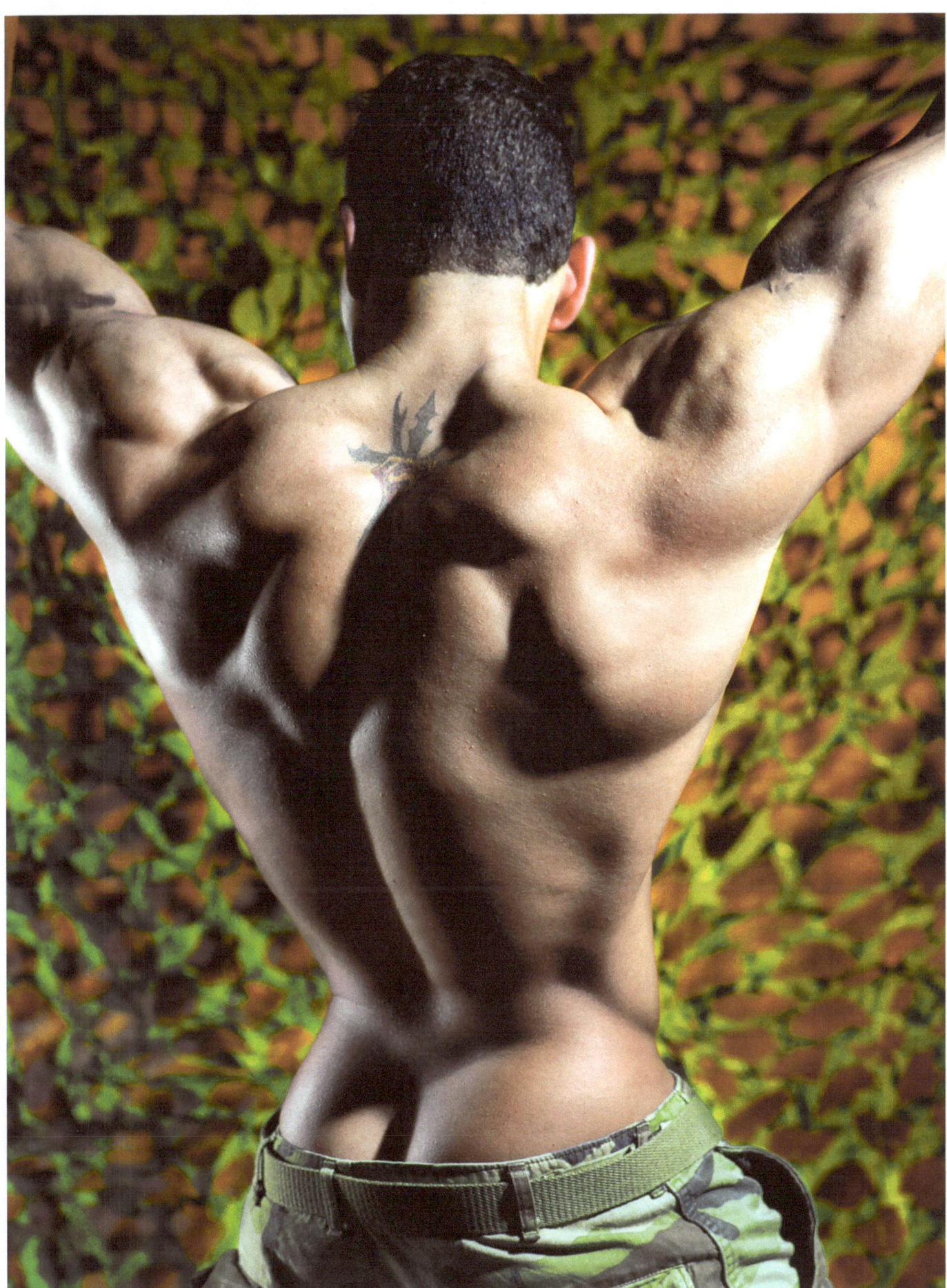

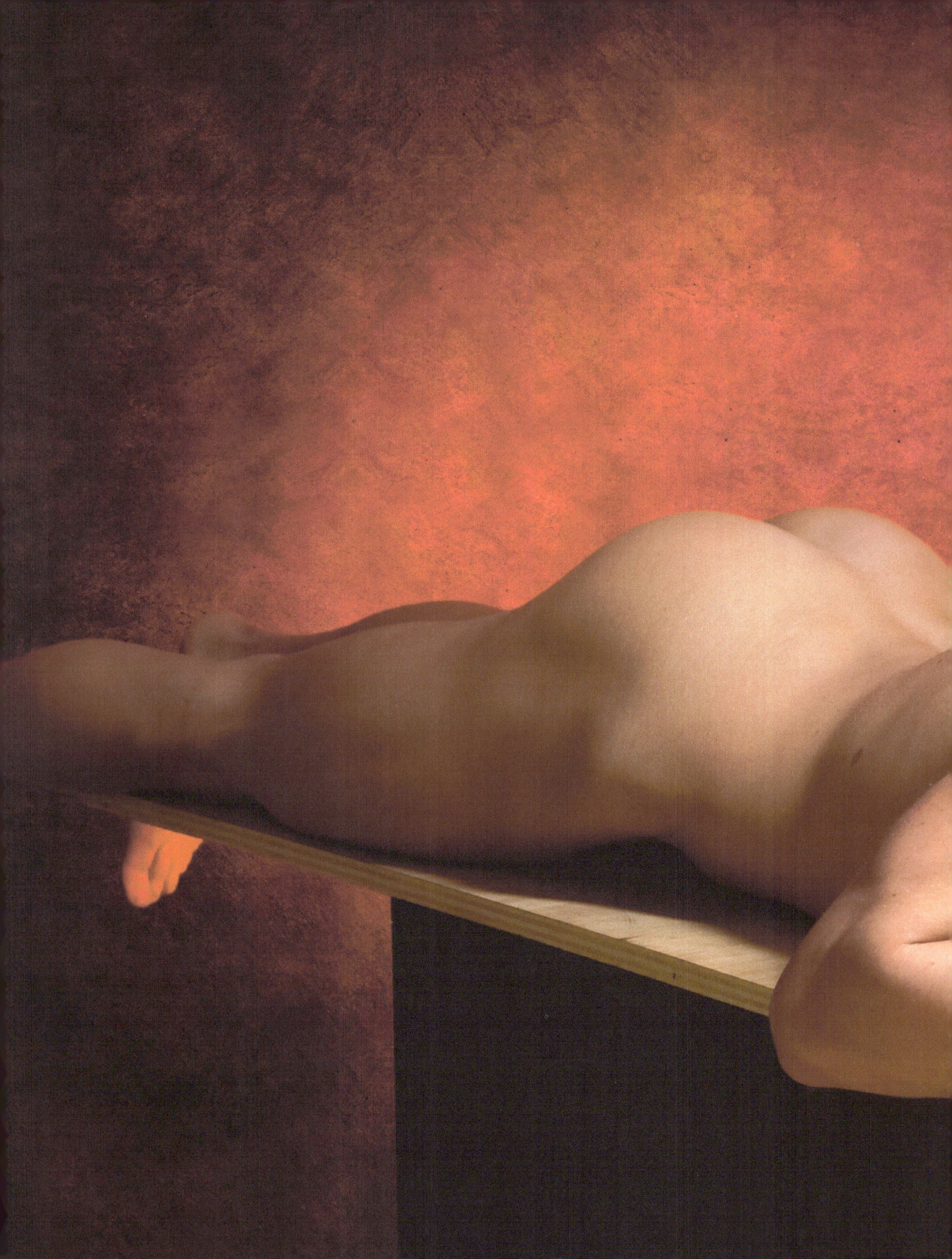

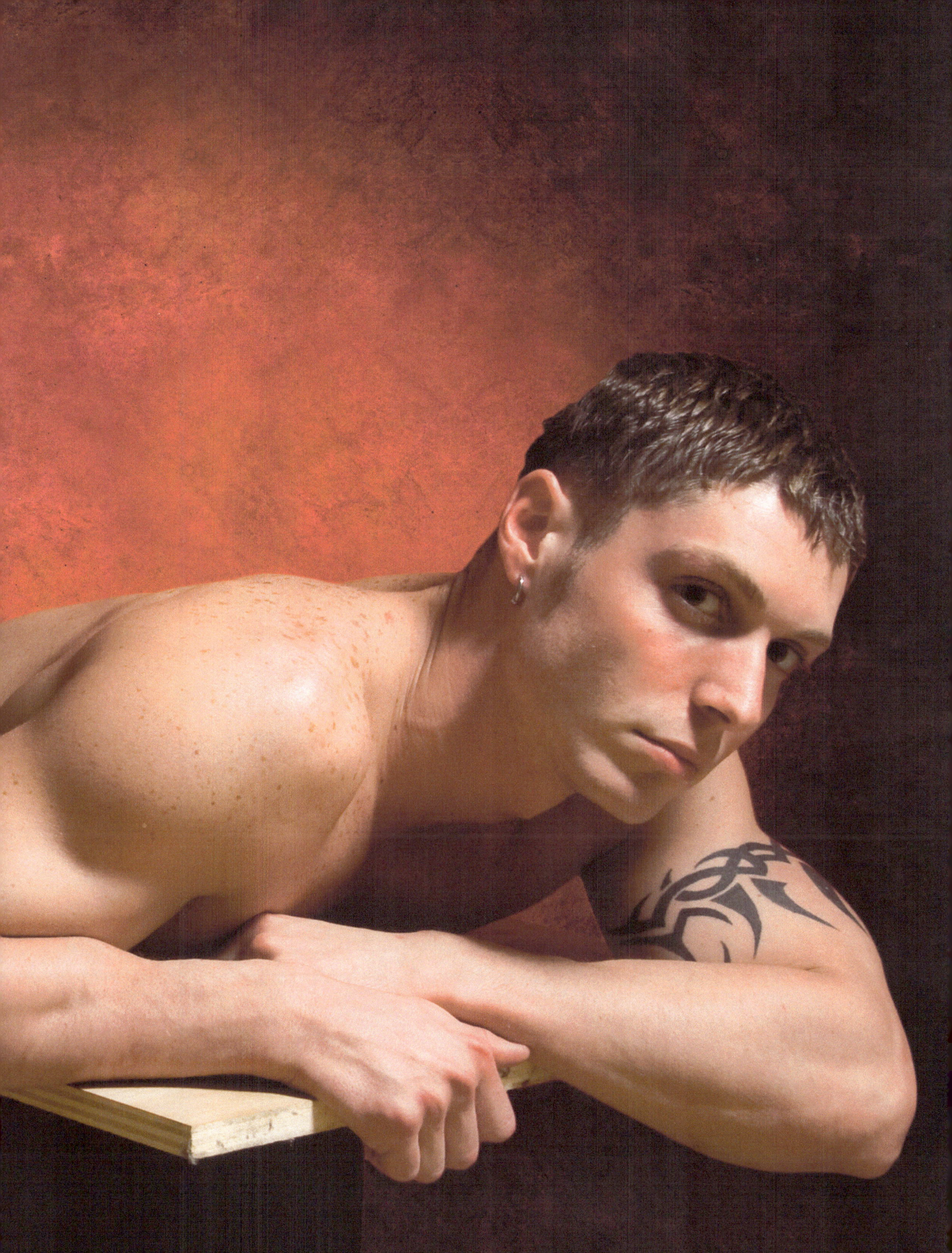

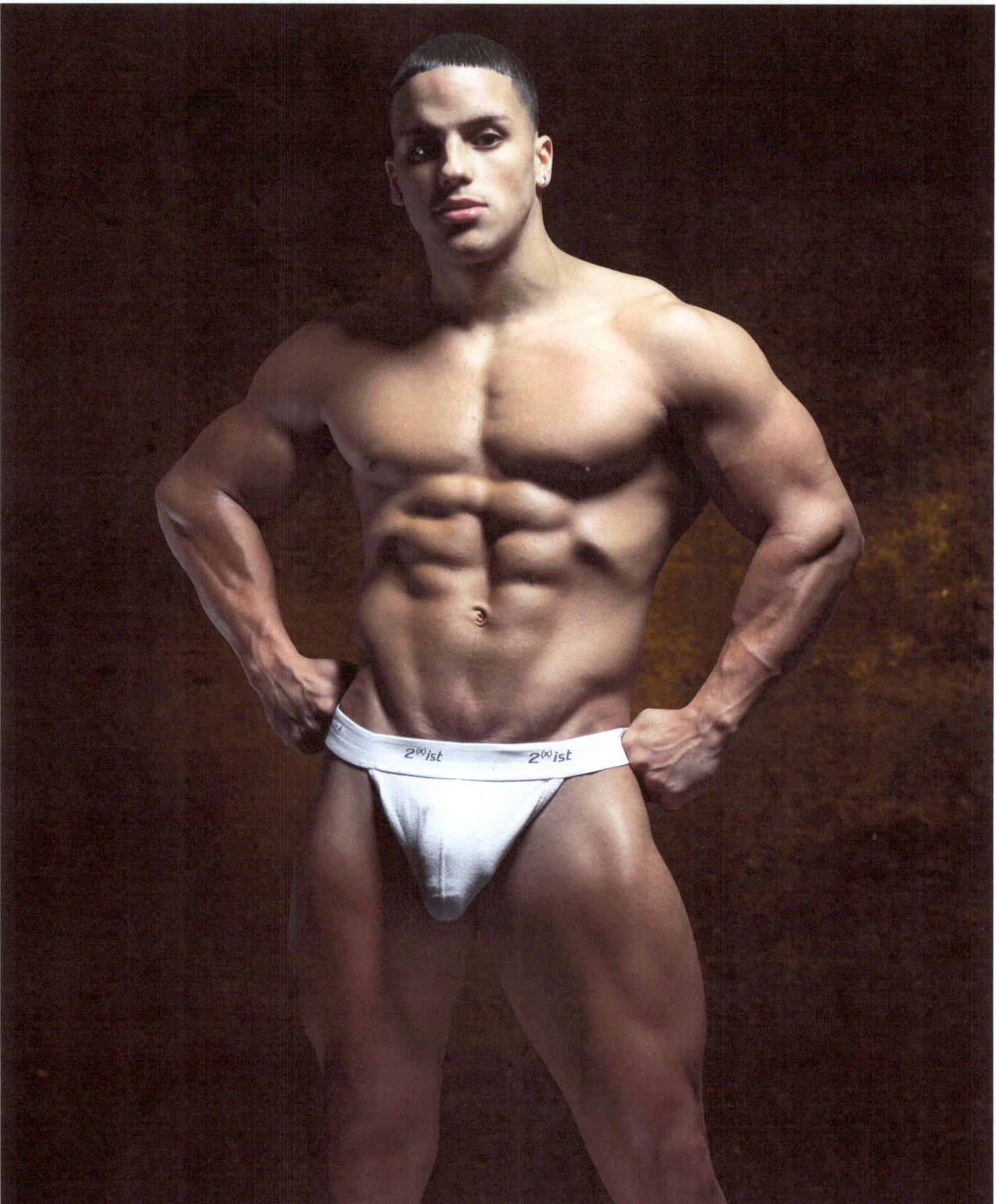

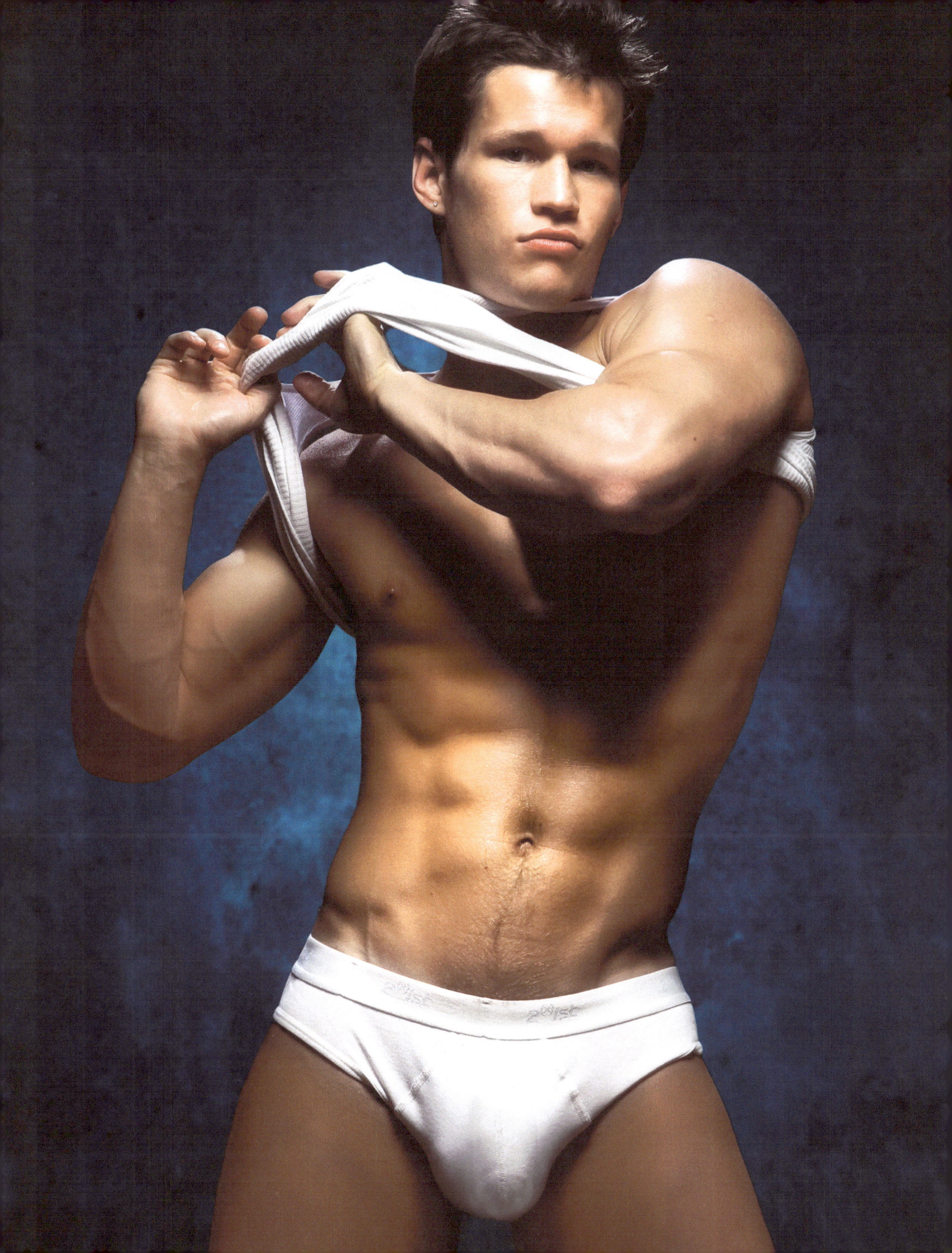

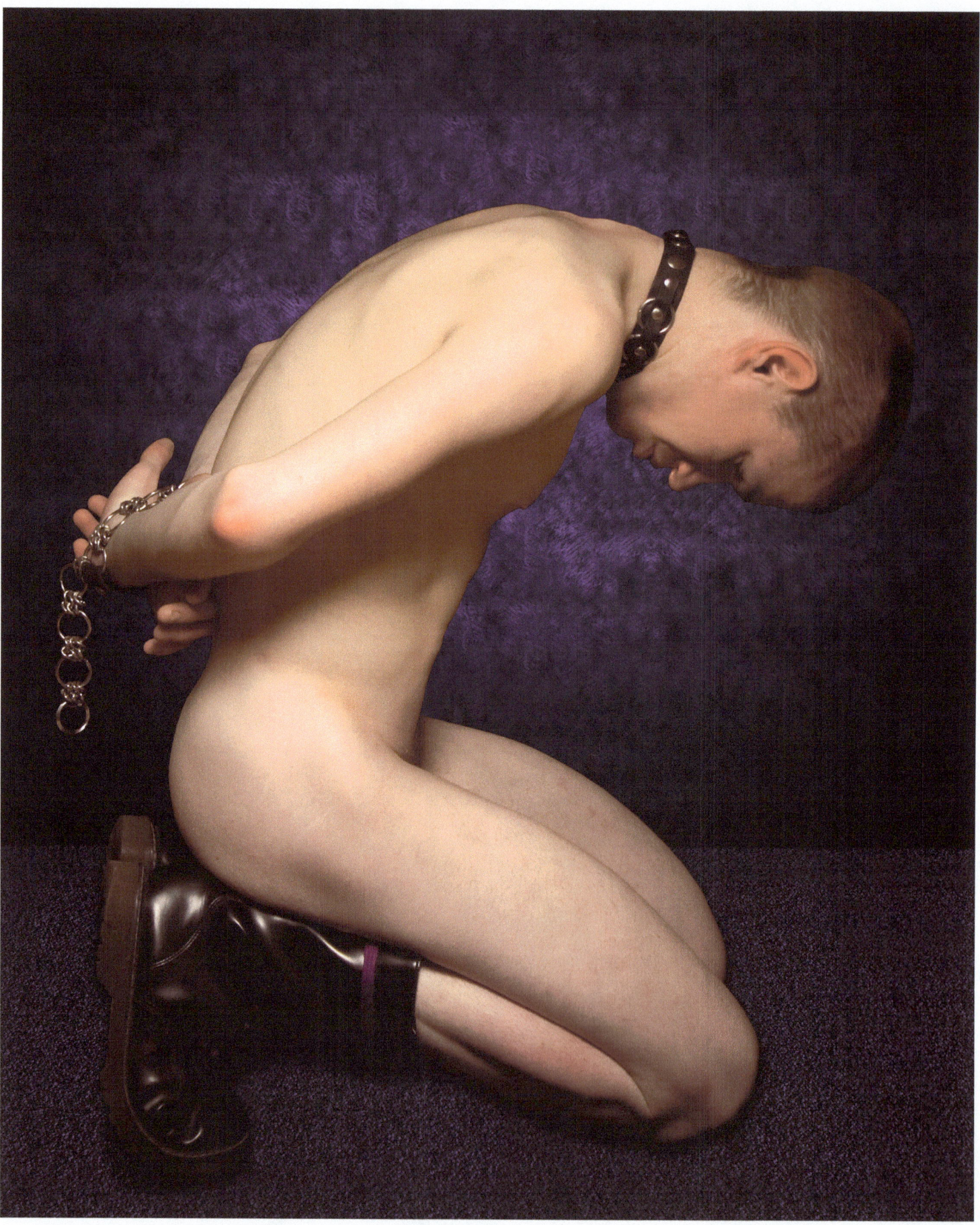

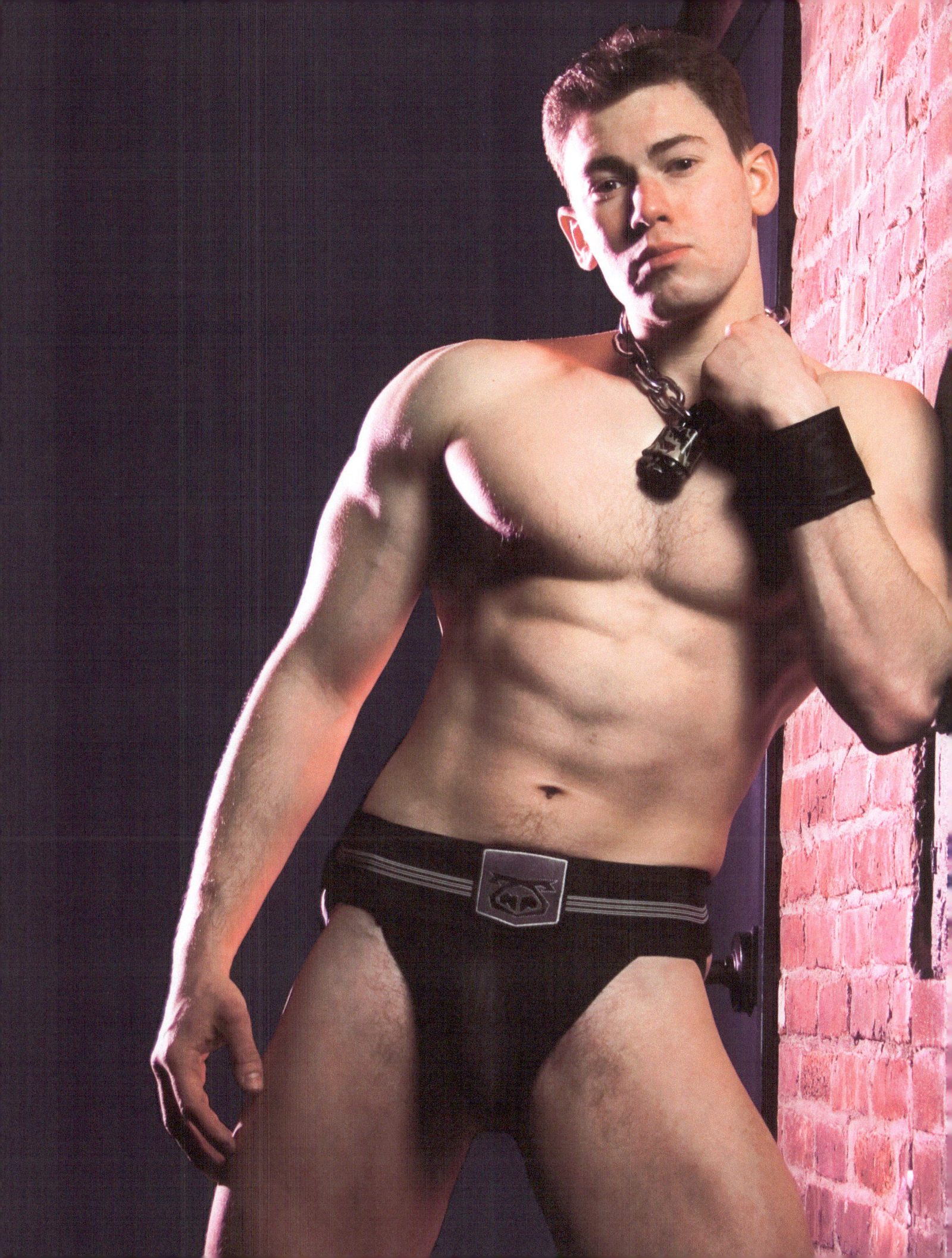

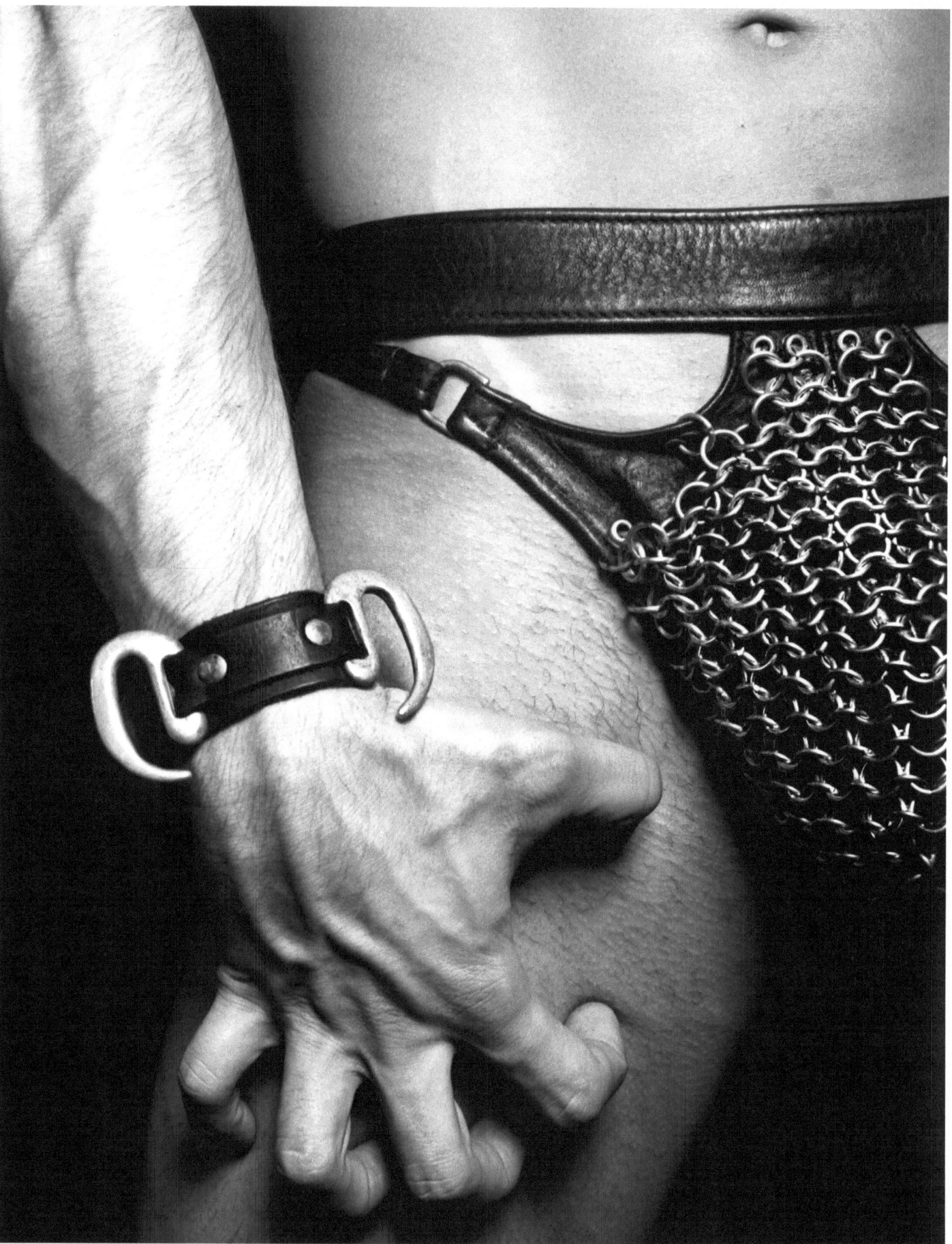

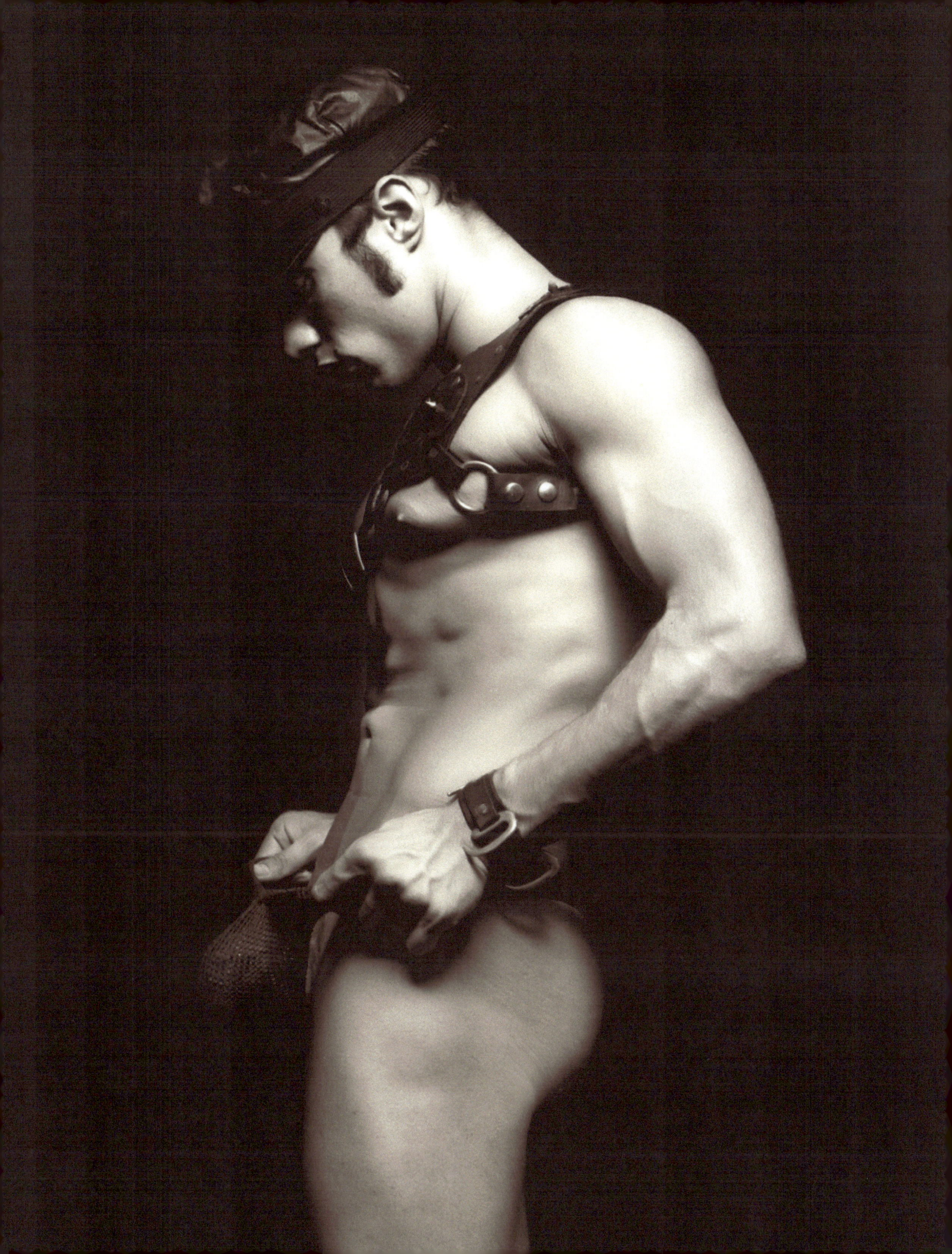

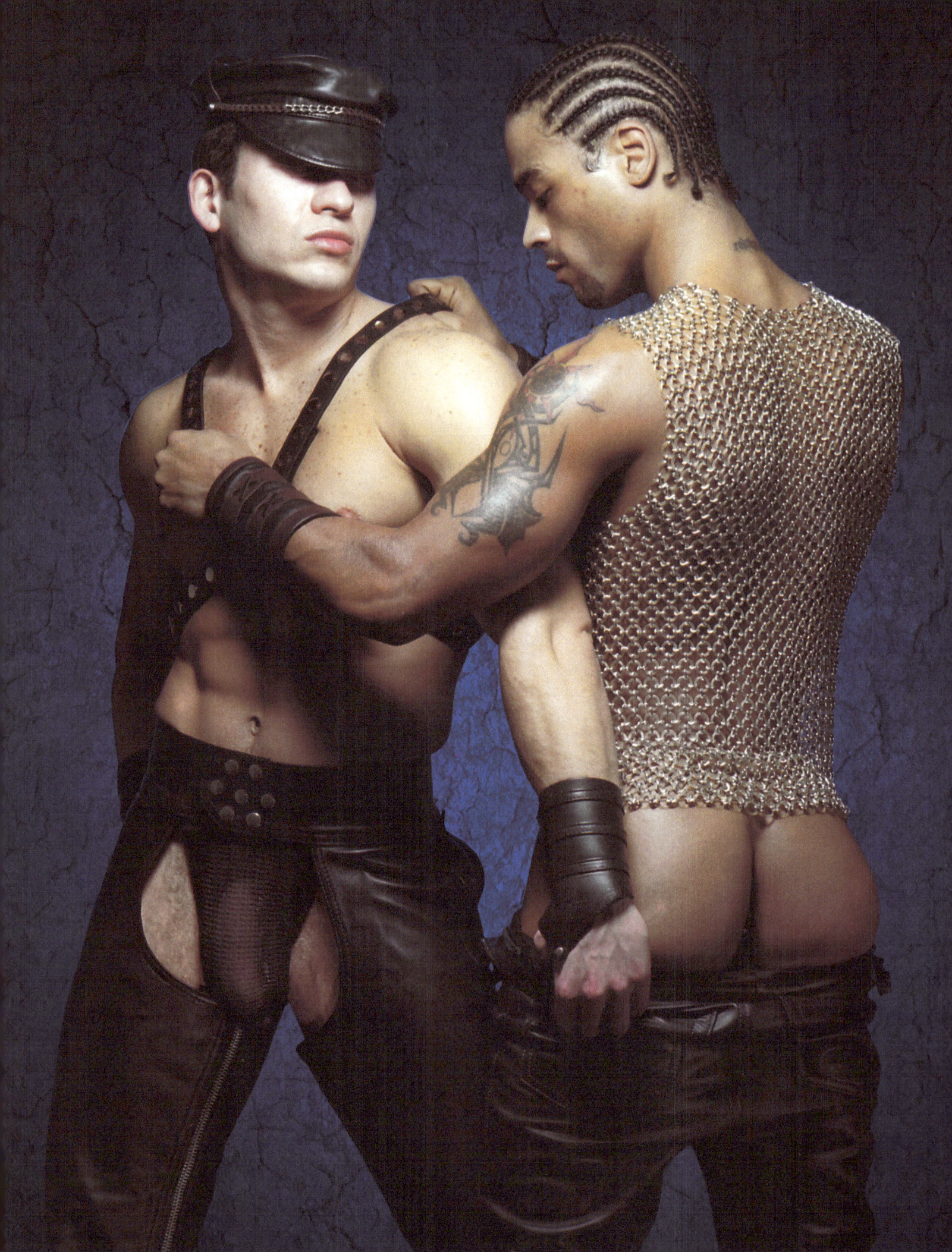

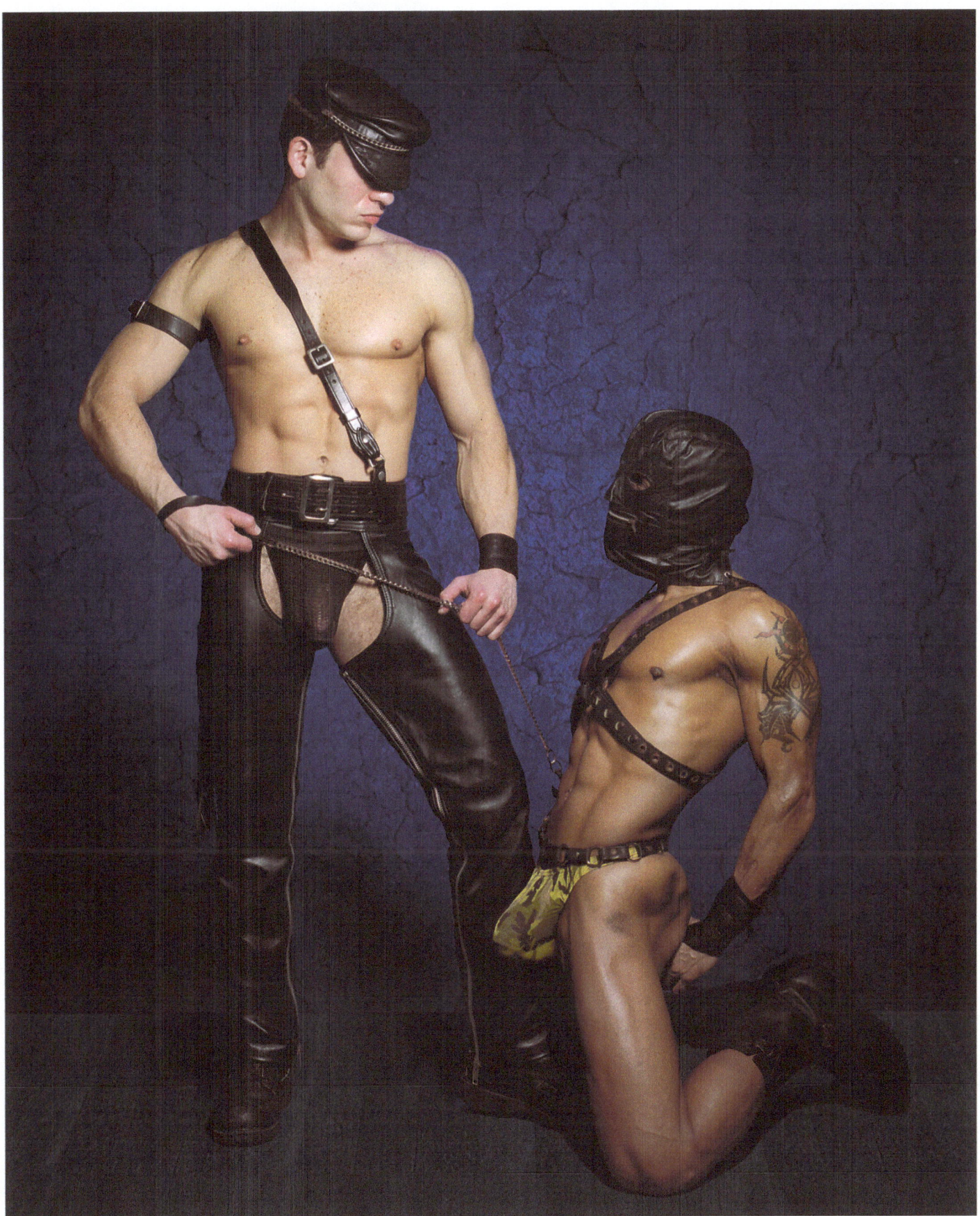

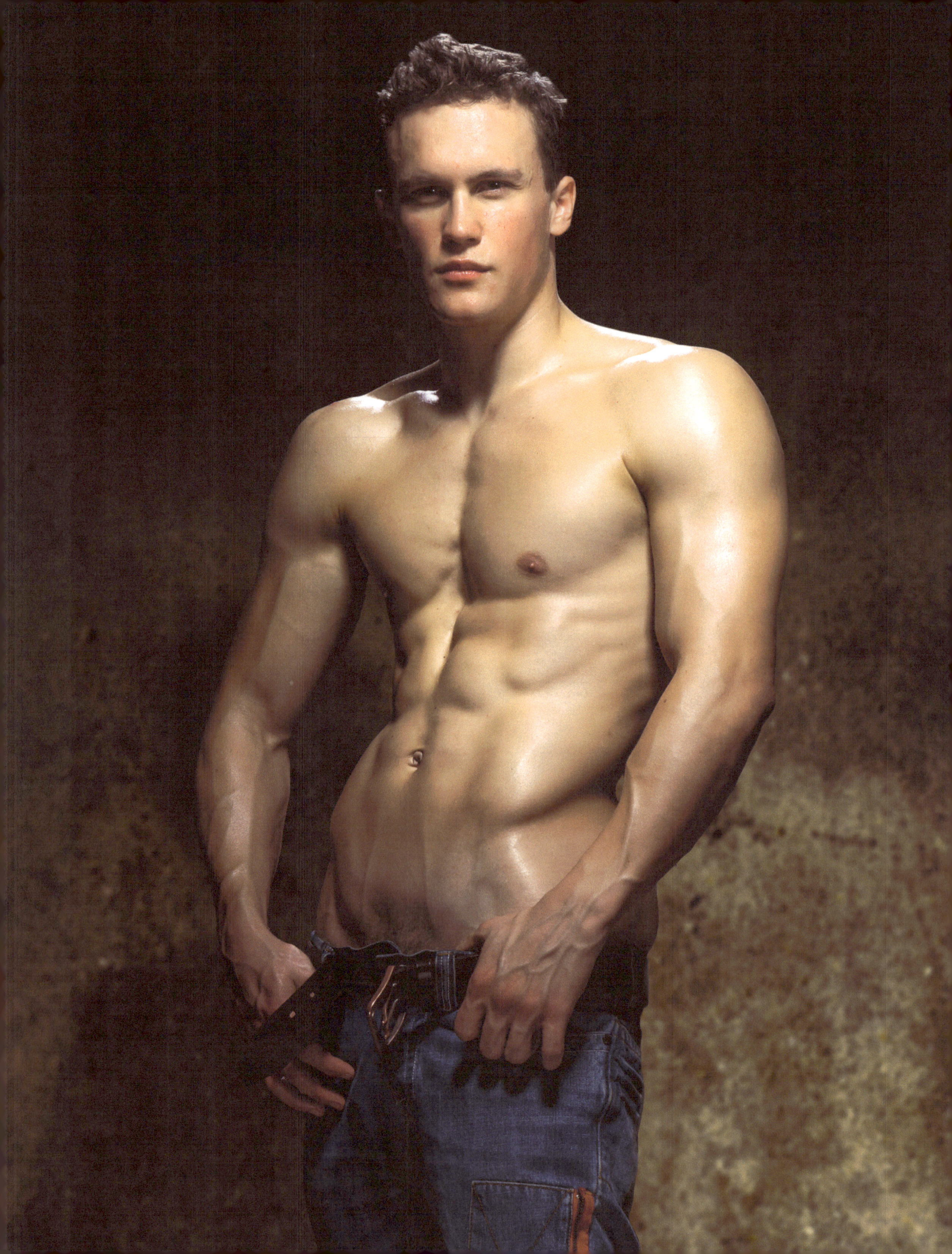

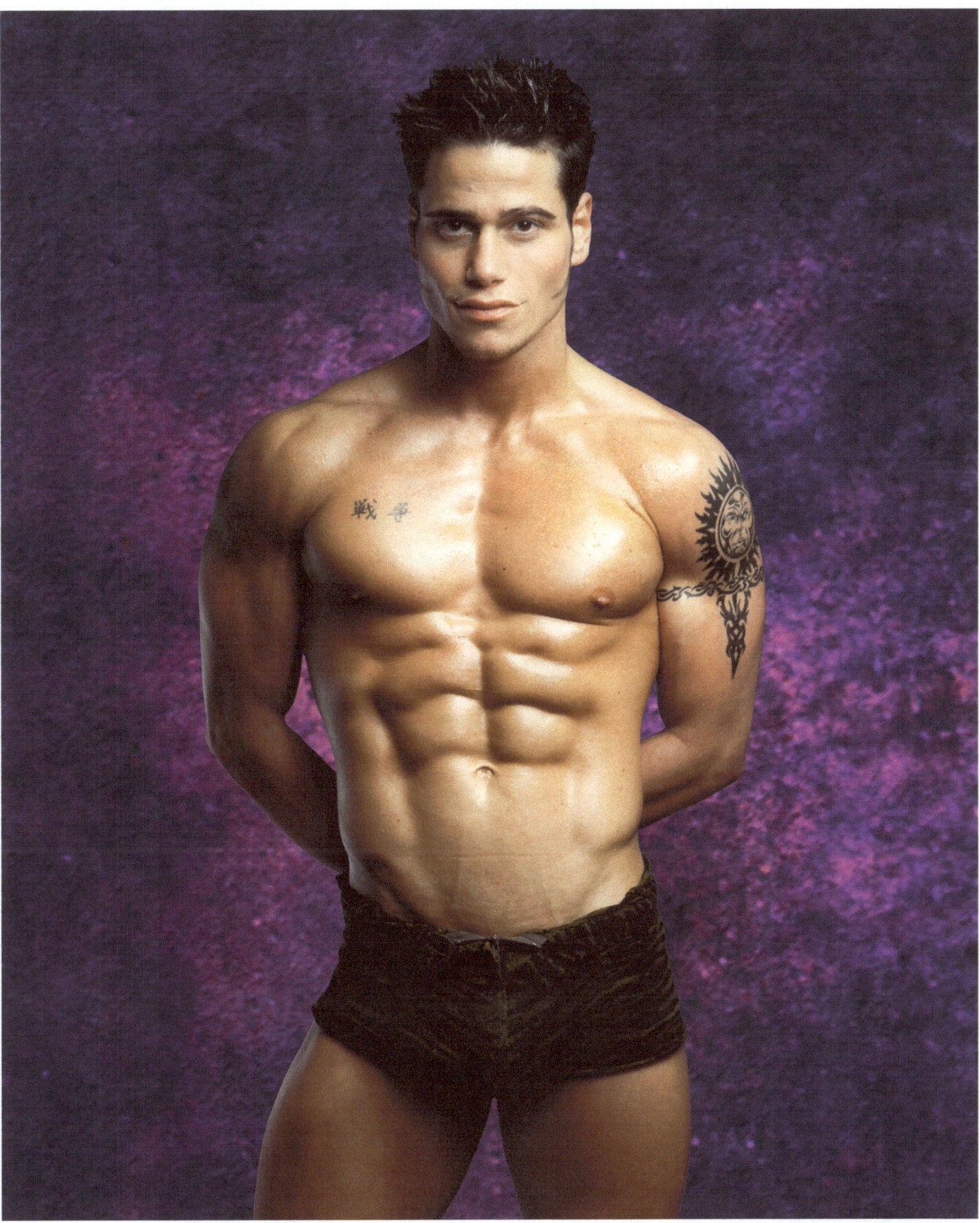

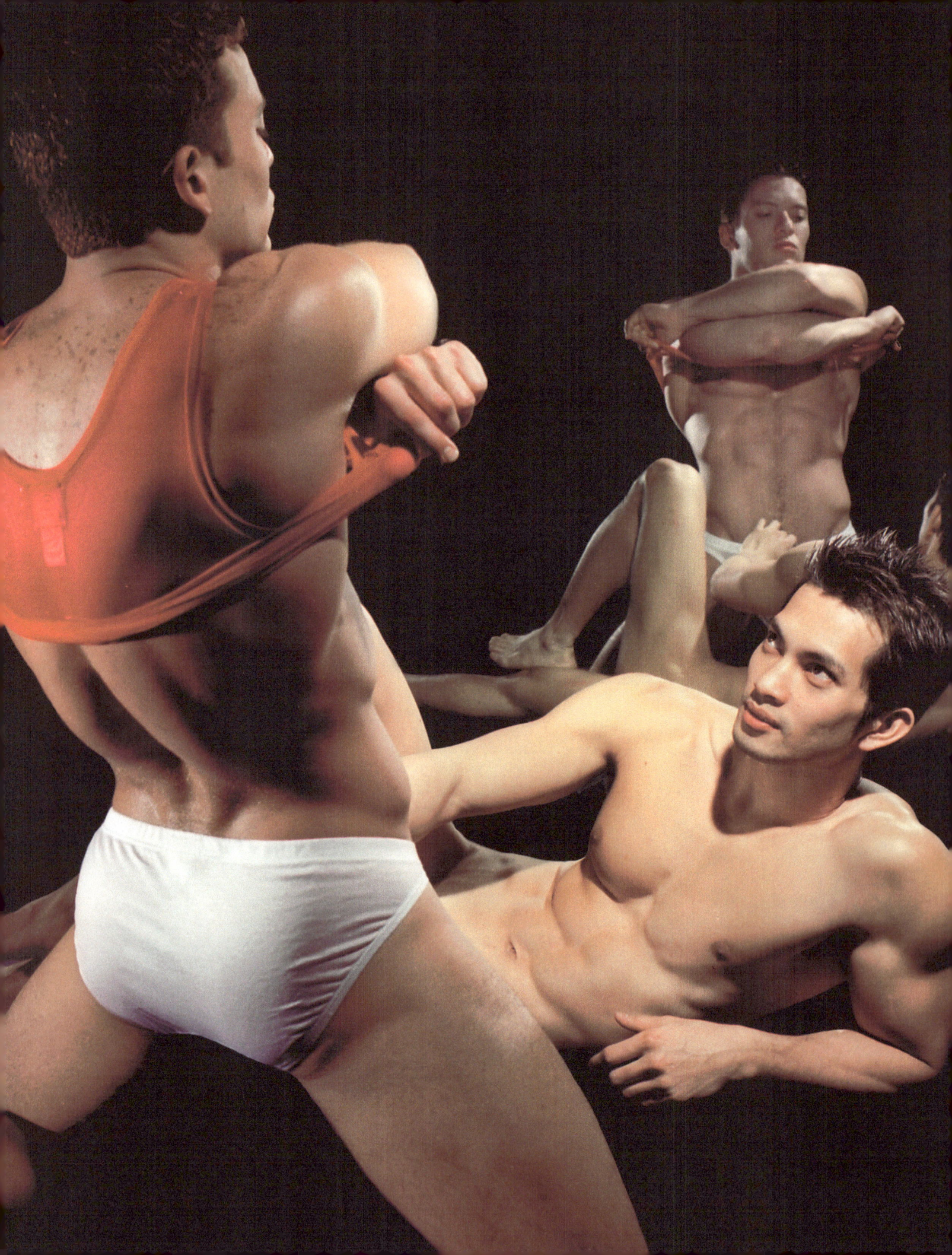

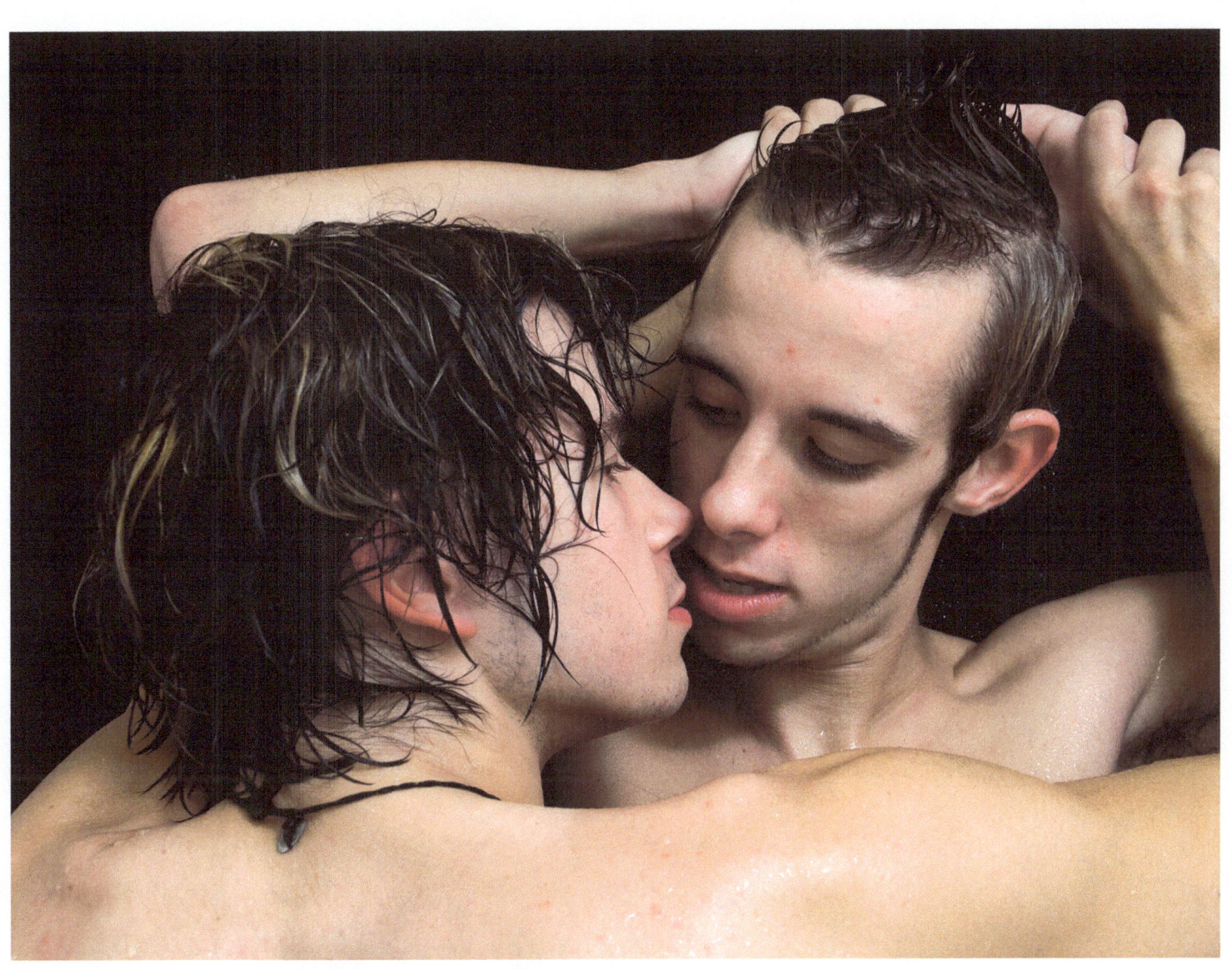

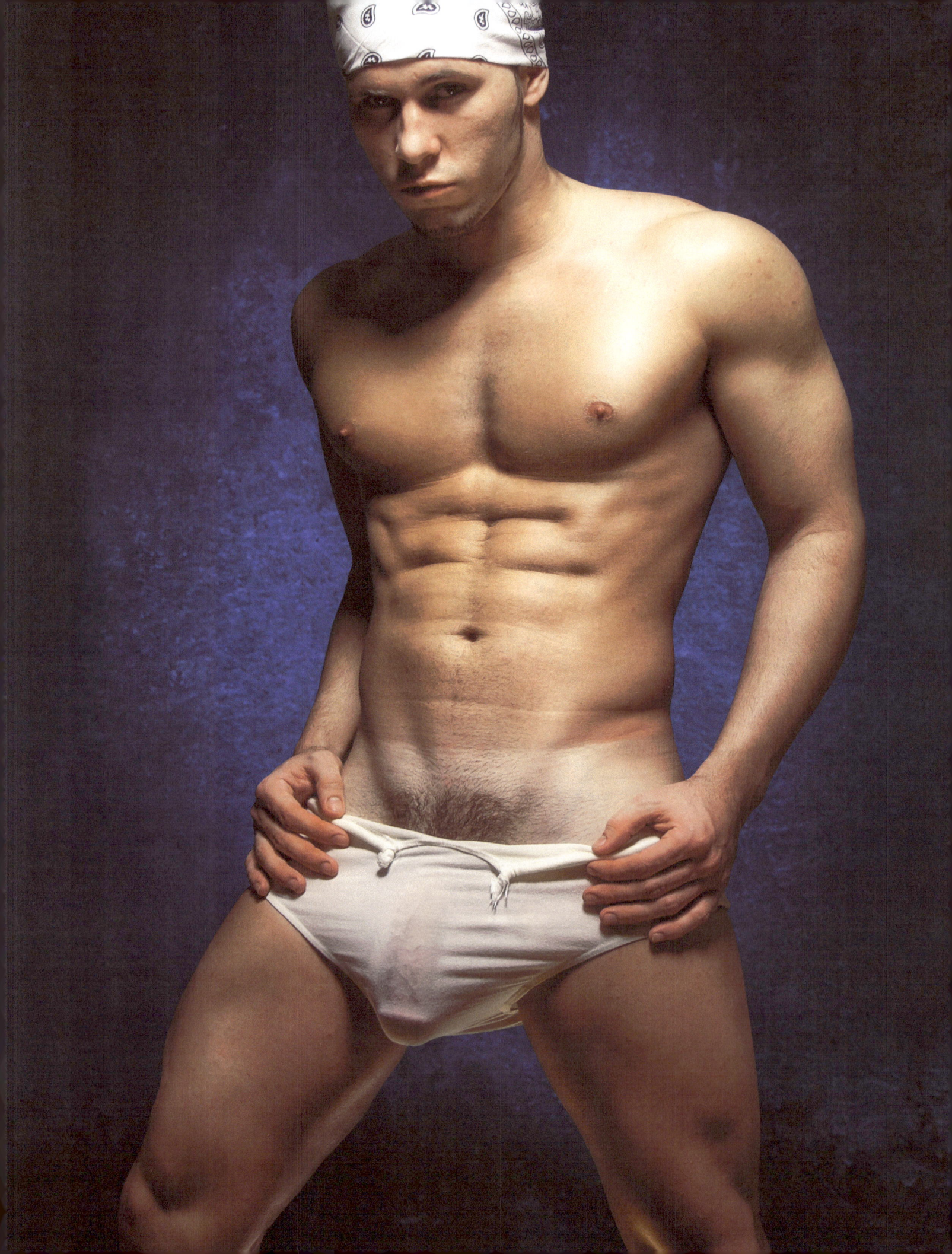

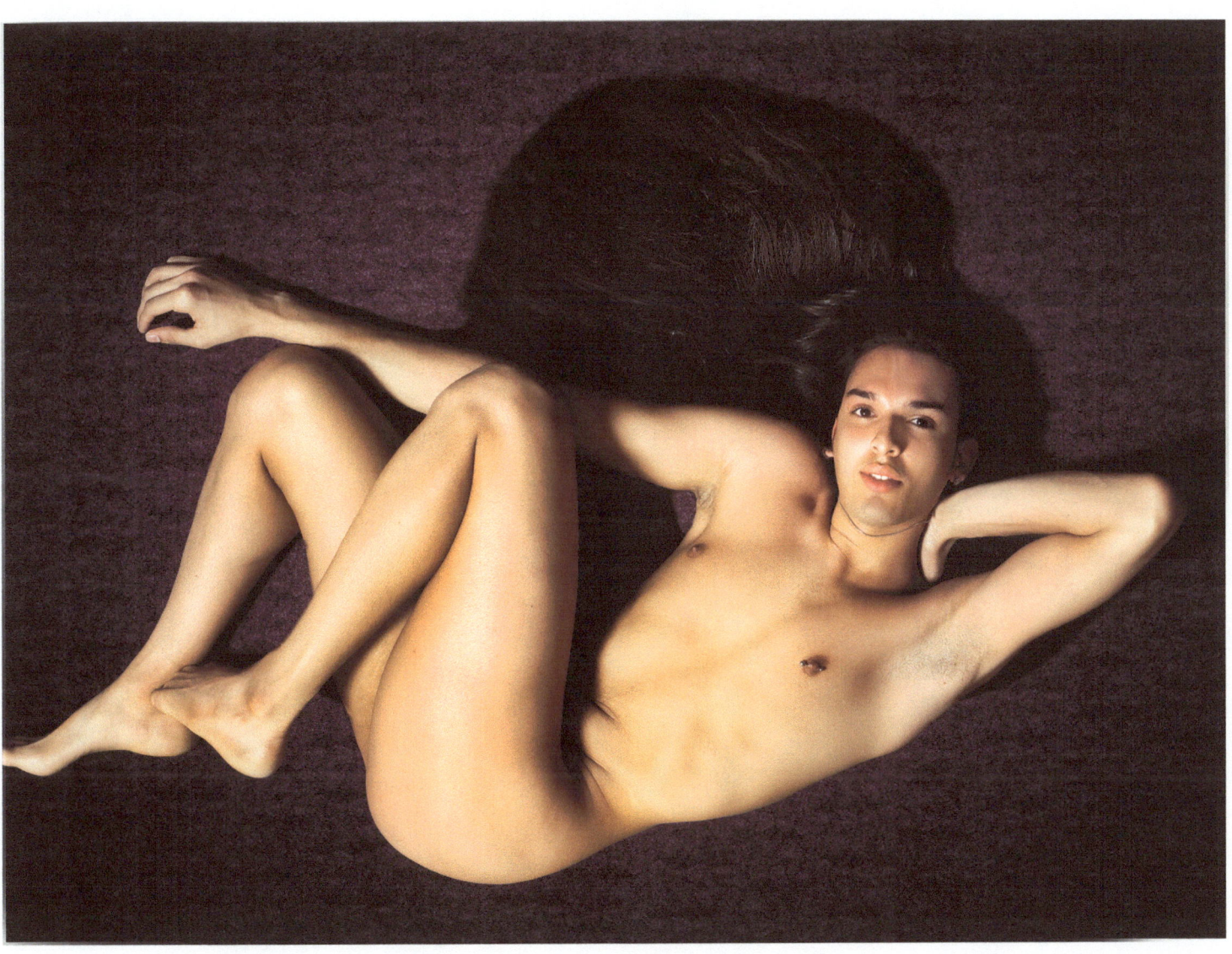

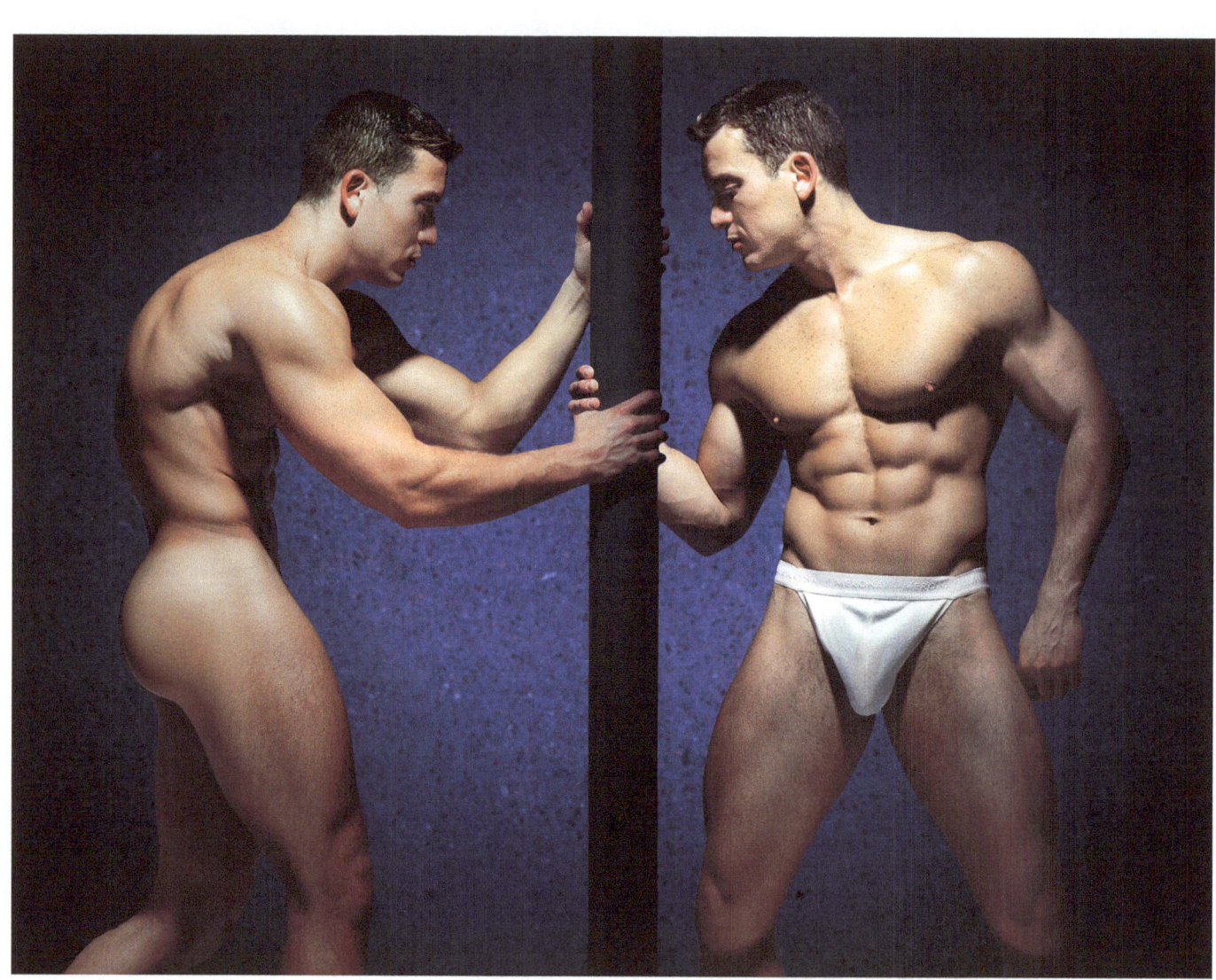

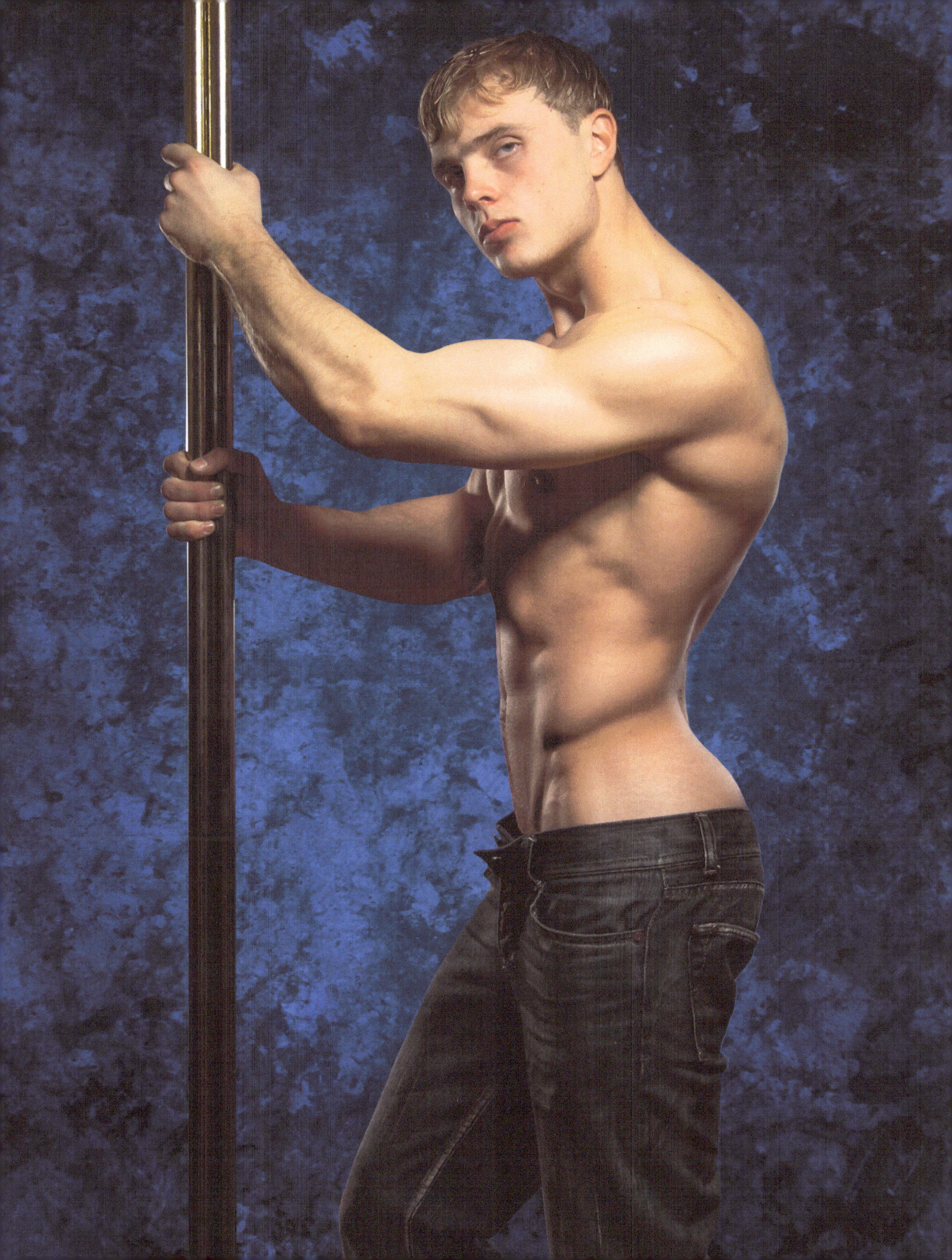

acknowledgments

Very special thanks to Arthur Lambert, Rick Harper
and Trevor Briggs Thanks also to all the Models and
Lucas Entertainment who were involved.